A Republican Europe of States

Combining international political theory and EU studies, Richard Bellamy provides an original account of the democratic legitimacy of international organisations. He proposes a new interpretation of the EU's democratic failings and how they might be addressed. Drawing on the republican theory of freedom as non-domination, Bellamy proposes a way to combine national popular sovereignty with the pursuit of fair and equitable relations of non-domination among states and their citizens. Applying this approach to the EU, Bellamy shows that its democratic failings lie not with the democratic deficit at the EU level but with a democratic disconnect at the member state level. Rather than shifting democratic authority to the European Parliament, this book argues that the EU needs to reconnect with the different 'demoi' of the member states by empowering national parliaments in the EU policy-making process.

Richard Bellamy is Professor of Political Science at University College, London, and Director of the Max Weber Programme, European University Institute. His previous books include *Political Constitutionalism: A Republican Defence of the Constitutionality of Democracy* (Cambridge University Press, 2007), which won the David and Elaine Spitz Prize in 2009, and, as co-editor, *The Cambridge History of Twentieth Century Political Thought* (Cambridge University Press, 2003).

A superb rethinking of the European Union, which both reveals the deep and continuing appeal of the project, scattering the Brexit fog, and motivates an arresting but sensible set of proposals for institutional reform.

Philip Pettit, Princeton University and the Australian National University

Bellamy's defence of the European Union's legitimacy as depending on democratic reconnection with its Member States will provoke and may displease both euro-sceptics and euro-enthusiasts. Making both groups think again is important right now, as the EU faces some of its biggest ever challenges.

Jo Shaw, University of Edinburgh

In this beautifully argued book, Richard Bellamy sets out why 'in a globalising world democratic states have compelling...reasons to create institutions that resemble the EU in key respects'. For political theorists, this is essential reading on legitimacy, democracy and justice within and beyond the state. For scholars of the EU, this is essential reading on the democratic deficit, on parliaments and the EU, on EU citizenship, on differentiated integration and on the reform of the Eurozone. For everyone, this is a book with important implications for Brexit.

Christopher Lord, University of Oslo

Richard Bellamy, a master of contemporary political philosophy in the republican-liberal tradition, is here presenting a comprehensive and systematic analysis of the potential justifications and normative limits of European government beyond the democratic nation state. Rejecting cosmopolitan legitimacy concepts that ignore the rootedness of rights-based norms in political processes of an established polity, and defending the legitimacy of the heterogeneous achievements of democratic self-government in existing member states, the book is compelling in its critique of present excesses of European legal and monetary integration and of normatively unsustainable proposals for further centralization. Its own vision of a republican Europe of sovereign states that respect their cosmopolitan obligations appears normatively most attractive – but also quite demanding under present conditions of rising intergovernmental tensions.

Fritz Scharpf, Max Planck Institute for the Study of Societies

A presentation and defence of the EU as an association of sovereign republican states by Europe's leading republican theorist.

James Tully, University of Victoria

Richard Bellamy is a political theorist who truly understands the constitutional strand in Europe's ontology. This gives added purchase to his challenging attempt to 're-understand' and rethink how to frame the ever-illusive European reality.

J. H. H. Weiler, New York University

Like the best work in EU studies, Richard Bellamy recognizes that insights only come from being both attentive to the Union's institutional detail and sensitive to its uniqueness. However, he alone does so by exploring Europe's rich heritage in political thought. This book is the most ambitious example yet of his considerable contribution to the field.

Damien Chalmers, National University of Singapore

A Republican Europe of States

Cosmopolitanism, Intergovernmentalism and Democracy in the EU

Richard Bellamy

CAMBRIDGE
UNIVERSITY PRESS

CAMBRIDGE
UNIVERSITY PRESS

University Printing House, Cambridge CB2 8BS, United Kingdom

One Liberty Plaza, 20th Floor, New York, NY 10006, USA

477 Williamstown Road, Port Melbourne, VIC 3207, Australia

314–321, 3rd Floor, Plot 3, Splendor Forum, Jasola District Centre,
New Delhi – 110025, India

79 Anson Road, #06–04/06, Singapore 079906

Cambridge University Press is part of the University of Cambridge.

It furthers the University's mission by disseminating knowledge in the pursuit of
education, learning, and research at the highest international levels of excellence.

www.cambridge.org
Information on this title: www.cambridge.org/9781107022287
DOI: 10.1017/9781139136303

First published 2019

Printed and bound in Great Britain by Clays Ltd, Elcograf S.p.A.

A catalogue record for this publication is available from the British Library.

Library of Congress Cataloging-in-Publication Data
Names: Bellamy, Richard (Richard Paul), author.
Title: A republican Europe of states : cosmopolitanism, intergovernmentalism
and demoicracy in the EU / Richard Bellamy.
Description: Cambridge, United Kingdom ; New York, NY : Cambridge
University Press, 2019. | Includes bibliographical references.
Identifiers: LCCN 2018041951| ISBN 9781107022287 (hbk) | ISBN
9781107678125 (pbk)
Subjects: LCSH: Democracy – European Union countries. | Legitimacy of
governments – European Union countries.
Classification: LCC JN40 .B45 2019 | DDC 341.242/2–dc23
LC record available at https://lccn.loc.gov/2018041951

ISBN 978-1-107-02228-7 Hardback
ISBN 978-1-107-67812-5 Paperback

For Sandra

Contents

Preface and Acknowledgements

Any British national writing about the European Union (EU) right now cannot avoid doing so under the shadow of Brexit – especially if the topic is democracy in the EU. Yet, although this book was completed in June 2018, two years after the fateful referendum, and addresses many issues pertinent to the debate over the UK's departure from the EU, its gestation and writing goes back much longer. Formally speaking, I embarked on this project in 2012–14 thanks to the award of a Leverhulme Research Fellowship, which also permitted me to take up a Fellowship at the Hanse-Wissenschaftskolleg (HWK) in Delmenhorst from 2013–14. These Fellowships allowed me to write a number of articles that sketched out the argument for a 'republican intergovernmentalism' that I advance here. I am grateful to both foundations for their funding and to UCL for granting me leave in 2012–14 and to the European University Institute for allowing me to delay the start of my Directorship of the Max Weber Programme to 1 May 2014, thereby enabling me to take them up. In many respects, however, the ideas developed in this book go back over twenty-five years to the Maastricht Treaty of 1992, when I first began to write about the EU. Several of the articles written over this twenty-five-year period, many co-authored with Dario Castiglione of the University of Exeter, are collected in our joint book *From Maastricht to Brexit* (Bellamy and Castiglione 2019), that forms to some degree a companion volume to this one. As readers of those pieces will see, although my ideas have evolved over these years, a certain continuity underlies my thinking.

Like many others, I feared that the step change in the integration process heralded by Maastricht risked outstripping what many citizens of the member states would, and should be expected to, regard as legitimate, unless these measures could be credibly subjected to democratic control aimed at preserving a degree of social as well as political equality. However, I also doubted the plausibility and justifiability of either simply scaling up the democratic mechanisms of the nation state to the EU level, or of adopting many of the proposals for alternative and more novel dispersed and deliberative mechanisms of democratic accountability of a transnational character. Political identification with the EU remains weak compared to national and sub-national identities, with the partial exception of some elite groups; an integrated public sphere likewise only exists in a highly fragmented and dispersed sense, and is similarly most common among mobile and educated professionals; and the intermediary structures of civil society necessary to support political mobilisation of a pan-European kind, such as a transnational party system, are also patchy and feeble and often created and financed by EU institutions. In these circumstances, enhancing the democratic authority of the European Parliament or other EU institutions merely deepens what, following Peter Lindseth (2010), I call the democratic disconnect with citizens. From this perspective, political integration creates a democratic deficit at the domestic level without resolving that of the EU level. That worry seems confirmed by the way the growing politicisation of EU integration has generally arisen at the domestic rather than the EU level, and been driven by antagonism towards the EU rather than motivating support for it (Kriesi 2016). Although Brexit represents an extreme case, Euroscepticism has been an increasingly salient feature of the domestic politics of almost all member states over the past two to three decades (Usherwood and Startin 2013).

As a result, this book offers a different approach – that of reconnecting the EU to the domestic democratic processes of the member states. I dub this approach 'republican intergovernmentalism'. I advocate this strategy for normative rather than purely pragmatic reasons: that is, as someone who regards democracy as necessary for the legitimacy of any political system, and sees some form of international cooperation of the kind represented by the EU as required for the equitable, as well as the efficient and effective, functioning of democratic states in a globalising and interdependent world. Only through such international arrangements can the peoples of democratic states retain a credible degree of control over the economic, social and political processes that shape their lives and meet their moral obligation as democrats to uphold the equal value of the democratic rights of the peoples of states other than their own. However, I see no need for the EU or similar international organisations to detract from the sovereignty of the member states and their peoples – rather, they can and should help preserve such sovereignty and will be the more justifiable and effective for doing so. As such, the EU is best characterised as what I call a republican association of sovereign states, with calls that it acquire sovereign powers and become itself a locus of democratic authority misplaced, and more apt to detract from the efficacy and legitimacy of the EU than to enhance it. However, I regard Brexit as similarly misguided – a political and moral as well as an economic mistake of major proportions. These failings have been amply demonstrated by the sheer difficulty the Brexit negotiators have encountered in successfully unravelling the UK from either its moral commitments, especially towards Ireland, or its political and economic undertakings in areas as diverse as defence, scientific research and data protection. As various commentators have wryly remarked (e.g. Barker 2017), the need for the UK to renegotiate numerous trading agreements covering the entire economy, and the myriad problems of doing so from a position of comparative weakness, has meant that the UK's negotiations to leave the EU have at times borne a remarkable similarity to its earlier negotiations to join it.

This argument will no doubt annoy many EU sceptics and a certain type of EU Federalist in equal measure. I console myself with the thought that others (myself included) may think that suggests I've got matters about right. Nevertheless, I have greatly benefitted from conversations and comments from many fellow academics, both those more sceptical about the EU than I and those (the majority) who for the most part are more favourable to traditional forms of political integration than myself, although as critical in their own ways of the EU's current arrangements. I am especially grateful to my current and former UCL colleagues David Coen, Jeff King, Cécile Laborde, Christine Reh and Albert Weale for many discussions of different arguments that greatly improved my thinking. I also benefitted hugely from the events I was able to organise on EU affairs as Director of UCL's European Institute, and am grateful to Uta Staiger, the Institute's Executive Director, and Sir Stephen Wall, who Chaired its advisory board, for their invaluable efforts in helping set it up and arranging its programme. At the EUI, I am grateful for the support of my wonderful colleagues in the Max Weber team – especially Ognjen Aleksic, Francesca Grassini, Valeria Pizzini Gambetta and Karin Tilmans and, of course, the brilliant Fellows I had the privilege to get to know over the past five years. I discussed early versions of Chapters 3, 4 and 5 with different groups of PhD researchers in the Legal and Political Theory working group, especially Elias Buchetmann, Oliver Garner, Sofie Møller and Eleonora Milazzo. I also tried them out in two of the Thematic Research Groups of post doctoral Fellows in the Max Weber Programme I co-organised and got helpful feedback from many of the Fellows in them, including Guy Aitchison, Or Bassok, Juliana Bidadanure, Chiara Destri, Christina Fassone, Diane Fromage, Christine Hobden, Pablo Kalmanovitz, Hent Kalmo, Steven Klein, Zoe Lefkofridi, Julia McClure, Eric O'Connor, Andrei Poama, Julija Sardelic, Florian Stoeckel and especially Lior Erez, with whom I co-taught a course on Political Theory and the EU. I also benefitted from the acute observations of Philippe Van Parijs on these chapters during his period as a Visitor at the Institute and from Dennis Patterson and Stefan Grundmann on Chapter 3, Hanspeter Kriesi and Adrienne Héritier on Chapter 4, and Ann Thompson, Nehal Bhuta and Rainer Bauböck on Chapter 5. The Max Weber Programme also provides an unrivalled opportunity to invite some of the leading figures in the historical and social sciences to give guest lectures and to discuss their ideas with them. With regard to this project, I am particularly grateful for the possibility afforded by the Max Weber Lecture series to discuss certain issues relevant to the book with Tom Christiano, Barry Eichengreen, Jan Werner Müller, Kalypso Nicolaïdis, Claus Offe, Philip Pettit, Thomas Piketty, Dani Rodrik, Quentin Skinner and especially Philippe Van Parijs, who used the occasion to present his own stimulating views on 'Just Europe'.

Four of these Max Weber Lecturers had long influenced my thinking and offered support and encouragement for my endeavours. Quentin Skinner and Philip Pettit, whose neo-Republican theory of freedom as non-domination inspires my overall approach, have been helpful as ever, with Quentin offering comments on an early presentation of Chapter 3 at a conference in Milan and Philip on lectures based on Chapters 4 and 5 at conferences in York and Prague. I am likewise grateful to Tom Christiano for similar commentary on a presentation of Chapter 4 at a conference in Barcelona and for conversation on the general argument, which also draws on his own work on the democratic legitimacy of international institutions. Finally, Kalypso Nicolaïdis is another person to whom I owe a significant intellectual debt, with my 'republican intergovernmentalism' being a version of the approach she has called 'demoicracy'. I am additionally grateful to her for some very incisive comments on the Introduction and an insightful suggestion regarding the title.

I also benefitted greatly from cooperating with Kalypso and Joseph Lacey, her colleague at Oxford and a former EUI PhD researcher, on a project on 'Europe's Borders' that gave rise to Chapter 6. Collaboration on a number of pieces with Joseph also fed into my revisions of Chapters 1 and 5. Others who have offered thoughtful commentary on different chapters and related papers at seminars across Europe and beyond that have helped shape, and undoubtedly improve, my arguments include Daniele Archibugi, Kenneth Armstrong, Katrin Auel, Luca Baccelli, Samantha Besson, Paul Bou-Habib, Vittorio Bufacchi, Seyla Benhabib, Damian Chalmers, Simon Caney, Carlos Closa, Ian Cooper, Francis Cheneval, Paul Craig, Ben Crum, Deirdre Curtin, Marc-Antoine Dilhac, Erik Oddvar Eriksen, Sergio Fabbrini, Adam Fusco, Maurizio Ferrera, John Erik Fossum, Andreas Follesdal, Valentina Gentile, Oliver Gerstenberg,

Gabor Halmai, Christian Joerges, Anna Kocharov, Jeff King, Beate Kohler-Koch, Justine Lacroix, David Lefkowitz, Chris Lord, Martin Loughlin, Carole Lyons, Sebastiano Maffettone, Giandomenico Majone, José Martí, Andrew Mason, Agustín Menéndez, David Miller, Margaret Moore, Andrew Moravcsik, Glyn Morgan, Niamh Nic Shuibhne, David Owen, Markus Patberg, Johannes Pollak, Pierpaolo Portinaro, Simona Piattoni, Uwe Puetter, Claudio Radaelli, Mario Riccardi, Sonja Puntscher Riekmann, Miriam Ronzoni, Richard Rose, Enrico Rossi, Andrea Sangiovanni, Emilio Santoro, Joanne Scott, Fritz Scharpf, Waltraud Schelkle, Antoinette Scherz, Frank Schimmelfennig, Jo Shaw, Stephen Tierney, Nadia Urbinati, Laura Valentini, Richard Vernon, Daniel Viehoff, Juri Viehoff, Neil Walker, Thomas Winzen, Daniel Weinstock, Andrew Walton, Jonathan White Michael Wilkinson, and Andrew Williams. My apologies for any inadvertent omissions. Needless to say, none of those thanked are responsible for any of the weaknesses of the book, which are entirely my fault for paying insufficient attention to their advice and criticisms. However, without their critical engagement, it would have been far worse.

This book has taken rather longer than anticipated and I am grateful to Cambridge University Press and especially John Haslam and Tobias Ginsberg for their forbearance. It would have taken even longer without the assistance of Sarah Drew Lucas in knocking the manuscript into shape. I am also grateful for the helpful comments of referees on the initial proposal and a first draft.

Finally, two people deserve a special mention. As I noted above, much of my work on the EU has been undertaken with Dario Castiglione who, along with the late Neil MacCormick – who I had the privilege of working with at Edinburgh in the late 1980s and early 1990s, and was another significant influence on my thinking on this topic – first got me interested in these debates. This is now the second book that we have started writing together and that I have ended up doing alone, but as before Dario has continued nevertheless as a ghostly collaborator in the development of much of this argument, with core elements of Chapters 1 and 4 originating in pieces we wrote together. Last, but very far from least, my wife Sandra Kröger has sustained me throughout the composition of this book, offering much needed emotional and intellectual support. More of an expert on the EU than I, we've discussed pretty much all the book's arguments over the years and elements of Chapter 4 and much of Chapter 6 were developed in articles we wrote together. I owe her more than I can say. This book is dedicated to her in gratitude and love.

Introduction: Democratic Legitimacy and International Institutions – Cosmopolitan Statism, Republican Intergovernmentalism and the Demoicratic Reconnection of the EU

It's the Politics, Stupid

This book proposes an account of the democratic legitimacy of global institutions in general and of the European Union (EU) in particular. That may seem at best a thankless and at worst an impossible task at a time when such organisations have come under increasing attack for undermining democracy at the domestic level without adequately compensating for this loss at the supra- or trans-national level. Yet, the unprecedented opposition to these post-war forms of international cooperation makes a reassessment of not just their functional but also their normative justification all the more urgent.

The creators of what was then the European Community (EC) sought to legitimise integration indirectly, providing it with so-called 'output' legitimacy (Scharpf 1999: 6–13) through what the architect of this strategy, Jean Monnet, referred to as 'concrete achievements' in the form of desirable policies, notably an end to war and improved economic well-being (Müller 2011: 142). Though they hoped popular endorsement would follow from the success of European integration in securing peace and prosperity, their strategy was in many respects deliberately technocratic and non-democratic. On the one hand, it reflected a reinforced liberal distrust of democracy in the wake of the rise of fascism prior to World War II (Müller 2011: 128), with the EC seen as a mechanism for constraining demands for popular and national sovereignty that were widely blamed for the catastrophes of the first half of the twentieth century. On the other hand, while potential democratic opposition at the member state level was to be circumscribed in the short term, in the long term the hope was that increased economic cooperation would steadily create the conditions for democracy at the supranational, EC, level. However, although this strategy aimed at weakening the sovereignty of nation states and their peoples, the acceptance and success of the supranational promotion of economic liberalism depended to a large degree on the democratically created institutions of these self-same states providing social protection for the losers of enhanced inter-state market

1

competition (Ruggie 1982) As Robert Gilpin (1987: 359) famously put it, 'Smith abroad' was rendered acceptable and even possible through being embedded within 'Keynes at home' (Isiksel 2016: 173). The trouble has been that far from acquiring the political capacity for Keynes across borders, the EU has strengthened a neo-liberal (mis)reading (Winch 1978) of Smith at home and abroad.

The economic downturn and domestic adoption of new right policies in the late 1970s and 80s gradually placed the post-war compromise under strain, with a free-market and libertarian view of Smith abroad being matched with, and increasingly reinforcing, a similarly neo-liberal version of Hayek at home (King 1987). Meantime, the Maastricht Treaty and the completion of the Single Market and move to Monetary Union created a step change in the EU's fostering of economic liberalisation during the 1990s that limited the possibility for domestic intervention even further, not least due to the progressive constitutionalisation of the EU's market regulations by a proactive European Court of Justice (Alter 2001; Grimm 2016: ch. 14, 2017; Isiksel 2016). Labour mobility from the less to the more successful economies became the main instrument of European social policy (Ferrara 2014; Isiksel 2016: 175–9; Scharpf 2010: 238; Streeck 2014: 178). It is against this background, made worse by the Euro crisis, that the problem of the EU's democratic deficit came to the fore. The 'output' legitimacy of economic success backed by the rule of law could no longer substitute for the absence of 'input' legitimacy offered by democratic politics (Bellamy 2006, 2010).

Most discussions of the democratic shortcomings of the EU turn on exploring the prospects of the EU evolving into a directly elected democracy, in which EU level decision-makers are both representative of and responsive to EU citizens as a whole (e.g. Follesdal and Hix 2006; Habermas 2001, 2015). These analyses regard the creation of some form of global or regional democracy of either a supra- (Held 1995; Archibugi 2008) or a trans- (Pogge 1992; Bohman 2007) national kind as the logical response to the functional weakening of national-level democracy by global forces, and the only way to address its related normative shortcomings. However, such proposals fail to address the concerns of those who see such a shift of democratic authority to the supra- or trans-national level as not only impractical and unlikely, at least in the short term, but also undesirable and unnecessary. After all, if disappointment with the EU's supposed democratic deficiencies has undoubtedly driven much contemporary criticism of the EU, so has antagonism towards the very aspiration to create an EU wide democracy (Grimm 1995; Hooghe and Marks 2009).

As the failure to get popular assent to the proposed Treaty establishing a Constitution for Europe in 2005 had already indicated, many citizens perceive such a move as creating rather than addressing the EU's democratic deficit precisely because it constrains the capacity for democratic decision-making within the member states by the different peoples of Europe. Although significant national variations in the degree of Euroscepticism exist, the centrality of the perceived costs or benefits of membership to domestic politics in determining popular attitudes to the EU is a general phenomenon (Kriesi 2016; De Vries 2018). The more citizens regard the EU as displacing and diminishing rather than supplementing and enhancing democracy at the member state level, the greater the likelihood that they will be antagonistic towards it. The domestic context of support for or opposition to the EU cannot be ignored, therefore. Those subject to the EU's authority must see it as the proper forum for resolving certain of their conflicts and promoting a particular set of their concerns. Legitimacy of this kind cannot be achieved by assertions of its functional or moral necessity if these are themselves to some degree matters of dispute. Nor can it be legitimately imposed from above by stealth. To be regarded as a legitimate locus of authority, the EU must be capable of answering to the commonly avowed reasons and shared interests of those subject to its authority in ways that reach beyond their differences and disagreements. In exploring this possibility, this book will argue that the EU can achieve the necessary general acceptance of its appropriateness at the level of states and their peoples but not, or at least not to the same degree, at the level of individuals. Moreover, there are good functional and normative reasons for this lack of fit related to the existence and preservation of the value pluralism represented by the diverse, and frequently divergent, economic and political cultures of the various member states.

The resulting account of the EU, and of global governance more generally, tries to square the circle between those who advocate demo-cratising global or regional institutions so they are directly authorised by and accountable to individual citizens, and those who object that in so doing democracy at the level of the nation state gets unjustifiably dimin-ished. I shall argue that this impasse rests on a false dichotomy. Rather than subverting democracy at the national level, global institutions are in many respects vital to its continuing effectiveness and acceptability in an interconnected world. Nevertheless, such institutions do require demo-cratic input legitimacy and to be viewed as producing suitably legitimate outputs. However, they can acquire this legitimacy not by becoming themselves sources of democratic authority but through being under the democratically authorised and accountable control of the states that have established them and regulate their interactions through them. I call such an arrangement a republican association of sovereign states. Drawing on the republican notion of freedom as non-domination (Pettit 2012), I argue that citizens will only enjoy such freedom when the following two conditions are met (Pettit 2010a): first, domestic democratic institutions must ensure political authority within a state is under their equal influence and control; and second, the state must be part of an association of democratic states in which the rules governing their mutual relations are under the equal influence and control of the elected representatives of those states. My claim will be that an account of the EU that conforms to these two criteria will be capable of possessing input and output legitimacy of an appropriate and valuable kind commensurate with what people broadly and reasonably conceive as the legitimate role of the EU as a whole in a globalising world.

The rest of the book is concerned with advocating this international arrangement relative to those that argue for some form of supra- or transnational global or cosmopolitan democracy, and detailing its institutional requirements with reference to the EU. This introduction seeks to indicate what is at stake in this argument: why it is important, what motivates the approach I take, and how it might be best realised. It closes with some reflections on method concerning how normative theorising about political ideals needs to relate to empirical political realities, before giving an outline of the book.

Democratic Legitimacy and International Institutions

Two Challenges to National Democracy: Globalisation and Cosmopolitanism

As I detail in Chapter 1, the argument is framed in the context of two challenges to democracy at the level of the nation state: the functional challenge posed by globalisation and the moral challenge posed by cosmopolitanism. It has become a commonplace that globalisation has weakened the capacity for nation states to frame independent socio-economic and security policies. Democratic decision-making at the national level either cannot fully address, or can be partially undercut by, transnational processes, such as cross-border financial movements; international activities, such as those of criminal and terrorist organisations; and certain democratic decisions of other nations, such as the lowering of corporate taxation or the weakening of environmental controls; all of which can originate in other states yet operate across states. To differing degrees, depending on the policy and the capacity of the state involved, they need to cooperate with other states through international legal frameworks and organisations in order to regulate many economic and social processes effectively and to provide adequate systems of defence and policing.

At the same time, most moral systems recognise a cosmopolitan requirement to treat all individuals as moral equals, regardless of where they live or come from. Of course, they differ greatly as to what that entails and when it becomes a relevant consideration. Some moral theories view this requirement in more minimal and restrictive terms than others, yet all reasonable moral codes recognise that certain moral aims, such as the protection of persons from serious and widespread violations of human rights, the alleviation of dire poverty and the avoidance of environmental catastrophe as a result of climate change, are, in Thomas Christiano's words, 'morally mandatory' at the global level (Christiano 2012: 388). Given that these aims can only be met through widespread cooperation across the world, the relevant duties to fulfil them potentially fall on all individuals whatever state they may happen to belong to. Indeed, most states have signed up to addressing a significant number of these aims through international agreements such as the Charter of the United Nations, the Millennium Declaration of the United Nations, the United Nations Framework Convention on Climate Change and the founding documents of the GATT and WTO (Christiano 2012). Nevertheless, the very division of the world into different states has been seen as itself a source of injustice from a cosmopolitan point of view. Not only are the citizens of wealthier states born with great advantages compared to those of the very poorest states – a fact many regard as difficult to justify morally, not least because this wealth often originates from past injustices perpetrated by these same states, but also these already advantaged citizens may use their democratic influence to push their governments to exploit their state's greater economic power to maintain and even increase these inequalities.

Taken together, these two challenges pose the question of how far, if at all, state-based systems of democracy can operate effectively and morally? The defenders of national sovereignty can appear to deny the need to meet either challenge, making their proposals seem unrealistic and immoral as a consequence. Indeed, many supporters of Brexit and of President Trump have been characterised in just such terms. Consequently, taking state sovereignty as a starting point, as I wish to do, might seem a doomed enterprise that can only lead to impotence in the face of the first challenge and be a source of injustice with regard to the second. At the very least, such criticisms suggest, addressing the global challenge requires state-based governance be supplemented by global or regional institutions and agreements, such as the UN, NATO, the WTO, NAFTA and the EU, capable of coordinating concerted action at the international level and providing regional or global regulatory frameworks. Meanwhile, to meet the moral challenge involves states being constrained by international law, particularly international human rights law such as the European Convention on Human Rights, which entrench the relevant morally mandatory norms. To the extent such bodies require democratic legitimacy, that is most straight forwardly and appropriately provided directly, so that all citizens subject to their authority – regardless of whatever state they happen to belong to – have an equal say in their operation. Either way, state sovereignty cannot avoid being diminished, and with it democracy at the national level, and rightly so.

Although I agree that meeting the two challenges requires that states supplement and constrain their actions through international institutions and law, I disagree that this necessitates, either practically or morally, any diminution of state-based sovereignty and democracy. I lay out my argument for thinking so in Part 1 of the book. What follows briefly sketches what motivates my reasoning.

The Need for Democratic Legitimacy

At the heart of my account are a set of interrelated arguments concerning the inescapable need for democratic legitimacy, the conditions that support it, and, underlying both, the plurality of values as an inherent part of the human condition that any plausible or acceptable global and cosmopolitan theory has to accommodate (Bellamy 1999: 3–13).

What John Rawls (1993: 54–8) termed the 'fact of pluralism' – the complexity of social life, the wide variety of interests and life experiences of different people, the range of moral claims of different kinds we may make of each other, and the limits of our practical reasoning when attempting to reconcile the conflicting perspectives to which these may all give rise – means that issues of any intricacy that require a collective decision may produce reasonable disagreements. Such disagreements are reasonable because, given the fact of pluralism and the consequent incompleteness and partiality of each person's point of view, they can occur even when all concerned are exercising their judgement in a conscientious, rational and well-intentioned manner. The rationale for democracy rests on its offering a fair system for legitimately resolving these disagreements when collective decisions among a group of people are believed or prove to be necessary.

As will be elaborated in Chapters 1 and especially 2, the 'circumstances of disagreement' occasion the need for an account of legitimacy that is distinct from appeals to the common good or to justice *per se*. Technocratic claims to provide 'good governance', which have frequently been invoked in the EU context (e.g. Majone 1996, 1998, 2001), lack legitimacy in this regard, even when they are justified not just on grounds of market efficiency but also on the basis of rights (Eriksen and Fossum 2004). Rather, legitimacy so conceived describes a valid source of 'content-independent' moral duties for a person or persons to comply with the decisions that are directed at them (Christiano 2015: 983). Democracy serves as a legitimate political mechanism of this kind (Bellamy 2006). Because the democratic process of majority rule based on one person one vote provides people's different views and interests a fair hearing, regardless of who holds what view, without prejudging which is the right answer (May 1952), democracy enables individuals to resolve their disagreements about the common good and justice when making collectively binding decisions in ways they all can accept as legitimate and hence have an obligation to obey. It provides a form of public decision-making in which citizens can regard themselves as possessing an equal status, whereby all have a duty to recognise the right of everyone else to be treated with equal concern and respect.

The above argument indicates why an account of democratic legitimacy in the international sphere proves inescapable for addressing the two challenges. The functional pressures for some form of global governance and the cosmopolitan moral pressures to treat all individuals justly cannot of themselves determine how they might best be met. These are matters of reasonable disagreement, so that any response requires democratic legitimation. Before tackling these challenges, therefore, it is necessary to confront the prior question of what would be the most appropriate structures whereby such legitimacy might be obtained. Chapters 1 and 3 argue that state sovereignty offers a necessary context for a democratic process possessing the features needed for it to be non-dominating. In particular, it serves to turn its individual members into citizens of a demos, capable of conceiving themselves as a public with a broadly equal stake in the maintenance of certain public goods and able to deliberate about how to do so in an open and public way that treats them as equals. In different ways, I argue that supra- and trans-national schemes of democracy confront a two-fold difficulty in meeting the conditions for such a legitimate democratic process. As a result, I propose an alternative scheme of international democracy based around a democratically credible process of mutual agreement among the governmental representatives of the different demoi of sovereign states.

Two Difficulties for Supra- and Trans-National Democracy

Supranational schemes involve scaling up sovereign political authority beyond the state. By contrast, transnational schemes seek to disperse that authority across a variety of different political bodies operating below and across existing states in a manner that makes states redundant and avoids any political body possessing the attributes of sovereignty.[1] However, as I detail in Chapter 3, both schemes confront certain generic difficulties in constructing free and fair decision procedures that avoid domination.

First, to formulate collective decisions that treat the members of large and extremely heterogeneous populations impartially and equitably, in ways that avoid various problems of oppression either of or by minorities, will require highly complex and non-majoritarian democratic mechanisms – not least because not all individuals will have an equal stake in all global collective decisions (Christiano 2006, 2011b), a point I develop with regard to the EU in Chapter 6. Yet, this complexity can become itself a source of inefficiency, ineffectiveness and inequity, which lacks the quality of public equality that gives democracy its legitimacy (Miller 2009, 2010). It will be harder for decision-making not only to be legitimate in giving a fair hearing to all, but also, due to the epistemic difficulties confronting individuals in such a vast system, to be seen to be so by individual citizens (Dahl 1999; Christiano 2006: 104–5).

Second, the citizens of already existing democratic states often have long established and distinct histories of self-government, which have given rise to different and frequently divergent collective agreements that command broad legitimacy among those involved. Imperfectly to be sure, but to an unprecedented degree compared to previous political arrangements, democratic states have managed to promote some of the core purposes of a political community by providing their citizens not only with a minimal degree of peace and security but also a range of other benefits – from a system of justice capable of regulating and enabling social and economic life in ways that moderate coercion and unfairness, to a degree of public education and health, and so on. In many respects, this achievement can be attributed to the incentives democracy creates for rulers to promote the interests of the ruled in a broadly effective, efficient and above all equitable manner (Christiano 2011a). States differ greatly in the ways and extent to which they promote their citizens' collective interests. True, these differences are often illegitimate. As I noted in passing above, many instances of states offering far less to their citizens compared to other states result from the injustices the more developed states have inflicted on the less developed through various forms of past

---

[1] Note that, following Pogge (1992) and Bohman (2005), I employ 'transnational' to denote a way of organising power that stands in sharp contrast to 'international'. If the first cuts across all state borders, rendering them redundant, the second operates between state borders. As I show in Chs. 3 and 5, this distinction yields quite different characterisations of the structure of the EU and the nature of Union citizenship.

and present domination and exploitation: from war, invasion and colonisation, to the imposition of unfair trade agreements. Yet, this diversity also reflects the pluralism of human ideals and interests, and the plurality of ways people may choose to pursue them.

At this point, the two difficulties come together. The difficulty confronting any democratic system operating above or across already existing democracies at the regional or global level is not simply that of fairly representing all individuals within collective decisions in a meaningful way, but also, and at the same time, that of allowing them the space to develop a suitable variety of different forms of social, economic and cultural life that respect the plurality of both human goods and values and of the ways these might be combined and pursued. Supranational and transnational schemes find themselves on the horns of a dilemma in this regard, with supranational accounts potentially meeting the first difficulty only to fall foul of the second, and transnationalist accounts doing better with regard to the second but at the expense of the first.

Advocates of supranational democracy contend that in principle it would be feasible to address the problems posed by the first difficulty (Archibugi 2008, Koenig-Archibugi 2011, Valentini 2014). However, the potential feasibility *per se* of such schemes is not the only objection made here. Even if such arguments are correct, and I voice various doubts on that score in Chapters 3 and 4 in particular, that does not mean such a development is likely, at least in the foreseeable future (Zürn 2016), or – and more importantly – is desired or justified. For many people, the predictable and tangible costs of transition to such a system outweigh any prospective, putative benefits. No international organisation, not even the EU, provides anything like the range of public services and goods offered by contemporary democratic states. These settlements have come about over a very long period of time; invariably as a result of considerable internal political struggles to establish and improve state-based democratic systems. It is natural that citizens will fear that in transferring political authority for the structures of their community upwards, beyond their particular states, they will lose a degree of control over the scope and depth of what gets supplied to them.

The second difficulty enters here. The democratic processes of existing states have given rise to considerable diversity in their economic and social systems – too much to be adequately accommodated within common norms, rules and institutions, even at the regional level (Hall and Soskice 2001, and Chapter 6 of this book). This diversity reflects not only very different degrees and forms of social and economic development, but also different political cultures and traditions. Meanwhile, states that are socially and economically heterogeneous and/or contain significant cultural and national minorities have generally had to grant significant self-government rights to various territorial and even some non-territorially based groups to accommodate the resulting diversity of values and preferences of their citizens on an equitable basis (Kymlicka 1995, 2001). From this perspective, reconstituting democracy at the regional, let alone the global, level cannot but be a diminishment of democracy. It clashes with the democratic desire for self-government according to norms and within political institutions citizens can identify with as theirs. After all, such processes of political transformation have hitherto involved war and coercion, not least because people have an attachment to their existing political cultures.

Transnational schemes that disperse political authority horizontally, across existing states (e.g. Cohen and Sabel 2005; Bohman 2007), potentially fare better with regard to this second difficulty of allowing for diversity. But they too entail disaggregating already existing democratic systems, thereby also threatening the provision of the goods they provide to citizens. As I show in Chapters 3 and 4, by distributing decision-making authority across a wide range of different levels and functions, this approach exacerbates the first difficulty by undermining the capacity to frame collective policies that give due weight to different views and interests or to assign responsibility to any given decision maker for the combined effects of disparate decisions. Instead, decisions get made in discrete domains without consideration for their knock-on effects for other decisions in other domains because no single sovereign authority exists for considering them as a whole.

In both respects, therefore, the standard framing of the democratic shortcomings of organisations such as the EU in terms of a lack of direct democratic accountability to individual citizens emerges as fundamentally misconceived. On the one hand, it risks replacing reasonably equitable and legitimate state-based systems of political authority with a much more complex system that is likely to be less equitable or legitimate. On the other hand, this approach ignores the legitimacy that already existing democratic systems possess for their citizens, and the value their civic cultures may have for them as products of successive generations of democratic struggle and decision-making. None of which is to deny that democratic systems may lack legitimacy through their external as much as their internal exclusions. The challenge is to see whether the problems posed by these external exclusions can be addressed in a way that avoids the disadvantages I've suggested confront schemes for supra- and trans-national democracy.

International Democracy? Republican Intergovernmentalism and the Demoicratic Reconnection of the EU

Republican Intergovernmentalism

Accordingly, this book adopts a different perspective. Instead of focusing on the present or prospective possibility of supra- or trans-national organisations becoming sources of democratic authority in their own right, it explores their role in supporting, extending and improving the functioning and legitimacy of the democratic systems of their constituent polities. Rather than viewing global institutions as supplanting certain functions of their member states, I shall argue that we need to conceptualise them as shared mechanisms through which associations of sovereign states can mutually regulate their interactions in normatively justifiable ways – a conception of international governance I term 'republican intergovernmentalism' (Bellamy 2013).

As I argue in Chapter 2, a democratic system that possesses the qualities needed for decision-making to be regarded by those involved as legitimate can be regarded as non-dominating in the 'republican' sense by ensuring legal and political authority is under the equal influence and control of those subject to it (Pettit 1997, 2012). The opening section of Chapter 5 indicates how the welfare democracies that emerged in western Europe post-1945 can be regarded as approximating such a republican regime. They established a degree of relational equality among citizens with regard not only to the process of making collective decisions but also the substance of the decisions themselves, not least through mitigating the inequalities that can result from market transactions through public systems of social security, health and education. However, in ways I noted earlier, a state may meet the threshold conditions for a non-dominating political system internally, but be dominated or itself dominate externally through a failure to address either the globalisation or the cosmopolitan challenges. In an interconnected world, involving multiple forms of mutual dependency resulting from the global challenge, external domination becomes ever more likely and possible, rendering the need to address the cosmopolitan challenge ever more urgent.

I shall argue that a republican association of sovereign states can overcome these problems through institutionalising a practice of consensual agreements among democratic states, in which governments must act credibly as the democratic representatives of their respective peoples and are under a moral duty to treat each other with mutual concern and respect on that account. The aim is for international decision-making to achieve the dual goal of avoiding governments dominating the citizens of the state they represent, on the one side, or the citizens of other states with which they interact, on the other side. In so doing, they can simultaneously meet republican criteria for non-domination both internally and externally when making collective agreements to regulate their interactions, including the possibility for citizens to move freely among the states of the association, and to secure justice and common goods at the regional or global level.

Demoicracy and the Democratic Disconnect

Part 2 sketches the institutional requirements of decision-making within such an association, taking the EU as a case study. I align 'republican intergovernmentalism' with what has been called 'demoicracy' (Nicolaïdis 2004). That is, it involves a form of democratic international governance among different peoples rather than the creation a supranational people (see Nicolaïdis 2013, with Lacey 2016 and Ronzoni 2017 offering useful overviews of the different versions of demoicracy). In my version, these demoi are located in states and their regions rather than formed of various hypothetical, and as yet largely artificially constructed (Kohler-Koch 2011; Kröger 2016), transnational groups (as in Bohman's 2005 scheme). Chapters 3 and 4 seek to show how republican intergovernmental decision-making among different demoi addresses the two difficulties with legitimate democratic decision-making at the international level that I identified earlier. Sovereign states provide a context that overcomes the first difficulty so that governments can coherently be said to represent their respective peoples, while democratically authorised and accountable intergovernmental decision-making overcomes the second difficulty in showing equal concern and respect to the diverse collective decisions made by different demoi.

So conceived, international organisations should not aim at becoming the focus of a larger democratic community in their own right, with their own demos. Rather, their purpose is to allow different democratic communities, each with their own demoi, to co-exist on mutually agreed and equitable terms. As such, these international organisations have to remain subordinate to their constituent members as a delegated authority under their joint and equal control. The problem of democratic legitimacy thereby changes from being one of a democratic deficit at the supranational level to that of a democratic disconnect between the peoples of the constituent states and the inter- and multi- national decisions their domestic representatives make in their name, including the creation and control of international regulatory bodies operating, like the EU, at the supranational level (Lindseth 2010: 234). Chapter 4 in particular explores how this disconnect might be overcome through the empowerment of national parliaments in intergovernmental decision-making.

Meeting the Two Challenges: Rodrick's Trilemma and Cosmopolitan Statism

Can such a demoicratic association of sovereign states meet the two challenges? I believe it can, albeit in slightly different terms to standard schemes for global and cosmopolitan democracy. In particular, this account seeks to advance on an equal basis the common good of individuals as citizens of different states rather than as individuals *per se*, but in so doing it shows equality of concern and respect for the various reasonable ways that different peoples have come to combine the plural interests and values pursued by human beings.

The global challenge can be formulated in terms of what Danni Rodrik has designated as 'the fundamental political trilemma of the world economy' (Rodrik 2011: xviii). Rodrik's trilemma concerns the impossibility of pursuing simultaneously democracy, national self-determination, and economic globalisation – one of these has to give (Rodrik 2011: xix, 200–5). As he explains – 'If we want to maintain and deepen democracy, we have to choose between the nation state and international economic integration. And if we want to keep the nation state and self-determination, we have to choose between deepening democracy and deepening globalisation' (Rodrik 2011: xix, 200).

It might appear that attempting to deepen democracy at the nation state level by trying to manage economic globalisation through a demoicratic association of sovereign states proposes doing precisely what Rodrick suggests is impossible. However, the alternative to going fully global need not be an even more impractical and objectionable retreat into national autarchy and the unbridled pursuit of national self-interest. Instead, the republican intergovernmental approach allows for what Rodrick calls 'smart globalisation', of a kind he contends characterised J. M. Keynes' design for the Breton Woods system after the war (Rodrik 2011: xix, ch. 4, and see Streeck 2014: 185–8 for a proposal to remodel EMU in these terms). It offers mechanisms that allow the associated states to regulate their interactions and cooperate in ways that reduce the transaction costs of international trade and support collective goods at the global or regional level, while at the same time being able to place a constraint on the type and extent of globalisation by allowing for variations in domestic economic policy that reflect the divergent economic and social circumstances of different states and their diverse democratic choices. Chapter 6 explores the advantages and demoicratic legitimacy of this approach through an examination of differentiated integration within the EU.

Republican intergovernmentalism also acknowledges the moral obligations following from the cosmopolitan challenge. A demoicratic association of this kind institutionalises what in Chapter 1 I designate as a 'cosmopolitan statism' – that is, a form of international governance in which states evince a cosmopolitan regard for the citizens of other states by treating them as moral equals to their own citizens. The claim is that is best achieved in a democratically legitimate manner by an appropriately structured two-level, demoicratic approach to international decision-making. A key point is that this moral equality is not between individuals who lie outside any political community but between individuals as citizens of different political communities. On this argument, even basic human rights are properly conceived as the entitlements of citizens rather than of individuals pure and simple. For, given these rights can be defined and secured in a reasonable manner in a number of different ways, the right to legitimately claim rights only comes through being a citizen of a suitably democratic political community (Bellamy 2007, 2012). Yet, that makes access to such political arrangements a right of all individuals – the right of rights. Therefore, all states have a moral obligation to uphold this right not only internally, by ensuring their domestic decision-making is adequately democratic, but also externally, by respecting and supporting the democratic structures of other states and the access of stateless persons to them. As such, they have a duty to establish suitable 'republican intergovernmental' mechanisms, with a responsibility to support this right either directly, in the manner of the European Convention on Human Rights (ECHR; on which see Bellamy 2014), or indirectly as the EU – bound as it is by its own Charter of Fundamental Rights – ideally should do.

A sympathetic critic might argue that 'republican intergovernmentalism' need only serve as a transitory stage towards more encompassing supra- or trans-national arrangements. So conceived, it would be best seen as part of what Christiano (2016: 222) calls a 'progressive cosmopolitan' involving a form of what Lea Ypi (2008a) has termed state cosmopolitanism, in which states act as agents of cosmopolitan reforms. As both Christiano and Ypi have argued, it could be justified as practically warranted to overcome the two difficulties mentioned above, yet be compatible with the achievement over time of a transition to a full-blown cosmopolitan democracy that all those subject to it regard as legitimate. The EU has often been viewed in such teleological terms. However, I shall contend there are principled reasons for avoiding such a transition linked to the incentives provided by an association of sovereign states towards promoting diversity and non-domination among its members. Contrary to what both many Europhiles as well as Eurosceptics believe, I shall also argue that the EU shares numerous features of such a republican association of states, and need not be regarded as some form of super- or post-state in the making. Nevertheless, the beliefs of supporters of Brexit notwithstanding, domestic democratic control within an interconnected world can *only* be retained within some sort of international institutional arrangement of this kind. Outside such an association neither of the two challenges can be met. Any hope of controlling global social and economic processes and inter-state interactions in a democratically legitimate manner will be lost, and with it the ability to realise either justice or rights (Bellamy 2018).

A Republican Europe of Sovereign States as a Realistic Utopia

The proposal that we should (re)conceive the EU, along with other forms of global and regional governance, as a republican association of sovereign states is developed in the spirit of what Rawls called a Realistic Utopia – that is, as 'an achievable social world' that nonetheless 'extends what are ordinarily thought of as the limits of practical possibility' (Rawls 1999: 6). That is not to deny that many features of the EU as it currently is, as with other international institutions, cannot be accommodated to this model, or that those aspects that can be conceived in these terms frequently fail at present to work as well as they might. The argument is merely that the EU, and global and regional institutions more generally, could and should be so understood, and reformed accordingly. Nevertheless, in seeking to show the feasibility of this proposal by relating it to a detailed discussion of the EU as it actually exists, some critics might accuse this approach of sacrificing utopianism to realism. Yet, in suggesting the EU and similar international institutions be reformed to meet certain normative ideals, other critics might contend it lacks realism and is too utopian. In this section, I briefly respond to both criticisms. I shall contend that political ideals cannot be imagined or coherently formulated without addressing the political realities that have made them conceivable and prove necessary to their realisation, while these political realities cannot be adequately described without reference to the political ideals that partly constitute them. Moreover, without mixing utopianism with realism, political proposals can never attain legitimacy – they depart too far from the concerns and preferences of people in the here and now.

Rawls aimed to follow Rousseau's opening thought in the *Social Contract* of 'taking men as they are and laws as they might be' (Rawls

1999: 7). To a degree, I adopt a similar line of thinking and likewise move from an existing system of states and their peoples to imagining a desirable set of institutional arrangements that might regulate their interactions. This exercise is sometimes characterised as a matter of balancing an ideal of the just society against the prevailing constraints of currently existing reality (Cohen 2003; Valentini 2012b: 658). However, since these constraints include many injustices, critics of this approach claim such realism involves too many concessions to the status quo. For example, Rawls's account of the law of peoples, which inspires certain features of the view of the EU proposed here, has attracted precisely this criticism and been charged with idealising, and thereby legitimising, an outmoded 'Westphalian' model of international justice in consequence (Buchanan 2000). Such critics suggest we should conceive of ideals independently of such contingent facts, only ruling out at a subsequent stage ideals that would be literally infeasible in any plausible human world – either because they involve logically incompatible demands or defy our best understanding of what might ever be possible given what we know about human nature and the natural world, such as travelling faster than the speed of light. Ideals so conceived serve as benchmarks for the evaluation of current social and political arrangements, to which real-world constraints can be factored in when considering how one might move from the non-ideal to the ideal (Estlund 2014).

By contrast, other critics accuse Rawls and those who follow him of not being realistic enough (Williams 2005). They argue that he overlooks a key aspect of human nature that is relevant to thinking about justice – the fact that we reasonably disagree about its nature and terms. Moreover, they contend that such disagreement leads to a need to tackle a number of intrinsically political issues related to achieving peace, security and legitimacy (Waldron 1999: 102; Sangiovanni 2008). These issues prove more fact dependent, since they cannot be satisfactorily addressed without taking into account factors such as people's beliefs, selfishness, corruptibility and actually existing power relations. For these realist critics, the Rawlsian preoccupation with justice, along with certain idealising assumptions he holds in formulating his account of it, such as full compliance, result in his appealing to unrealistic moral standards for judging contemporary societies. These offer little if any guidance for how we should act in a less than ideal present, while ignoring the political sources of much oppression (Valentini 2012b: 658–60).

A realistic utopia clearly needs to avoid the twin dangers highlighted by these critiques of being either so close to existing reality as to inadvertently justify injustice by adopting an uncritical status quo bias, or too utopian and appealing to contentious and implausible ideal standards that have little purchase on how we might tackle injustice, not least by ignoring the political circumstances in which we must confront such questions (Ypi 2010). As it happens, I believe neither set of criticisms applies to Rawls's theory. However, my concern here is not to defend Rawls's views so much as to advocate a general approach inspired by his work that builds reflectively on the principles of legitimacy immanent in the public culture of democratic societies, on the one hand, and of those international institutions, such as the EU, governing their mutual relations, on the other.

As I argue in Chapter 2, and have already noted above, legitimacy takes priority over considerations of justice because, as realists typically note, conflicts of interest and differing points of view generate disagreements about the nature of justice. As a result, a need arises for impartial political structures that allow individuals to reach collective decisions about justice despite disagreeing, and that can secure the rights resulting from these decisions in a stable fashion. To provide the peace and stability justice requires, these political structures will need to be accepted as legitimate by the individuals subject to them. As not only Rawls (1993) but also his realist critic Bernard Williams remarked (2005: 10), within modern societies, characterised by a high degree of value and social pluralism, the most likely candidate to gain such acceptance is some form of political liberalism that conceives citizens as free and equal, and obliged to relate fairly towards each other within a scheme of social cooperation. The related notions of freedom, equality and fairness belong to the public political cultures that have emerged historically within liberal democratic states, such as those that comprise the member states of the EU. As a result, these values need not – and probably could not – be presented as timeless or foundational metaphysical truths. Indeed, they have been cashed out in a variety of ways within the diverse public cultures of different liberal democracies. However, they have a common focus in referring to the relations among individual citizens who together form a demos through being subject to the power of a particular state. In other words, as I argue in Chapter 3, political legitimacy so conceived proves intrinsically related to the necessity of being subject to the sovereign authority of a state. A sovereign political authority makes politics possible: that is, it makes possible the resolution of disagreements in a political way, rather than through either the application of pure force or by assuming all will somehow agree on, and defer to, the 'right' point of view.

As many commentators have pointed out, a distinctive feature of the EU lies in its *not* being a super state (Weiler 1998b). It has polity-like characteristics but does not itself possess sovereignty or coercive, as opposed to persuasive, powers. These latter remain with the member states, which implement EU decisions. Consequently, I follow Rawls

(1999; Rawls and Van Parijs 2003) in regarding the EU as being, as the Treaty on European Union puts it, a union among 'the peoples of Europe'. Therefore, the focus for a theory of legitimacy for the EU is not the provision of fair terms of cooperation among free and equal individual citizens but among free and equal peoples. Moreover, given these peoples are not themselves subject to a single coercive power, these terms have a different scope to those at the domestic level. In particular, they constrain a cosmopolitan or, in this case, a European egalitarianism that looks to a global or a European redistribution among individuals or the formation of a global or a European *demos*. For in this account, individuals will always figure as citizens of particular states, with this status – as is the case with Union citizenship – mediating their relationship to any inter- or supra-national organisation and to the citizens of other contracting states within it (Sangiovanni 2007).[2]

It will be objected that this approach falls foul of the charge of conservatism noted above. However, to ask what renders a state system such as we know it legitimate is not by any means to regard everything existing states do as meeting these criteria. Not only can states be criticised for failing to live up to the acknowledged standards regulating the system, but also the implications of these standards can be developed in radical ways that extend existing practices. As Rawls noted (1971: 20–1), the process of philosophical reflection he termed 'reflective equilibrium' operates in just this fashion by first systemising and developing the general principles that lie behind our firm convictions with regard to relatively settled particular cases, such as the obligation of states to observe their treaties and undertakings or not to go to war for reasons other than self-defence, and then extending them to those less settled cases where we seek guidance, in the case he considers to 'a duty of assistance' to help societies burdened by natural disasters or dire poverty (Rawls 1999: 35–43). For reasons expounded in Chapter 2, I follow Philip Pettit (2014) in suggesting that a particularly compelling way of characterising how the core values of freedom, equality and fairness cohere as features of both domestic and international political legitimacy is in terms of the republican notion of freedom as non-domination. Yet, as I try to show in Chapters 4–6, while this provides a lens that makes sense of certain salient

---

[2] In Cheneval 2008, 2011 and Cheneval and Schimmelfennig 2013, Francis Cheneval has argued that demoicrats should modify Rawls 1999 to include individual citizens as well as state peoples. However, for the reasons just given, I regard this modification as inappropriate and to a degree redundant. After all, peoples are constituted and limited by a contract among individuals, which carries over into any subsequent agreement among these peoples so that any association of state peoples must show equal concern and respect for the rights of the individual citizens of its members. I explore this reasoning further in Ch. 5.

normative features of international arrangements in general, and of the EU in particular, it can also be extended into supporting more extensive obligations associated with ensuring all peoples can be self-governing and guarantee citizenship to their members.

Nevertheless, some will protest that the statist starting point rules out the possibility of the EU either itself becoming a state (Mancini 1998; Morgan 2005) or providing a model of a post-state and post-sovereignty form of political association (MacCormick 1999; Bohman 2004b). In Chapter 3 in particular, I offer both empirical and normative reasons for questioning the plausibility and desirability of both these possibilities. Concentrating coercive power at the regional, let alone the global, level has long been regarded as raising issues of feasibility and the risks that such a supranational political authority will be too remote to be either effective and efficient, not least by being insufficiently attentive to local peculiarities, or able to adequately represent or be influenced and controllable by a diverse and plural population. As I noted in the previous section, it also ignores the value the public cultures of different political and juridical orders possess for those subject to them, the role such diversity can play in stimulating competition and comparisons that promote innovation and best practice, as well as offering choices to individuals and checks and balances on the deployment of power by these orders over each other and their respective citizens (Rawls 1999: 36; Kant 1796: 113–14). Dispersing sovereignty might be thought to offer these advantages. However, it is unclear that a completely horizontal distribution of power could provide individuals with peace and security or assure them of a coherent set of basic rights across all social domains. Such a system also has difficulty explaining any of the basic concepts of existing international law, all of which assume states – even human rights conventions aimed at defending a set of universal individual entitlements – do so by virtue of encouraging conformity to certain standards on the part of domestic legal systems. As soon as it is accepted that individuals necessarily belong to particular coercive orders, then it will be impossible to specify an individual's basic rights and liberties without reference to his or her location within a particular sovereign territory (Wenar 2006: 106–10).

Given these constraints, I shall argue it becomes hard to conceive of the EU as a realistic utopia other than as an association of sovereign states. However, that does not mean that such an association need operate only at the margins. Assuring fair cooperation among states and their citizens in ways consistent with their peoples being non-dominated involves encouraging considerably more mutual respect and deliberation among their different demoi than typically exists at present. Indeed, I shall argue that only an organisation possessing many of the features of the EU can make this possible, although it requires a number of reforms to be fully legitimate.

Plan of the Book

In developing this argument I bring together three different literatures. The first consists of the normative literature on global justice and democracy, characterised by the debate between statists and cosmopolitans. The second comprises the literature on European integration, and most particularly the theories of liberal intergovernmentalists and neo-functionalists. The third involves the growing body of work exploring the contribution of a republicanism grounded in a conception of liberty as non-domination (Pettit 1997, 2014; Skinner 1998) to both these literatures.

While, broadly speaking, statism gets related to liberal intergovernmentalism and cosmopolitanism to neo-functionalism, neither normative theory is presented, or should be understood, as simply the ideological rationalisation of the corresponding explanatory theory. Rather, linking the two sorts of theory highlights the degree to which ideal theories often draw on certain empirical assumptions, on the one hand, and real world theories make ideal assumptions about the ideational motivations of various actors, on the other. To paraphrase Kant (1781, 1787: 193–4), if ideal theories without some real assumptions would be 'empty', real theories lacking any ideal assumptions would be 'blind'. Bringing the two together supports a certain systematisation of broadly held ideals through reflection on whether and, if so, how they can be understood to have credible and desirable implications when applied to empirically plausible circumstances.

Republicans agree on the need to situate the achievement of distributive justice within a broader understanding of political justice (Laborde and Ronzoni 2015), a point developed in Chapter 2. However, they can be found in both the statist and cosmopolitan camps and espouse correspondingly diverse views of the EU (compare Bellamy 2013, with the supranationalist and transnational accounts of Marti 2010 and Bohman 2004b respectively). Hitherto, republican accounts of the EU and global justice more broadly have tended to develop what Pettit (2012: 12) calls, albeit somewhat contentiously (Bellamy 2016), the Italian-Atlantic tradition of Machiavelli and Madison (e.g. Fabbrini 2007; Ladvas and Chryssochoou 2011; Bohman 2004a). The position developed here is distinctive in defending what Pettit identifies as the alternative Rousseau-Kant tradition of republicanism and the link it makes between non-domination and popular and state sovereignty (Pettit 2012: 12–17). However, as I indicated above, I do so in ways that serve to bring together both statism and cosmopolitanism in a position I dub 'cosmopolitan statism', on the one hand, and liberal intergovernmentalism and neofunctionalism in a version of 'demoicracy', which is often seen as a 'third way' between these two, I term 'republican intergovernmentalism', on the other. The result is a position of broadly Kantian inspiration that sees what Kant termed 'a system of public right' as the product of a balance between domestic right, or the right of a state over its citizens; international right, or the rights of states vis-à-vis each other and their mutual relations; and cosmopolitan right, or the rights individuals can claim on grounds of humanity alone (Kant 1797: 136–7).[3] On this view, cosmopolitan right only becomes conceivable through the domestic right of sovereign states, which implies in its turn both international right and cosmopolitan right to be fully just (Flikschuh 2010: 487). Developing this account within the languages of contemporary political theory and political science, and updated to address our present circumstances, I shall argue that the EU is best seen – both normatively and practically – as an association of sovereign states that seek both internally, in their domestic arrangements, and externally, in their interactions with each other and the citizens of other states, to govern their relations in terms of the republican norm of non-domination.

The book elaborates this argument in two main steps. In Part 1, the normative literature predominates. Chapters 1–3 serve to develop the general argument that we should conceive organisations such as the EU in terms of an association of sovereign states, which have as their basic raison d'être to secure a condition of non-domination within and between their respective peoples. Chapter 1 compares statist and cosmopolitan arguments and tentatively argues for a mixed account I call cosmopolitan statism in which states recognise certain cosmopolitan obligations towards each other. Chapter 2 then relates the debate between statism and cosmopolitanism to a republican concern with legitimacy and non-

---

[3] Of course, there are many cosmopolitans who adopt avowedly neo-Kantian views (e.g. Beitz 1979 and Moellendorf 2002), though they tend to depart from Kant in regarding cosmopolitan right as incompatible with international right. Meanwhile, it is also true that in *Perpetual Peace* Kant is ambivalent over whether he regards international right as best institutionalised by a coercive supra-state authority or a voluntary federation of states (Kleingeld 2004). I am not qualified to enter into the details of Kantian scholarship and interpretation and fortunately need not do so. It suffices to note that I follow the interpretation of Flikschuh (2010) and Stilz (2009) on this matter, and the emphasis they place on the 'Doctrine of Right' (in Kant 1797), but elaborate it – most especially in Ch. 3 – in my own terms as an independent argument capable of being detached from its Kantian origins.

domination. I shall contend that the conflicts of interests and values associated with the fact of pluralism, along with the reasonable disagreements that result from them mean that we cannot avoid putting politics first. As a result, cosmopolitanism cannot but be statist in the sense of assuming a suitable institutional framework. At the same time, it becomes necessary to determine the normative qualities a suitable set of political institutions need to possess for them to provide a legitimate forum for individuals to debate and decide on the rules of justice that should regulate their interactions with each other. This chapter then defends the republican notion of non-domination as providing the requisite normative standard.

Chapter 3 closes Part 1 by exploring which set of institutional arrangements might best support non-domination in the context of the EU, or more generally globally, and argues against both a supranational state and the transnational dispersal of sovereignty, and in favour of an association of sovereign states. A cosmopolitan statism capable of sustaining non-domination among citizens and states requires democracy within states and mutual respect for the demoi of other states, with international agreements meeting the normative standards of a two-level game. Parallel considerations also govern the relationship between the EU's legal order and the national constitutions and legal systems of the member states, while qualifying arguments for a global or cosmopolitan constitutionalism more generally. Notwithstanding judicial doctrines of the primacy and direct effect of EU law, I shall argue that the EU legal order is best understood as having been created in accordance with, and being subject to, the constitutional requirements of its constituent parts, and periodically reviewable by them (Grimm 2016: ch. 13). As such, it should not, and need not, be conceived as an encompassing supranational legal order of an analogous kind to the constitution of a sovereign power, as a number of legal scholars have believed necessary (Mancini 1998; Lenaerts and Gerard 2004; von Bogdandy 2005). It has a different function and basis (Weiler 1999; Eleftheriadis 2007). At the same time, it does not presage a new kind of transnational cosmopolitan legal order either – at least, not one that can be detached from its basis in the domestic and international order of sovereign states which gives rise to it and renders it feasible, as has also been suggested (e.g. Kumm 2009).

Chapter 3 concludes by offering four criteria that such an association of sovereign states should satisfy. First, the associated states must be democratic states, which meet a threshold of non-domination in their domestic political and legal arrangements, and their mutual relations must be non-dominating of their domestic systems. Second, as a result, their joint governance arrangements must not only be established according to norms that are equally agreeable to both the state governments and to each of the peoples they represent, but also embody this dual requirement in their normal functioning. Third, the various states should avoid dominating the citizens of the other states, not least in allowing them to move freely between them without discrimination, provided they show equal concern and respect to each other's systems of domestic governance. Finally, such arrangements are voluntary. They reflect a moral obligation on the part of each of the associated states that follows from their claim to moral authority over their citizens by virtue of securing their equal freedom through the provision of an appropriate civic order. As such, the involvement of a democratic state in any international association of states ought to reflect its interest and capacity to participate with other states on equal terms in the production of suitable collective goods. Consequently, most associations will involve a degree of differentiation in the involvement of states.

Part 2 shifts the emphasis to the analysis of the EU and to the literature on European integration, and explores how far the EU does and could meet these four criteria. As I outlined in the opening section, linking the normative argument of Part 1 for a particular form of cosmopolitan statism to an appropriate account of European integration leads to a position I term 'republican intergovernmentalism'. On this view, a legitimate EU requires that member states possess a democratic system of a kind that keeps governments under the equal influence and control of their citizens, even in the area of foreign affairs, and that governments negotiate with each other in ways that oblige both each other and those they represent 'to hear the other side', as the republican slogan puts it, in ways that promote mutual respect for each other's right to self-government. So conceived, a 'republican intergovernmentalism' belongs to the family of theories Kalypso Nicolaïdis has called demoicratic, which view the EU as a '[U]nion of peoples who govern together but not as one' (Nicolaïdis 2013: 351). This position is not federalist in the sense commonly evoked in political debates about the EU, especially in the UK, to suggest a concentration of certain key sovereign powers at the EU level that have a hierarchical supremacy over those held at lower levels and that are directly accountable to EU citizens. However, it can be aligned to a much broader federal position, associated with Kant (1796: 102–4) among others, whereby states can and should create formal political and legal mechanisms for the regulation of their mutual interactions without ceding sovereignty to them (Kant 1797: 165).

Chapter 4 describes how the institutions comprising the EU's system of decision-making might be understood and partly reformed to meet the first two criteria, stressing the role national parliaments in particular can play within it. Chapter 5 notes how many features of EU citizenship as currently configured support the third criteria. Suitably developed, this status offers a practical response to many cosmopolitan criticisms of a statist perspective that appears to uphold the arbitrary advantages or disadvantages stemming respectively from birth into a stable and wealthy country or an unstable and poor one. Freedom of movement within an association of sovereign states can preserve the integrity of national citizenship while removing certain injustices that derive from its inherently exclusionary nature. It also has implications for how such an association should treat third country nationals, and in particular refugees in the context of the current migration crisis. Chapter 6 then explores how the EU can meet the fourth criteria. It provides a demoicratic justification for the already existing elements of instrumental, constitutional and legislative differentiated integration as normatively required for collective decision-making to be fair, impartial and equitable given the high degree of both socio-economic and political-cultural heterogeneity between the member states. This chapter also tackles what might be thought to be a major challenge to this account stemming from those legal scholars who claim that EU law has to be uniform and equal for all, a requirement inherent to the 'acquis communautaire' – the body of common rights and obligations that is binding on all the EU member states and to which they must accede and be capable of fulfilling to join the EU. I contest this view and offer an alternative demoicratic account of EU law drawing on the tradition of political constitutionalism (Bellamy 2007). I conclude by addressing the challenge of the Euro crisis. I argue that it serves as a cautionary tale of ignoring the heterogeneity of the EU that generates the demand for differentiated integration and produces the requirement for demoicratic structures to provide the EU with legitimacy. Rejecting calls for both fiscal and political union, I suggest ways whereby monetary union can be reconciled with retaining fiscal policy at the member state level.

In keeping with the Rawlsian notion of a realistic utopia described above, the resulting account of the EU seeks to be able to make sense of many aspects of the EU as it is, while offering an attractive and plausible account of how it could be, one that extends many of its underlying principles. The conclusion offers an indication of some of the advantages of this approach by outlining how it provides a response to the legitimacy problems raised by the growing 'constraining dissensus' (Hooghe and Marks 2009) within the populations of the member states, of which the vote for Brexit was the most extreme example.

Part 1

Cosmopolitanism, Statism and
Republicanism: Democracy, Legitimacy and
Sovereignty

1   Cosmopolitism and Statism: Global Interdependence and National Self-Determination

Introduction

Two apparently contradictory trends characterise contemporary European politics. On the one hand, there has been both a widening of the EU to include the countries of central and Eastern Europe, and increasingly the Baltic and the Balkans as well, and calls for its deepening – especially in the wake of the Euro crisis – with greater political unification promoted in many quarters as a necessary complement to monetary union and the single market. On the other hand, there are growing pressures towards devolution and secession within many established states as minority national groups in Scotland, Catalonia and elsewhere reassert a desire for self-determination. There is also mounting disaffection towards the EU across Europe, with rising support for Eurosceptical populist and radical parties of both the right, such as the UK Independence Party, Alternative für Deutschland, the Lega, and the Front National, and the left, such as Syriza and Podemos – a trend that has culminated in the recent UK referendum to leave the EU.

This second trend often gets compared somewhat negatively to the first, to which it is seen as an anachronistic and regressive reaction. From this perspective, the second trend represents an ultimately doomed attempt to escape the realities and obligations of an ever more interconnected world associated with the first trend, and to withdraw into the parochial and divisive nationalisms of the past. This analysis has both an empirical and a related normative aspect, reflecting respectively what I referred to in the Introduction as the functional and the moral challenges, whereby the process of globalisation raises the need and possibility for more global forms of legal and political organisation grounded in cosmopolitan principles that recognise the equal moral status of all individuals, regardless of their national, ethnic, religious or cultural affiliations (Held 1995). The move towards greater European integration is alleged to reflect this new reality. The EU may often fail to meet these emerging global challenges and cosmopolitan ideals, but for a number of its most prominent political and academic advocates it is the belief that only a body such as the EU has the potential to do so effectively that provides the best rationale for the integration process.

The empirical and functional aspect of this way of thinking was well expressed by the former President of the European Council, Herman von Rompuy, when asked his opinion on what was then only a proposed referendum on Scottish independence:

Nobody has anything to gain from separatism in the world of today which, whether one likes it or not, is globalised . . . We have so many important challenges to take and we will only succeed if we can pool forces, join action, take common directions. The global financial crisis is hitting us hard. Climate change is threatening the planet. How can separatism help? The word of the future is union. (von Rompuy 2012)

In a similar vein, the philosopher Jürgen Habermas has remarked how, in his view, 'financial markets' and 'more generally, the functional systems of world society, whose influence permeates national borders, are giving rise to problems that individual states, or coalitions of states, are no longer able to master' (Habermas 2012: xi). As a result of this 'need for regulation' on a global scale, he contends 'the *international* community of states must develop into a *cosmopolitan* community of states and world citizens' (Habermas 2012: xi).

As Habermas's remark indicates, the empirical and functional aspect of the integrative thesis has been considered as intimately associated with the normative and moral aspect. This position has also figured prominently in the discourse of EU officials. For example, former President of the European Commission José Barroso declared at a seminar on 'Global Constitutionalism':

The present crisis has shown the limits of individual action by nation states. Europe and the principles of the Treaty need to be renewed. We need more integration, and the corollary of more integration has to be more democracy. This European renewal must represent a leap in quality and enable Europe to rise to the challenges of the world today by giving it the tools it needs to react more effectively and to shape and control the future. (Barroso 2012)

In other words, he contends the functional need for more integration has as its by-product a moral spill-over that both allows for and requires more democratic decision-making at the European and ultimately at the global level. On this account, global problems can only be legitimately tackled by invoking global norms, that themselves imply enhanced global legal and democratic arrangements. The EU provides the most developed example at the regional level of such a supra- and post-national arrangement. Once again, Habermas provides a good academic example of this line of argument. He maintains the very idea of human rights involves 'an implicit claim that equal rights for everyone should be implemented on a global scale'. Moreover, this 'cosmopolitan claim' is not just a moral claim that motivates the critique of global injustice but also a legal claim for the constitutionalisation of international law, since 'human rights rely on finding institutional embodiment in a politically constituted world society' (Habermas 2012: xi–xii). As a result, he contends that the 'sustained political fragmentation in the world and in Europe is in contradiction to the systemic growth of a global multi-cultural society' (Habermas 2012: 7). In Habermas's view, the just and effective resolution of the Euro crisis requires a move towards a new form of social and political solidarity built on a commitment to human rights and the concomitant rejection of the outmoded categories of national identity and state sovereignty that he believes block moves towards a Union based on democracy and social justice rather than simply a single market.

Both the functional and moral strands of these arguments for greater EU integration have undeniable force. Any empirically plausible or normatively acceptable account of politics must acknowledge both the global issues currently confronting contemporary societies and the moral responsibilities owed to non-nationals. In an increasingly interconnected world, problems such as global warming, the fair regulation of international trade and severe poverty in developing countries cannot be ignored. To the extent that many Eurosceptic arguments appear to do so, they seem practically deficient and morally reprehensible. Yet, it would be wrong to regard all arguments that seek to understand the EU and global governance more generally in broadly international rather than cosmopolitan terms as indifferent to either global problems or norms of global justice and human rights. Rather, they seek to combine respect for these issues and values with forms of legal and political organisation that also give weight to some of the concerns underlying the second trend noted above, and the associated desire to retain power at, or possibly devolve it below, the level of established nation states, rather than to transfer it to a supranational body above them.

A more sympathetic reading of this second trend notes that it too can be linked to empirical features of contemporary societies and supported by normative values that reflect the self-understandings of liberal democratic states. From this perspective, the second trend arises from the importance of self-government among people who are mutually interdependent in a number of significant respects, share various common interests and norms, and seek to promote trust and support for collective arrangements that make sense to them as appropriate and are responsive to their interests and values (for this 'civic' or 'liberal' nationalist perspective, see Tamir 1993, Miller 1995, and

Moore 2001). As the quotes given above illustrate, many of those who regard the EU as a necessary functional response to globalisation also contend it allows for new forms of self-government that can satisfy these demands through the democratic control of processes that increasingly operate between and across states. Yet, continuing complaints about the EU's democratic deficit indicate how difficult this contention has proven to put into practice. More importantly, it also ignores the tensions that can arise between regional integration and the historical political identities and forms of communal self-rule that have developed within each of the member states – a tension that has become increasingly prominent in recent years (Hooghe and Marks 2009).

This chapter explores the twin challenges thrown up by the two trends of globalisation and cosmopolitan justice, on the one hand, and the continued demands for forms of national self-determination that combine popular with polity sovereignty on the model of the nation state, on the other. The EU is often seen as awkwardly placed between the two, its governance structures caught between representing citizens and representing states (Friedrich and Kröger 2013), developing a trans- or supra-national public interest and reflecting the mutual interests of the component nation states (Bellamy and Castiglione 2013). Many supporters of European integration believe that this situation is impractical and incoherent. They contend the only plausible and justifiable solution is to resolve the second trend into the first and to make the EU the primary locus of political identity and self-determination for European citizens (e.g. Hix 2008; Duff 2011; Van Parijs 2016). By contrast, I wish to suggest that these two trends can be brought together in a less reductive way whereby the second can be rendered consistent with the first, providing the necessary political framework for addressing the issues raised by global interdependence in a manner compatible with a concern for cosmopolitan justice. I shall argue that the EU can and should be conceived in these terms, providing the model of how sovereign states ought to cooperate in a global context.

The analysis is organised around a distinction between what can be called a civil and a civic model of political community. These two models represent contrasting ontological positions rather than rival ideological or policy proposals (as per the 'ontological'/ 'advocacy' distinction made by Taylor 1989: 159–60), which offer different understandings of the normative and empirical basis for broadly egalitarian and democratic values. I shall argue that the one favours an instrumental view of political community, the other an intrinsic view (see Mason 2012: chs 1 and 2).[1]

According to the civil model, both the design and competences of democratic institutions and the size and location of the political communities in which they operate should be determined by whatever scheme proves most appropriate to deliver effective and equitable policies in the most efficient manner (Van Parijis 2013). Cosmopolitans have typically adopted this model (e.g. Pogge 2008: 174–201; O'Neill 2000: 174–85; Beitz 1994: 124–6). Though some grant the modern nation state may prove convenient for certain purposes (Goodin 1988), others regard both state and popular sovereignty as undermining impartial principles of justice and favour their radical dispersal across a variety of political units (Pogge 2008). Analogous reasoning informs the neo-functionalist interpretation of the integration process which underlay the Monnet method and still provides the background assumptions behind much of the Commission's thinking. According to this thesis, the acquisition of competences by the EU induces a spill-over effect linked to functional efficacy, which both leads the EU to move into ever more related policy areas and in time encourages the shift to the European level of political institutions and ultimately people's allegiances and identities as well (Haas 1958).

By contrast, the civic model favours an intrinsic account of political community that regards the good of being an equal member of a democratic polity as possessing an independent value. In such a political community, citizens participate as equals in making those collective decisions in which, taken as a whole, they have an equal stake. The terms on which they participate are formally and to a degree substantively the same for all, and they treat each other as equals within the process of decision-making. Statist and liberal nationalist theorists have standardly invoked such a view of political community. For example, the intrinsic model of political community informs David Miller's advocacy of national self-determination (Miller 1995: 49–80 and 2009). It rests on a degree of mutual identification stemming from shared interests and values among its members, qualities that are fostered by mutual interactions between them.

---

[1] Although the 'civil' and 'civic' models overlap to a degree with the division between 'liberal' and 'communitarian' schools of thought made by analytical political philosophers in the 1980s and 1990s, these terms mislead – as Taylor noted – to the extent they suggest that the latter is in some way 'illiberal'. I follow Taylor's lead in seeing these models as offering different understandings of the socio-cultural basis of a liberal politics committed to both democracy and justice.

If one applies this distinction to the two trends outlined above, it may be that the empirical and normative arguments made by the EU officials and philosophers cited earlier offer a case for an instrumental political community at the European level, but they fall short of justifying an intrinsic political community. That might be thought unimportant. As we saw, some cosmopolitan advocates of global justice regard such an intrinsic community as outmoded, unnecessary and in certain respects unpleasant and unjustifiable as well as impractical. However, I shall claim that abandoning the second model for the first would incur a normative cost, including a loss of the sense of social solidarity and political engagement needed to sustain a collective commitment to meet our cosmopolitan moral obligations. Meanwhile, the civic model may not only be difficult to create at the global level, but also the attempt to do so would deny the value of the diverse civic cultures of already existing liberal democratic states. As a result, it proves more appropriate to reframe cosmopolitan obligations as duties on states to show equal concern and respect towards the civic cultures of different peoples by fostering rather than constraining the capacity of their respective peoples for self-government. Consequently, the most normatively desirable and empirically feasible way of conceiving the EU is in terms of what I shall call cosmopolitan statism – a term I use in deliberate contrast to Lea Ypi's statist cosmopolitanism (Ypi 2008a). Yet, that still leaves the tasks of defining what 'equal concern and respect' in this context entails, and specifying the institutional structures appropriate to realise it. These tasks are undertaken in the rest of Part 1 in Chapters 2 and 3 respectively, and then applied to the EU in Part 2 in Chapters 4 to 6.

The Statist Ghost in the Cosmopolitan Machine

This section outlines more fully than above the normative and empirical strands running through the cosmopolitan and statist arguments. As we shall see, these two strands determine the model of the EU each school of thought regards as desirable and feasible respectively. The differences between the two views relate in their turn to the contrasting ways cosmopolitans and statists conceive of the relationship of rights and citizenship, on the one hand, to popular and state sovereignty, on the other. Whereas cosmopolitans adopt the civil model of community and seek to divorce the former from the latter, statists appeal to the civic model and contend the latter necessarily frame the former.

Cosmopolitan Globalists and Civil Federalists

Following Brian Barry, one can define the normative basis of cosmopolitanism as resting on three elements: that individual human beings have ultimate value; that each individual human being has equal moral value; and that these two conditions apply to all human beings (Barry 1999: 35–6). Most cosmopolitans are keen to distinguish moral from legal and political cosmopolitanism. For example, Charles Beitz has written that 'cosmopolitanism need not make any assumptions at all about the best political structure for international affairs' (Beitz 1998: 831). Nevertheless, these claims notwithstanding, cosmopolitans do seek to constrain the ways political institutions, however configured, operate so as to ensure they treat 'every human being' as having 'global stature as an ultimate unit of moral concern' (Pogge 2008: 175). This argument has taken a number of forms, and is compatible with both a utilitarian and a deontological, rights-based morality, amongst other moral doctrines.

The significance of this constraint can be seen if one considers what might be ruled out by this approach. Clearly, it rules out valuing people according to features such as their race or gender. Yet it also has been held to rule out a partiality to compatriots or according value to collective entities such as states. The argument goes that being born into a given country is a matter of simple good or bad fortune and as morally arbitrary as having a certain colour or being born into a given class (e.g. Beitz 1983: 593, 595; Pogge 1994: 196, 198; and Moellendorf 2002: 78–80). As Simon Caney remarks, 'this reasoning is, I believe, either explicitly or implicitly present in almost all defences of cosmopolitanism' (Caney 2001: 115 n. 3). The difficulty such arguments face is spelling out what exactly they mean in practice (Miller 2005: 55–79). They are held to suggest that we should value all individuals equally, but exactly in what ways – be it through global equality of opportunity, global equality of resources or global equality of some other good – is unclear.

Two reasons explain this difficulty. The first, examined further in the following section, is that the significance of particular resources and opportunities is subject to different evaluations within different cultures or in different circumstances, rendering it hard to make the meaningful comparisons between different societies that are required to decide whether they are equal in some relevant respect or not (Boxill 1987: 143–68; Miller 2005: 60–3). The second and related reason, explored below, is that the claim that all individuals should be treated as moral equals, and the assertion that national belonging is as morally arbitrary as hair colour, does not in itself explain in what ways, if at all, they should be treated equally. As David Miller notes, a person with congenital disabilities suffers from differences that are morally arbitrary, but most would regard this circumstance as providing grounds for special, and hence unequal, treatment that is not morally arbitrary. A substantive reason is needed to show why national belonging is like hair colour rather than disability, and what that entails in practice (Miller 2005: 68–9).

The standard substantive counter-argument for nationality *not* being morally arbitrary in determining the opportunities and resources that are open to people has been that people in national political communities have special relationships to one another that they do not have to others elsewhere. Indeed, a cosmopolitan notion of equal respect might even justify acknowledging that citizens of a community should give priority to equalising the conditions of their co-nationals over equalising conditions between members of different, even very unequal, countries (Miller 1998). As a result, some cosmopolitan theorists have wished to suggest that relationships among people at the regional and global level are becoming more like relations between people within nations.

These considerations in part motivate Pogge's well known proposal that we should cash out the implications of cosmopolitan morality in institutional rather than interactional terms (Pogge 2008: 176–7): as applying to the rules and procedures of certain institutional schemes, rather than as pertaining to the actions of individual persons and agencies (for an interactional account of the kind criticised by Pogge, see Caney 2005: 78). He notes how the interactional case is practically weaker than the institutional in a number of respects. Take the case of rights, from which he argues. The perfect obligations necessary to uphold negative rights of non-interference can be conceptualised in global terms reasonably easily, since in principle at least they are costless and simply require individual forbearance. It is much harder to assign a global responsibility for positive rights to care and welfare that appear to rely on special obligations. Indeed, in the absence of any causal relation for the potential or actual harms involved, it is difficult even to justify positive action to secure negative rights world wide, through the supply of peace-keeping forces and the like.

This negative view has appealed to those who have wanted to associate cosmopolitanism with a neo-liberal advocacy of a global free market, requiring little more than minimal legal regulation to govern it and a consequent withering away of the necessarily coercive and inegalitarian redistributive apparatus of nation states (e.g. Nozick 1974). Of course, others retort that this view derives its plausibility from a very narrow account of rights. Our obligations look differently if one asserts a human right to subsistence (Shue 1996; Jones 1999), or even more radically to an equal right to the world's resources (Steiner 1994: 235–6).

The problem is that these and other claims, no matter how sophisticatedly elaborated, ultimately rest on rival moral intuitions that may lack universal appeal. They offer valuable contributions to a debate about justice, but, as will be argued in Chapter 2, it seems somewhat presumptuous to treat them as defining what just conduct dictates regardless of what others may think or where they may be located (e.g. as Luban 1985: 209 proposes).

The institutional view attempts to partially respond to this dilemma, since it potentially links us to a whole range of unknown others and provides a duty even to safeguard those negative rights we have not personally violated. The focus here is no longer on what relations ought to pertain between individuals, whatever they believe or wherever they are, but on the justice of the practices and arrangements within which people are involved and for which they are jointly and severally responsible. However, this institutional argument is contingent on the possible or actual existence of a global institutional scheme within which we all participate to some significant degree.

The socio-political strand of the cosmopolitan argument comes in here (Held 1995: chs 5 and 6). Global socio-economic forces are held to have created a greater degree of interconnectedness within the world than ever before. Technological advances have internationalised production, distribution and exchange and transformed financial markets. Multinational Corporations (MNCs), even when they possess a regional or national base, are said to organise their affairs on an international scale and respond to global market pressures. This internationalisation of markets is even more apparent in the financial sector, where new information technology has radically increased the mobility of economic units and to a large degree tied the world's major banking and trading centres into a single integrated network. New communications systems have also rendered ordinary people more aware of these global developments than ever before. The media, according to proponents of this thesis, have altered the 'situational geography' of social and political life by giving people direct access to distant events and creating new experiences, commonalties and frames of meaning that do not require direct physical contact – popular reactions to Tiananmen Square and the plight of the Kurds in the aftermath of the Gulf War being good examples of this phenomenon. A series of common cultural references – from the banality of soap operas through to greater popular awareness and knowledge of world events – have allegedly generated new solidarities as evidenced in transnational social movements such as Greenpeace and Amnesty International.

The above mentioned processes are claimed to have weakened in turn the capacity of nation states to provide for the security and welfare of their citizens, and led to the creation of a number of international power blocks, agencies, organisations, regimes and networks to facilitate their continued ability to do so by managing various areas of transnational activity. These institutions range from collective security arrangements such as NATO, through a variety of other intergovernmental bodies of different degrees of formality aimed at controlling various aspects of economic and social policy. Some are purely technical agencies and limited in scope, like the Universal Postal Union or the World Meteorological Association, others more politically contentious organisations with a potentially profound impact on core domestic policies, such as the IMF and World Bank. Some constitute international regimes with very broad competences and complex governance structures, such as the UN, the Council of Europe and the EU, others more informal global networks, such as the G7. All these organisations modify the freedom of action of states to one degree or another and undercut their capacity to operate as sovereign units. Consequently, their right to act as the agents of the sovereign will of their people has been likewise eroded. Effective decision-making and the sources of identification have in many cases passed elsewhere, or so at least it is alleged.

Finally, this move beyond the sovereign nation state is reflected in the body of international law that has grown up in the wake of these developments. Here individuals are gradually replacing states as the main subjects of the law. On the one hand, it has been recognised that individuals have rights and obligations that are independent of and go beyond those duties and entitlements they have as citizens of particular states – a point made most strikingly in war crime trials. On the other hand, the legitimacy of states has come to rest as much on the justice of their rule as on their *de facto* hold on power. The post-war international declarations of rights have reinforced this shift from state to individual, as have challenges to the notions of 'immunity from jurisdiction' and 'immunity from state agencies' that have hitherto operated as central principles of international law.

This global positivisation of individual moral rights brings the normative and empirical strands of the cosmopolitan thesis together. As we saw, it informs Habermas's view of the EU as a stage towards the embodiment of human rights in a legally and politically constituted world society. In fact, at least two broad possible views of the EU can follow from this perspective. One version holds that the forces described above have undermined the nation state, but that a centralised federal Europe, that is itself not unlike a nation state writ large, can fill the gap (Duff 2011).

Another, more truly cosmopolitan, version is not so much supra-national as post-national in orientation (Ferry 1992; Habermas 1999: 105–27 and, more generally, Habermas 2000), viewing moves towards federalism as an alternative to, rather than a new form of, the unitary sovereign state (Beaud 1995). By and large, political scientists – especially those of a neo-functionalist disposition – have been drawn towards the first position. They have advocated the strengthening of the Union's supra-national features – particularly the European Parliament and the Commission – and the phasing out of intergovernmentalism, and have welcomed the move towards common policies in the spheres of domestic justice and foreign affairs in addition to economic and social matters (George 1991; Hoffman and Keohane 1991; Eriksen 2009; Giddens 2014). Lawyers, by contrast, have been the principal advocates of the second position. They have drawn inspiration from the gradual development of a single legal framework by the EU's Court of Justice, noting with approval its increasing tendency to appeal to human rights and its claims of Primacy over the domestic law of member states and Direct Effect with regard to their citizens (Mancini 1989; Kostakopoulou 2008; von Bogdandy 2012). Needless to say, the reality falls far short of either version of the cosmopolitan ideal – a fact that statists are not slow in pointing out (for the difference between the legal and political science paradigms of the EU in this regard, see Haltern et al. 1995: 24–33; Wincott 1995: 293–311).

Statists and Civic Nationalists

Statists of a civic nationalist hue question both the normative and empirical aspects of the cosmopolitan thesis. With regard to the normative aspect, they dispute the global egalitarianism of the cosmopolitan case. That does not mean that they do not believe there are great injustices that arise from huge disparities in wealth between rich and poor countries and that these ought to be diminished. However, as I shall argue in Chapter 2, these disparities need not be decried on global egalitarian grounds. Among other reasons, they can be criticised as facilitating the domination of some states by others. Rather, what such statist theorists object to is the coherence of pursuing policies that accord intrinsic value to reducing equality according to some metric, such as resources or opportunities, between individuals across the globe.

As I noted above, such metrics prove impossible to operationalise because they are interpreted differently within different cultural contexts. Take the notion of equal opportunity, understood as granting individuals of similar talents and motivations an equal chance to achieve certain positions regardless of which state they come from. Assuming that not all political communities have been merged, so that the provisions available worldwide are identical in all respects, this principle must mean that individuals in different countries have equivalent opportunities. Within nation states, agreement is reached on certain sorts of resource and opportunities being important, and rough equivalents exist to match regional variations. Equal access to sporting opportunities may be thought important, say, but that can mean cricket pitches in England and rugby pitches in Wales, for example. But when one makes cross-national and cultural comparisons, the exercise becomes much more complicated. For the priorities may be very different. The measure of a good education in country A may not be the same as in country B – they value different skills and operate in different contexts (Miller 2005: 61–3).

Of course, there are also differences of opinion within national communities. However, there is an overarching social context within which they can be debated. The ways we view each other as equals is a function of the character of the society and the culture in which we live, and the goods we share (Walzer 1981). Therefore, the crucial factor is that we possess political equality in deciding and deliberating on the shape of that shared culture. A link is thereby established between national, popular and state sovereignty. Nationality defines a common political culture and identity, that to be subjected to democratic control has to be tied to a state which allows a people to determine for themselves the relevant ways they are alike and unalike, and so deserving of equal or different treatment within the public sphere (Miller 1995: 81–118; Walzer 1983: 28–9).

Statists also contest the second, empirical, element of cosmopolitanism, questioning both the degree and consequences of the processes of globalisation and interconnectedness. It is possible to dispute, for example, the extent to which MNCs truly operate at a transnational level. As Hirst, Thompson and Bromley have shown (Bromley et al. 2009), core capital, basic Research and Development, and management personnel and structures are mostly located within a main national base. The various political bodies and non-governmental agencies that have developed to cope with global problems of security and welfare tend to be inter-national and inter-governmental rather than supra-national. The UN, for example, far from representing a nascent form of cosmopolitan governance, as is sometimes argued (Held 1995), remains very much an instrument of the sovereign states which compose it – not least the superpowers, whose hold on the security council effectively blocks any move that might damage their interests (Zolo 1995: 27–8). Indeed, the major powers' effective control over the purse strings enables them to manipulate most important, and hence costly, initiatives requiring inter-state cooperation, and to stop those that do not meet with their approval – witness the sabotaging of UNESCO by Britain and the United States (Jones 1995a). More generally, the evidence that economic globalisation has rendered the capacity of governments and states to make autonomous decisions that impact on the welfare of their citizens seem open to ques-tion. The share of global GDP consumed by states has never been greater, with state income expenditure actually positively correlated with eco-nomic openness rather than the other way round (Hay 2007: 123–52).

Cosmopolitans also are said to overlook the differential impact of global forces on different countries and the imbalances in the degree and nature of the interdependence that they create. By and large, the wealthier and more powerful nations are net beneficiaries from global market forces, for example, whilst poorer states are either locked out of many of the networks or are subordinate partners and often damaged by global trade, becoming sources of cheap labour and resources, rather than developing strong economies of their own. Global environmental, health, security and other dangers that are no respecters of state borders are said to bind the peoples of the world together as sharing a common fate. However, they rarely affect all of them to an equal extent. When joint actions have shared consequences, such as the depletion of fish stocks, cooperative action may be possible, although here too the standard free-rider problems that arise with all public goods and bads mean that many countries will attempt to evade their responsibilities. Because the advan-tages and disadvantages are not usually mutual even with shared activities or problems, the incentives for cooperative behaviour are usually lop-sided (Jones 1995b: 75–7). Even within the EU, the substantial differ-ences in economic performance, social standards and political interests between the member states have rendered the formulation of common policies far from easy, a point discussed in detail in Chapter 6. Britain's acrimonious attempts to reduce the massive financial transfers to other EU states via the CAP reflect a genuine problem, which potentially weakens the commitment to the Union of all the main contributors (Bromley et al. 2009: 191–227; Jones 1993: 87–110). The differential impact of the financial crisis within the Eurozone has revealed this pro-blem in even more dramatic fashion, most notably in the on-going ten-sions between the creditor and the debtor states.

Although nations do form blocs for certain limited purposes, it is also important to note that these often have the goal of preserving state autonomy rather than diminishing it. Alan Milward's account of the European Community (EC), the forerunner of the EU, as a 'rescue' of the nation state is highly pertinent in this respect (Milward 1992). By extension, the EU emerges from this analysis as being, in part at least, a reaction against the forces of globalisation. Although the EU has drawn increasing criticism from those of a social democratic persuasion for promoting neo liberal market policies that undermine domestic welfare and social corporatist measures (Scharpf 2009), it has aroused parallel criticism from neo liberal defenders of the free market on account of the social chapter, environmental and similar regulation (Rabkin 1998). Arguably both views underestimate the EU's responsiveness to domestic political pressures in both directions, and the degree to which the core policies involving high government expenditure – social welfare provision, defence, education, culture and infrastructure – have hitherto remained outside its remit (Moravcsik 2004: 351).

For related reasons, more homogeneous consumption patterns and a greater awareness of world affairs has not necessarily produced as much convergence in political identity amongst the general population as cosmopolitans assert. People distinguish a humanitarian concern with famine or other disasters in countries other than their own from the sort of formalised responsibilities they have for co-nationals. They may support initiatives such as Band Aid or give to Oxfam, but that is a long way from condoning increased taxation to expand the development aid budget, say. Television, social media, faster communication systems, greater job mobility and the like, may have broadened people's horizons in certain respects and encouraged them to identify with a wider community, but the identification may not be as deep as the solidarities of old, based as they were on continuous, direct contact and personal involvement. As Will Kymlicka notes in relation to the impact of the EU and NAFTA on the citizens of their respective member states, 'despite being subject to similar forces, citizens of Western democracies are able to respond to these forces in their own distinctive ways, reflective of their "domestic politics and cultures"'. Eurobarometer polls for the EU consistently suggest that the overwhelming majority of EU citizens identify with their member state rather than the EU, supporting Kymlicka's observation that 'most citizens continue to cherish this ability to deliberate and act as a national collectivity, on the basis of their national solidarities and priorities' (Kymlicka 1999: 115).

Just as I distinguished two different versions of the cosmopolitan ideal with regard to the EU, so two broad positions can be associated with statist thinking. On the one hand, there are conservative Eurosceptics of the British variety who think in terms of narrow national interests and often conceive the nation in quasi-ethnic terms, resulting in a particularly hard line position on immigration for example (Malcolm 1991). On the

other hand, there are civic nationalists. These can be more social democratic in ideology and influenced by republican notions linking patriotism
with democratic participation, as in the French tradition (Thibaud 1992,
though see Miller 1995: ch. 6 for a British version of this argument). They
can allow, and even welcome, a liberal intergovernmental understanding
of the EU (Moravcsik 1993). After all, a civic nationalism is compatible
with a liberal framework that regulates interaction between states in ways
that keeps their pursuit of national self-interest and self-determination
within liberal and civic constraints (Keohane et al. 2009). However, they
would dispute any shift in a federalist direction. Until such time as
a global identity and public culture develops, moral weight has to be
given to the self-determination of different peoples. Attempts to force
the pace will be seen as unjustified, but certain moves of a cosmopolitan
kind are possible – even if the total transcendence of the nation state
remains highly unlikely (Miller 2008).

Two Views of Rights, Citizenship, Democracy and Sovereignty

Cosmopolitans and statists hold two different views of the nature of
rights, citizenship, democracy and sovereignty and the ways they relate
to each other. These differences partly reflect in their turn the aforementioned contrast between a civil and instrumental view of political community and a civic and intrinsic account.

Cosmopolitans see rights as essentially self-standing. Their justification
is independent of their recognition by any given society or culture and do
not rely on democratic endorsement for their validity. Their scope and
application is uniform and universal with individuals as their subjects.
Citizenship and sovereignty are regarded as potentially antithetical to
rights to the extent they link rights to membership of an already existing
state rather than regarding them as attributes of human beings as such.
Rather than being the source of rights, citizenship and sovereignty need to
be refashioned to reflect rights (Pogge 2008: 184).

Democracy plays an important role in this refashioning. On this
account, democracy follows from a right to an equal opportunity for
political participation (Pogge 2008: 191). Where and with whom that
right is exercised, and over what, should be matters of individual choice
constrained by feasibility criteria. Thus, Pogge suggests that political
units can be shaped and reshaped by a majority or supermajority of the
inhabitants of contiguous territories provided the new and any remaining
units remain viable and 'of reasonable shape', while any subgroups can
reject membership of the new unit, form their own or merge with some

other unit subject to these same criteria (Pogge 2008: 196–7). At the same time, he advocates the vertical dispersal of sovereignty across a number of governance levels, from the international to the local. Again, rather loose, largely functional, criteria govern this dispersal of decision-making power. On the one hand, inclusiveness favours a centralisation of power, so that all significantly affected by decisions may be included. On the other hand, effective and equal participation in decision-making favours the decentralisation of power, so that individuals have the time, knowledge and opportunities to influence the social and political conditions that most immediately shape their lives (Pogge 2008: 184, 186 and 191–5). He regards the EU's system of multilevel governance as partly reflecting such a democratic vertical dispersal of sovereign power, with the reconfiguration of its constituent political units the natural next step (Pogge 1997 and 2008: 301, 282fn and 386fn).

Such moves depend on what might be termed the 'regime' features of a political system, that constitute its mode of governance, being separable from its 'polity' features, namely the territory and people to whom a regime applies (for the 'polity'/ 'regime' distinction, see Bellamy and Castiglione 2003). Cosmopolitans contend a variety of different transnational and supranational democratic decision-making processes can emerge that are respected simply because they reflect cosmopolitan norms. Such norms can be grounded in international law, particularly human rights law. Indeed, Habermas argues this is already the case within the EU. He notes how the Court of Justice claims 'competence-competence' to decide issues of European law and their impact on the member states but has no power to enforce its decisions other than through the courts and administrative bodies of those same states. Many of those decisions, such as those relating to Union citizenship, establish transnational rights for individuals, including political rights to participate in EU elections wherever they reside. He regards this development as part of the process whereby law and democracy have become detached from state sovereignty, understood as a monopoly of coercive power over a given territory. Instead, he contends Court of Justice decisions are accepted because they are 'right' (Habermas 2012: 23–8).

By contrast to this position, statists regard rights as being framed and upheld by citizenship and sovereignty. Given rights need to be interpreted and enforced, their stable and successful enactment and establishment requires some agency that can do so in assured and impartial ways. That proves particularly true of property rights, which are partly conventional. All rights, but especially those property rights that are in land, create the need for a territorially based sovereign power. This power must possess a monopoly of coercive force not only within its borders but without them,

in order stabilise the system of rights, including those of property ownership, and defend them against incursions from other powers (Stilz 2009:
35–7).

I shall return in Chapter 3 to the role of territorial and political sovereignty
as defining features of a polity capable of sustaining a democratic regime
within which free and equal individuals can collectively define their rights.
Here I wish merely to note two consequences of this move. The first consequence is that so long as an individual's rights depend for their specifica-
tion and protection on being subject to a territorially based sovereign
political unit, then it will not be possible to fully stipulate those rights
without reference to the individual's territorial affiliation in at least some
instances. For example, with regard to issues of war and peace, the individual right to self-defence will be modified to involve the right to retaliate
against an invading enemy army and – to the extent their activities support
that army – the civilian population of an enemy (Wenar 2006: 108–9). Note
that the civically minded statist does not dispute that individuals are in the
ultimate analysis the holders of rights, on that point they agree with cosmopolitans, merely that the holding and exercise of these rights arise in the
context of a specific political unit.

The second consequence follows from the first, in that the basis, nature
and limits of an individual's obligations towards this unit become a key
issue from this perspective. Civic nationalist statists contend that coercive
institutions must operate on terms that make sense to those subject to them
(Walzer 1983: 28–9). If political institutions are to operate in non-arbitrary
ways, they must appear acceptable to all reasonable citizens as reflecting
the public political culture of the society concerned. Within these accounts,
a political society cannot be regarded simply as a voluntary association of
convenience among a group of individuals that are sufficiently co-located,
numerous and wealthy for their being members of the same political unit to
be plausible in functional terms. These individuals must relate to each
other in ways that make them a 'people' (Pettit 2006). As I shall explore
further in Chapters 2 and 3, a people arises in part from having certain
shared interests through participating in what Rawls's calls 'a cooperative
venture for mutual advantage' (Rawls 1971: 4). In other words, their
interactions and dependence on each other has a certain intensity of
a kind that gives them a roughly equal stake in the collective good of the
political society. Meanwhile, as important in shaping their social cooperation as shared interests, are shared ideas or a set of common reasons about
the appropriate ways to order the collective organisation of their affairs.

Neither shared interests nor shared ideas imply a lack of conflict about
either. merely that a basis exists for a people to reach agreement or agree
to disagree through fair and equitable democratic procedures. On the

civic account, democratic decision-making is as much about deliberation on the common good as a mechanism for the aggregation of individual interests. If democratic processes are to possess this quality, they must operate among a people or *demos* possessing the two qualities described above. For, the sense of a common fate and purposes promoted by mutually beneficial reciprocal interactions, help facilitate compromise and the avoidance of a purely self-regarding stance. As a result, minorities are more disposed to accept majority decisions, for example, and, perhaps most importantly, majorities to take into account the opinions and concerns of minorities rather than excluding them altogether (Miller 1995: 96–9; 2009).

Democracy so conceived operates as a forum of principle (Walzer 1981). The interests and values of diverse groups can be expressed on an equal basis, and the implications of different claims and views placed in the context of the whole range of policies being undertaken by the government and the wider needs and wishes of citizens. For example, conflicting accounts of rights can be weighed and balanced against each other in ways that show equal concern and respect for the individual autonomy of others. So can different conceptions of social justice that seek to determine what is owed to whom by whom, and in which circumstances. The crucial factor, though, comes from these collective decisions being perceived by those on all sides of the argument as somehow 'theirs' – as decisions made in common because those involved are more or less equally affected by the totality of the outcomes, if not each and every decision; draw on a common stock of norms when discussing and evaluating them, even if they disagree about their respective weighting and interpretation; and possess a degree of mutual solidarity as fellow citizens in a shared social enterprise (Sandel 1987).

It is no accident that the two paradigmatic examples of constitution-making, namely France and the United States in the eighteenth-century, were simultaneously instances of state- and nation-building as well. In the terminology I have been using, the polity dimensions stemming from state sovereignty and a people provided the context for establishing a regime characterised by democracy and the rule of law. Law and democracy cannot boot-strap and provide the source of their own polity conditions. They imply a people who are entitled to make and enforce decisions within a given domain. As a result, the statist ghost of already existing civic political communities always lurks within the cosmopolitan machine.

When rights and obligations are nested within particular political communities in this way, their cosmopolitan reach will be affected. To the extent that our understanding of basic rights is coloured by the culture of our particular political community, there are likely to be conflicts between the priorities and publicly recognised needs of different societies. State support for certain religions or languages may be important in some communities and regarded as illegitimate in others, for example. Even when the same rights are acknowledged, variations in local context may lead them to being interpreted and balanced in contrasting and not always compatible ways. In addition, there will be a feeling that 'charity begins at home' that will set limits on how much people will commit themselves to helping outsiders when that clashes with programmes, also motivated by rights considerations, of a domestic character. Thus, statists regard it as legitimate that a more generous national social security system, say, might be established at the cost of less spending on foreign aid overseas (Miller 1995: ch. 3, and 100–3; 2007).

Support for national and state sovereignty need not entail a view of international relations as an anarchic and amoral Hobbesean state of nature. Claims to self-determination for one group imply recognition of similar rights by others – including non-aggression and limited aid (Rawls 1999). Globalisation can be expected to produce forms of inter-state cooperation in those areas such as defence, the environment and the economy, where the capacity of states to act in autonomous ways has been seriously impaired. To the extent that global interdependence does link states within institutional networks, then they will have the sorts of obligations cosmopolitans advocate. Nonetheless, the absence of agreed metrics as to the value of resources or the relative worth of various rights and liberties will make arguments for a global redistribution of goods and services hard to cash out in practice – especially as such schemes can conflict with as well as support the autonomy of national communities.

Following Michael Walzer, one can characterise the difference between the two schools of thought in terms of a distinction between 'thick' and 'thin' moralities (Walzer 1994: ch. 1). In his terms, universal human rights represent a 'thin', 'minimal' morality that all societies ought to uphold. But they do so in numerous 'thick', 'maximal' ways. Moreover, the individual rights bearers are similarly contextually defined. That is not to deny value-individualism, as is sometimes implied, but it is to reject those versions of methodological individualism that ignore the social dimension of personal identity and the development of autonomy (for a critique, see Tamir 1993: ch. 1). According to this thicker, more civic view of rights and the individual, a pure cosmopolitanism offers an inadequate account of moral agency. For the cosmopolitan, universalist agents are supposed to act on the basis of rational considerations of pure principle that abstract from their sense of identity as persons holding certain convictions and possessing particular attachments. By contrast, the statist believes that both the principles and the moral motivations and character of those who follow them need to be fleshed out with natural sentiments and 'thick' concepts such as courage, honesty, gratitude, and benevolence that arise out of specific ways of life.

On its own, cosmopolitanism cannot generate the full range of obligations its advocates generally wish to ascribe to it. For the proper acknowledgement of 'thin' basic rights rests on their being specified and overlaid by a 'thicker' web of special obligations. Welfare states, for example, have typically arisen in societies where there are strong feelings of social solidarity (Offe 2000). These reinforce the formal obligations that arise from being members of an institutionalised scheme of political cooperation as citizens of the same state. Essentially, they create a sense of identification amongst a given group of people between whom it comes to be felt both legitimate and plausible that collectively binding decisions about the distribution of burdens and benefits should take place. That sense of commonness does not determine what its precise implications or content should be, but it does provide the basis on which such determination takes place. It defines the *demos*, as it were, for whom a form of democratic rule appears appropriate and plausible and among whom a process giving each an equal say in overcoming their disagreements will be understood as both legitimate and legitimising.

Nationalism has traditionally provided the ideological glue necessary to define a relatively circumscribed group of people and unify them around a set of shared institutions and practices that were sovereign over a well-defined territory. Political loyalty, accountability and legitimacy were tied in this way to state power and authority. Indeed, nationality was typically the creation of states and political elites seeking to consolidate their hold over their populations. Cosmopolitans deny the necessity and desirability of such attachments. They may, as Thomas Pogge does, grant them a certain empirical weight but not any moral significance. A mixture of voluntarist and utilitarian considerations of a broadly functional kind provide the only normatively relevant considerations so far as people's obligations to any particular polity are concerned (Simmons 1979). By contrast, the earlier sketch of the statist and civic nationalist argument suggested that largely unchosen commonalties of history, belief, geography and civic culture *do* have an ethical relevance. They supply the feelings of reciprocity, trust and commitment needed to supplement the ties of mere mutual advantage that result from individuals acting on the basis of rational self-interest alone. Such moral qualities have an important influence on the character of political life, since they increase people's willingness to engage in cooperative behaviour by raising their expectations and confidence in others. They provide the preconditions for a civic political community. For, as David Miller has argued (Miller 1995: ch.

2), far from encouraging self-interested and partial behaviour, the lessening of the tension between personal and collective goals within a group is likely to make an impartial stance more acceptable.

Conclusion: A Cosmopolitan Statism?

Does this situation create a stand-off between cosmopolitanism and statism? Does it mean that 'thicker' ties neither should nor can be extended beyond the state? I do not think it necessarily does. As we have seen, it is mistaken to regard the two as inherently at odds with each other, with the latter anti-liberal, anti-rights and anti-individualist, as certain commentators have claimed (e.g. Holmes 1993, and for a helpful critique of this assumption, see Blake 2013: 38–43). Rather, they offer contrasting accounts of how we should think about individuality, rights and their relationship to the political societies that embody them. Moreover, I have also suggested that the two need to take account of each other to some degree. On the one hand, cosmopolitan norms cannot be taken as given, with political structures – as in the civil model – their instruments; to be configured in whatever way best secures their implementation. Not only do the claims and the resulting obligations stemming from these norms need to be specified in ways that make sense to, and can motivate those involved – as in the intrinsic political structures of the civic model; but also they already have been so, often in different ways, within the democratic systems of existing states. On the other hand, statists cannot ignore cosmopolitan norms. In an interconnected world, states trade and interact in other ways with each other that will impact on their capacity for self-government. Consequently, they have reasons to regulate their interactions in equitable and fair ways that indicate a cosmopolitan regard for the citizens of different states. Yet that raises the original dilemma all over again: for, how are states to agree on which of their different interpretations of cosmopolitan norms should prevail?

How might we get around this impasse? Four possibilities present themselves – non-cosmopolitan statism, post-state cosmopolitanism, statist cosmopolitanism and cosmopolitan statism – each of which comes in what could be called a 'thin' and a 'thick' version. I shall describe each briefly in turn.

The 'thin' version of pure statism consists of a world of largely self-sufficient states with minimal or no interaction. In this scenario cosmopolitan norms would be redundant, though members of other states might still have a humanitarian and pragmatic concern with whether these states oppressed their citizens or not. In practice, though, autarchy has long ceased to be an option. As the example of North Korea tragically illustrates, states cannot supply for their citizens needs effectively, and the attempt to do so requires considerable oppression of the citizenry to keep them from interacting with outsiders or simply leaving. It also drives them to the 'thick' version of an aggressive, imperial strategy, whereby they seek to oppress and even occupy neighbouring states. I shall not pursue this possibility further.

Post-state cosmopolitanism has greater appeal, superficially at least, gathering support from many cosmopolitans of a liberal egalitarian disposition who regard state sovereignty as the key cause of domestic as well as global injustice. The 'thin' version is a variety of philosophical anarchism, that denies the possibility of, or need for, any particular obligations to a specific state other than those that we choose to undertake with specific individuals (Simmons 1979: 31, 69; Caney 2005: 78). To the extent we have moral duties to uphold people's natural rights or promote their well-being, we owe them to individuals everywhere (Simmons 1979: 194; Caney 2005: 72). Yet, whether such natural rights involve merely refraining from coercion (Nozick 1974) or extend to rights to welfare (Shue 1996) remains at this stage unspecified – a point we shall see in Chapter 2 to be problematic. It allows that a legally regulated free market of a neo-liberal kind might satisfy a pure 'thin' cosmopolitanism. The 'thick' version accepts that we may need to create political structures to particularise these obligations, but suggests we can do so by creating a network of post-sovereign self-constituted civil organisations, whose members have joined on a purely voluntary basis (Pogge 1992; Bohman 2005).

Statist cosmopolitans develop this last point by accepting the need for state institutions to secure and motivate cosmopolitan norms. However, they regard states as operating in an instrumental way in this regard, to be employed by a cosmopolitan minded avant-garde (Ypi 2011, ch. 7). In the 'thin' version (Ypi 2008a), the world is still divided into separate states but largely for contingent reasons of efficiency and to reflect a degree of cultural diversity (Goodin 1988). However, in principle this could be simply a transitionary phase to a 'thick' version involving the creation of a world state with a cosmopolitan purpose (Cabrera 2004; Nili 2013; Ulas 2015). The 'thickest' version of this position ultimately involves developing a cosmopolitan state, or at least a civic political community capable of sustaining a cosmopolitan democracy, at the global level (Koenig-Archibugi 2011).

By contrast, cosmopolitan statists see the system of states as intrinsically linked to the promotion of cosmopolitan norms. A 'thin' cosmopolitan statism involves a system of states that merely uphold certain basic rights that are respected when making purely international agreements (Miller 2007). Instead, on a 'thick' version of this view, states can form a civic association involving some delegation to a supranational authority, within which they can regulate their interactions through cosmopolitan norms they formulate on joint and equal terms while retaining their status as separate sovereign political communities.

We can map these four positions, along with their respective two variations, onto different models of the EU deriving from the literature on European integration.

	Statism	Cosmopolitanism
Cosmopolitan	**Cosmopolitan Statism** 'Thin' – Civic/liberal nationalists, but who believe states have humanitarian obligations to uphold but are sceptical of seeing EU as anything but a limited international organisation.	**Cosmopolitan Globalism** 'Thin' – World market and international law based on human rights – comes in both neo-liberal and left libertarian variations.
	Liberal Intergovernmentalism 'Thick' – A civic association of European democratic nation states, involving supranational institutions and some variable geometry. Demoi-cracy, 'Republican' Intergovernmentalism	'Integration through law', based on the constitutionalisation of the Treaties by the CJEU. 'Thick' – Post-state, functional parcelling out of sovereignty across networks of local and transnational civil society organisations. Multi-level governance
Statist	**Pure Statism** 'Thin' – Autarchic system of states – deeply Eurosceptic, as advocated by some extreme-right nationalist and extreme-left parties. 'Thick' – An imperial 'Napoleonic' conception of Europe.	**Statist Cosmopolitanism** 'Thin' – A step-by-step move towards supra- and post-national federalism. From Liberal Intergovernmentalism to Multi-level Governance 'Thick' – The creation of a post-national civic European super-state or Federation. A European version of cosmopolitan democracy. Neo-functionalism

Figure 1.1: Models of the EU (adapted from Bellamy and Castiglione 2004: 187–93) plots all eight of the combinations sketched above.

These positions can be characterised as 'ideal types' and involve both pro- and more sceptical and even anti-EU positions. Moving anticlockwise from the bottom left, pure statist, box, one can characterise each of these views and their respective 'thin' and 'thick' versions as follows:

1) The 'thin', pure statist version is that of a Europe of separate, largely independent nation states (for moderate versions, see Malcolm 1991, Tuck 2016), possibly characterised by ethnic nationalism (Scruton 2016), while the 'thick' version is that of an imperial Europe of a similar autarchic nature vis-à-vis the rest of the world (the Napoleonic Europe criticised by Constant; Constant 1813: 73–7). Both are more theoretical than real possibilities, though the 'thin' version gets advocated by some extreme right and extreme left parties.

2) The 'thin' statist cosmopolitan argument can be aligned to a certain form of liberal internationalism or, in the EU context, intergovernmentalism, that views democracy and the state's system as instrumental to upholding individual rights and interests, and justifiably constrained in its operations when majorities threaten rather than support these liberal goals. International organisations are promoted via liberal democratic processes by elites so as to constrain domestic democratic majorities in liberal ways, both internally and externally (Moravcsik 1993). As such, they bolster the liberal legitimacy of states (Keohane et al. 2009), not least by gradually increasing the complexity of collective decision-making and the various checks and balances to which it is subject (Moravcsik 2002). From this perspective, the EU offers an emergent, multilevel, post-national system of European states (Ypi 2008b). The 'thick' version of this position suggests in neo-functionalist fashion (Haas 1958) that greater European functional integration in the economic sphere will ultimately spill over into a need for greater legal and political integration that can be married to cosmopolitan human rights norms. The result will be the creation of a post- and supra-national European federal state (Habermas 2012).

3) The 'thin' version of pure cosmopolitanism sees Europe as constituted through law and respect for human rights. In some versions, this moves the EU towards a form of cosmopolitan democracy and even to a European state, though one constituted by human rights, thereby dovetailing with the 'thick' statist cosmopolitan view (Held 1995: 278 et seq.; Archibugi 1998: 68, 98 et seq; Mancini 1989; Von Bogdandy 2000). Others see human rights law and European citizenship as being divorced from democracy and the state (Kochenov 2014). A 'thicker' version sees the EU as offering an alternative to any form of state, and emphasises the emergence of transnational non-governmental

organisations as the basis of a network of a post-sovereign, purely voluntary and self-constituting, global civil society (Pogge 1997; Bohman 2004b; Brunkhorst 2002; Müller 2003).

4) Finally, the 'thin' version of cosmopolitan statism envisages a Europe of nation states bound by international agreements that respect human rights (Miller 2008), a position compatible with a moderate form of liberal intergovernmentalism (Moravcsik 1993). However, a thicker version adopts what could be called a form of republican intergovernmentalism. This account stresses the democratic character of the integration process, in which governments must act as the duly authorised and accountable representatives of their peoples. On this view, the EU forms a civic association of European nation states, involving the devolution of authority to some supranational bodies that remain under their joint and equal control and a degree of variable geometry (Bellamy 2013).

Once again, these models combine empirical and normative aspects, and so can be evaluated for their plausibility and desirability. So far, I have only rejected the options in the bottom left box of 'pure' statism as clearly implausible and undesirable, though some reservations regarding the top right box of pure cosmopolitanism have also been registered. My claim, developed over the next two chapters, will be that cosmopolitan morality only makes sense to the extent that it is embedded within a statist frame-work: the position I categorised above as cosmopolitan statism, that occupies the top left box, and that only the 'thick' version proves empiri-cally and normatively defensible. However, to substantiate this claim we need criteria by which to assess the various possibilities in a coherent and hopefully convincing fashion. Chapter 2 turns to that task, with Chapter 3 providing the assessment.

As will emerge, the endorsement of cosmopolitan statism follows from a more general point, already noted in this chapter, whereby agreement on specific norms of justice implies a social and political context that reflects a web of mutual relations, such as are standardly found in demo-cratically organised nation states. Chapter 2 relates this condition to the broader need for processes of legitimation to adjudicate among reason-ably differing cosmopolitan norms of justice. This requirement shifts the focus of cosmopolitanism away from justice *per se* to the political precon-ditions for free and fair agreement among different persons and peoples in the context of an interconnected world. I shall put forward the republican notion of non-domination as a criterion for evaluating different global political arrangements and argue in Chapter 3 how this favours the version of cosmopolitan statism characterised above as a civic association of democratic nation states.

On this account, it is the possibilities for domination that represent the main challenge posed by globalisation and interdependence. Bodies such as the EU can only be agents for promoting non-domination and avoid being dominating themselves to the extent that they meet a dual standard of gaining the non-dominated endorsement of both the governments of democratic states and of the citizens they represent. In other words, they must conform to the normative standard of a two-level game (Savage and Weale 2009). As I remarked above, this position can be located within the EU literature as a form of 'republican' intergovernmentalism, the main features of which are developed and defended in Part 2 over Chapters 4–6.

2 Justice, Legitimacy and Republicanism: Non-Domination and the Global Circumstances of Legitimate Politics

Introduction

Chapter 1 presented cosmopolitanism and statism as divided along two main, if related, dimensions. On the one hand, cosmopolitans argue for the global application of egalitarian theories of justice, whereas statists deny this possibility and insist that such theories can only apply within a political community of the kind that does not exist at the global level. On the other hand, cosmopolitans contend that international law provides the basis for a transnational democratic regime divorced from any given polity and that separates popular from state sovereignty. By contrast, statists contend that a democratic and legal regime is necessarily embedded within a polity that combines popular and state sovereignty, and that most international law is consequently best understood as inter-state rather than cosmopolitan law. As we have seen, these two models give rise in their turn to quite different images of the EU. Whereas the first suggests it provides a new kind of post-, trans- or supra-national regime without a polity, the second suggests that it must either develop polity-like characteristics or remain an essentially intergovern-mental regime.

In this chapter, I wish to suggest that it is possible to bring these two models at least partly together by showing how the second proves neces-sary for the articulation of the concerns of the first. The last chapter associated their differences with two different ways of understanding political community – the civil and the civic models. This chapter pro-poses that underlying these two models are two different ways of relating justice to legitimacy. The argument below shall maintain that justice has to be located in an account of legitimacy, so that politics comes first (Pettit 2012: 24–5). By extension, the identification of and commitment to cosmopolitan norms of justice cannot be separated from the specifica-tion of a type of political community that would allow these norms to be debated and decided upon by those to whom they will apply in ways they can regard as legitimate.

As with the two models of political community, I adopt a broadly egalitarian conception of the two concepts of justice and legitimacy (Valentini 2012a: 593–5). In formal terms, one can define justice as giving each their due according to a given principle, and legitimacy as indicating that institutions are recognised as rightfully ruling over those to whom they apply. While related, in that the perceived justice of a regime is likely to be a contributing factor to its legitimacy, the one cannot be regarded as providing criteria for the other. Beyond the formal contours of the concept of justice, however, I shall contend that considerable reasonable disagreement exists as to what giving some one his or her due entails (Waldron 1999). Different theories of justice, even within the same family of theories – such as Rawls's and Dworkin's respective liberal egalitarian accounts – offer different views of what a person is owed from the state and other citizens. Nevertheless, states have to institute and enforce some view or set of views.

The notion of legitimacy arises at this point. The state's right to rule involves that those subject to it accept its authority. Many criteria might be given for such acceptance, including a historical and cultural identification with a given political community. Within liberal democracies, though, such acceptance has typically rested on the state providing citizens with reasons to believe that it treats them as equals. In the absence of any commonly accepted epistemology capable of giving objective reasons for a given group of people to accept a given set of policies as equitable, these accounts conclude that the available reasons will be those linked to their having participated on equal terms in a political process to determine those policies. Therefore, a legitimate state will need to sustain democratic practices. As a result, the commitment of citizens to a political community takes on an independent weight – it cannot be instrumental to serving ends that it plays an intrinsic part in determining. The grounds for political community will need to be investigated in their own terms, as raising separate normative and empirical conditions to those that might justify their possible reconfiguration or collaboration to tackle issues related to globalisation and justice.

What I called statist cosmopolitan theorists conceive institutions as instrumental to the realisation of a certain ideal of justice. Consequently, they focus on identifying and justifying a suitable global distributional principle capable of treating all individuals equally, regarding the question of the most appropriate global institutional order as a subsequent and subordinate step orientated to discovering a fitting arrangement for realising that principle. By contrast, the cosmopolitan statist accounts incline towards a focus on the equal right of individuals to live inside an institutional order possessing the intrinsic qualities necessary for legitimising a view of justice entitled to inform collective public policies for those concerned. An upshot of the analysis below will be that only the cosmopolitan statist account proves normatively and empirically justified.

This account gives rise in its turn to an alternative way of conceiving injustice that I shall maintain can be best formulated in terms of the republican notion of non-domination. From this perspective, a legitimate political process for determining a collective policy on justice will be one that instantiates non-dominating relations among those involved in, and subject to, it. This approach centres not on social and economic inequality *per se*, so much as the power relations lying behind such inequalities through which certain agents and agencies can dominate other agents and agencies both within and across state borders. With regard to the global order, it leads to a distinctive form of cosmopolitan statism that highlights not so much problems of global *distributive* justice, at least not directly, as problems of global *political* justice that result when one state's capacity to be democratically legitimate gets undermined by the dominating actions of another state or some other organisation based within another state or states (Macdonald and Ronzoni 2012).

Such considerations prove crucial to any investigation of the current and prospective democratic legitimacy of the EU. They shift attention away from asking which institutional arrangements might best realise a preconceived notion of justice and towards considering which arrangements might best sustain the conditions of civic equality needed for people to decide collective issues relating to justice in non-dominating ways. To the extent member states already instantiate such conditions to some degree, and have settled on various collective policies that embody particular conceptions of social justice, they are entitled to be treated in non-dominating ways. Indeed, the central purpose of the EU can and should be conceived as being to achieve precisely this goal.

The rest of this chapter explores the distinction between justice and legitimacy, and the role of a republican notion of non-domination in securing the latter. I shall argue that the legitimacy of particular conceptions of justice can only be determined by political communities with sufficient intrinsic qualities to be able to support a democratic regime. Yet, that need not suggest that to arrive at a cosmopolitan conception of justice we need a more encompassing democratic political community. Not only may such an encompassing community be less able to sustain the necessary conditions to arrive at such a conception in a legitimate way, but also, as I observed above, it devalues and risks dominating existing communities.

This chapter thereby sets the scene for Chapter 3, where I shall argue that the most normatively desirable and empirically feasible way of conceiving the EU is in terms of what I called 'thick' cosmopolitan statism. According to this position, states regulate their interactions and those of their citizens in ways that conform to the republican norm of non-domination. Such a political ontology treats the EU as a republican association of European sovereign states and peoples, each of which possesses a cosmopolitan regard for tackling the problems of a globalising world in non-dominating ways that mutually support the capacity of the different *demoi* of the association to sustain a democratic political community.

From Justice to Legitimacy

In this section I seek to delineate the two concepts of justice and legitimacy, note their complementary and conflicting aspects, and then show why the first must be situated within the second.

Justice and Legitimacy: Conflicting or Complementary?

As I remarked at the start of this chapter, justice indicates the moral entitlements of individuals, and hence what they are owed by others and, more especially, by the political institutions to which they must submit. By contrast, legitimacy concerns not what individuals are entitled to but rather what entitles political institutions to rule or exercise power over them. Though distinct, both justice and legitimacy can be construed as different responses to a common normative demand that a political system should show those subject to it equality of respect though being in principle justifiable to all citizens qua free and equal agents (Valentini 2013: 178–9 and 2012a: 595–6; Kymlicka 2001: 4). Justice requires that individuals are treated as *substantively* equal in some respect, be it with regard to access to opportunities, resources, or, more minimally, and in a way that need not be egalitarian except in largely formal terms, with regard to certain basic rights. Legitimacy requires that individuals are treated as *procedurally* equal in some respect, maximally in each consenting to a given arrangement, more minimally in each having an equal say in influencing and accepting it. Both forms of procedural equality can be realised via some kind of democratic process.

At one level, therefore, one can regard justice and legitimacy as complementary. They not only express an identical moral requirement to show individuals equal respect, but also serve a matching purpose in justifying coercion. A political system that claimed the obedience of citizens while failing to give them what they are owed substantively and procedurally as moral equals would be unjust and illegitimate. At another level, however, justice and legitimacy can conflict. One can regard laws as legitimate – as having been made according to a due process – but unjust, as failing by one's standards to give each person his or her due. Likewise, one can view laws as just without necessarily being legitimate – as in the case of a benevolent (or not so benevolent) dictatorship that manages to make at least some decisions one regards as substantively justifiable.

Certain justice theorists (Rawls 1993), including many cosmopolitans (Buchanan 2004), find this potential tension between justice and legitimacy problematic. They seek to resolve it by treating legitimacy as a sub category of justice. On this account, a system is legitimate to the extent that it satisfies certain minimum substantive distributive standards, including those required for the exercise of certain procedural rights. Moreover, a system becomes illegitimate to the extent democratic procedures violate these basic standards, which thereby need to be locked in through a legal constitution capable of trumping democratic decision-making. Yet, treating legitimacy as a component of justice raises a number of potential problems in its turn. For example, how are we to distinguish those elements of justice that provide the threshold for legitimacy from those that are either unnecessary or insufficient to generate it? And does that mean that democratic decision-making that respects that threshold ought to be accepted as just, even if the decision itself is in other respects unjust?

Laura Valentini (2012a: 598–601) has proposed a resolution of these problems by suggesting that a certain minimal account of justice can be agreed on as stipulating those conditions the denial of which would on any reasonable view prove inconsistent with showing people equality of respect. She associates those demands of justice that form a *sine qua non* of equal respect with the basic rights found in international charters such as the European Convention on Human Rights (ECHR). However, beyond this minimum she allows that reasonable disagreement exists as to which account of a growing number of accounts of justice offers the best account of equal respect. No epistemic grounds exist for preferring one over the other, for regarding Dworkin's argument for 'equality of resources', say, as preferable to Sen's equality of capabilities. At this point, issues of legitimacy take centre stage, and attention must turn to principles of political justice that are sensitive to disagreement and conflict, including our disagreements about principles of distributive justice. Being subject to reasonable disagreement, substantive egalitarian theories of distributive justice cannot serve as guides to the design of institutions either domestically or globally. They can only inform the debates of individuals within just institutions. Instead, the structure of institutions belongs to the domain of theories of legitimacy and has to be informed by considerations of procedural equality.

Valentini makes a case for a version of what I called 'thin' cosmopolitan statism. Those who adopt this position accept all persons deserve to be shown equal respect regardless of their place of birth, but deny that as a matter of social justice they are obligated to anything more than a commitment to basic human rights and a general duty to assist the poor (Rawls 1999; Nagel 2005; Miller 2007). Contrary to cosmopolitans (Pogge 1992; Caney 2005), they deny that egalitarian justice can be extended globally. Like Valentini, they contend such extensions to be misconceived. The novelty lies in her reasoning for this conclusion. On her account, given pervasive reasonable disagreement about justice, institutions that guard against unreasonable infringements of equal respect by protecting human rights are '*as just as they can be*' (Valentini 2012a: 601). As a result, the debate about both domestic and global inequality needs to shift from a concentration on justice to a concern with legitimacy and to ensuring democratic institutional structures exist that allow individuals to confront and decide between competing theories of justice. She contends a politically just global order of this kind would uphold universal basic rights but need not necessarily imply either a global state and institutions of cosmopolitan democracy or a world of just but independent democratic states. The most plausible and normatively attractive arrangement might be something in between.

My account overlaps in certain respects with Valentini's in foregrounding global political justice, and of those statists, such as Miller (2007), who adopt a parallel view if not identical reasoning and conclusions. However, it differs in two key respects. First, it insists on the primacy of politics even on matters of basic justice, wrapping these latter into the notion of political legitimacy. Second, it is not based directly on a principle of equal respect but rather on non-domination, where issues of inequality of power are crucial. As a result of these two differences, the intrinsic importance of democracy goes all the way down. I shall elaborate the first below and the second in the following section on republicanism.

The 'Circumstances of Legitimacy': Responding to the 'Circumstances of Justice' within the 'Circumstances of Politics'

In developing her argument, Valentini appeals to a distinction between the 'circumstances of justice' and the 'circumstances of legitimacy' (Valentini 2012a: 598), the latter reflecting what Jeremy Waldron has referred to more broadly as the 'circumstances of politics' (Waldron 1999: 159–60). As Rawls, following Hume, noted, the 'circumstances of justice' indicate the need for a collective distributive rule in a condition of moderate scarcity, so not everybody can have everything they want, and limited altruism, so all cannot be expected to spontaneously honour their obligations to others when required to do so (Rawls 1971: 126–30). However, as Waldron pointed out, we perforce must reach agreement on a just distributive rule in circumstances of pervasive disagreement about justice and, it might be added, uncertainty and fallibility in implementing any rule we may agree on. It is precisely these circumstances that give rise to politics and the need for political mechanisms to decide between our conflicting views. She then puts the two together to suggest that while justice requires we acknowledge that human beings have rights and deserve equal treatment, legitimacy responds to the fact of political disagreement about justice and requires that we have an equal say when collectively deciding on which rights and what kind of equality are appropriate for us and apply to given cases.

I agree with much of her argument. However, politics reaches further down than this. Any claim of justice – even of the most basic kind that Valentini contends it would be unreasonable to disagree with – can only be legitimately made within a political context. Ascertaining the validity of a claim and what it practically entails cannot be decided by the claimant alone but implies its acceptance by those against whom the claim is being made (Bellamy 2012a: 452–3). If such claims are to be impartially adjudicated and enforced, then that cannot be achieved by the assumption of a pre-political 'reasonable agreement' among the parties. As Rawls noted, our practical reasoning is attended by what he called 'the burdens of judgement ... the many hazards involved in the correct (and conscientious) exercise of our powers of reason and judgement in the ordinary course of political life' (Rawls 1993: 55–6). These burdens range from the different life experiences people bring to the assessment of a situation, to the multiple normative considerations likely to be involved and the difficulties of relating them to often complex empirical evidence. One aspect of these burdens is that we are inevitably partial in our judgments. Even with the best will in the world, it will be impossible not to be biased towards our own interests and experience. Not only are these what we know and appreciate best, but also our knowledge of the interests and experiences of others will necessarily be limited and cannot accommodate everyone. As such, a constant danger exists that a successful claim will involve a claimant imposing his or her view on others. Moreover, to successfully sustain that claim over time will ultimately require the threat of force. Consequently, the risk is that right will simply be might or the rule of the most persuasive and strongest. Avoiding such partiality, therefore, involves establishing some impartial form of arbitration and enforcement – in other words, some sort of political authority.

As a result, the circumstances of politics go all the way down because the need to provide an effective and stable political authority capable of resolving disagreement forms what Bernard Williams called 'the first political question'. As he explained, it is the first question because a satisfactory and successful answer to it 'is the condition of solving, indeed posing, any others' (Williams 2005: 3). However, as Williams also noted, an adequate answer must meet what he termed the Basic Legitimation Demand (BLD). To do so, the response to the first political question must offer 'an "acceptable" solution', one that can provide a justification of the political system's right to rule to each person subject to it. As Williams conceded, the BLD is a moral principle but not one that is 'prior to politics'. Rather, 'it is a claim that is inherent in there being such a thing as politics: in particular, because it is inherent in there being a first political question' (Williams 2005: 5). Williams argued that coercion is by definition anti-political, since it denies the need for rulers to justify their authority to others as an alternative to a state of war – it merely institutionalises a bellicose state between rulers and ruled. As such, it does not answer the first political question so much as restates it. To avoid such a restatement, therefore, a political authority must be capable of achieving the non-coerced acceptance of those subject to it.

From this perspective, even basic rights cannot be conceived as pre-political constraints upon politics. Rather, they are implied by, arise within, and must be decided and enforced through politics. Outside politics, there can be no rights or justice, but merely competing and conflicting *assertions* of rights and justice, and their successful or failed imposition by their claimants on others. As we shall see in Chapters 4 and 5, this argument challenges cosmopolitan-inspired attempts to ground European citizenship and the validity of the legal decision-making of the EU in a set of putatively fundamental European rights (Habermas 1992 and 2001). For, on the account given here, the legitimacy of the EU can only rest on its *political* constitution and the democratic mechanisms through which that constitutive process proceeds (Bellamy 2007: 260–3).

We cannot legitimately respond to the global 'circumstances of justice', therefore, by constructing a global civil political community of some kind on the basis of certain cosmopolitan norms, as statist cosmopolitans suggest (see Miller's parallel critique of Ypi's notion of avant-garde agency in Miller 2013: 93–7). For, these norms lie themselves within the 'circumstances of politics'. Consequently, legitimacy cannot be derived from a given political arrangement being instrumental to the achievement of certain putatively just, or even supposedly efficient, outputs (Bellamy 2006). Instead, we need a global civic political community of some kind capable of supporting an intrinsic form of politics through which people can debate different norms of justice and decide on and define those that should apply to them. To the degree already existing states enshrine such a politics, then any change to the current global political order would need to be one that their peoples could accept through these domestic mechanisms. In this respect, cosmopolitanism will be unable to transcend a statist and civic framework in which issues of justice and legitimacy can be related. Indeed, if an appropriate political regime assumes a polity with the characteristics associated with statism, then cosmopolitanism will always need to have a statist cast of some kind – be it in the form of a global state or some kind of global association of states.

To assess the intrinsic qualities of different political arrangements in this regard, we require a different criterion to their capacity to promote justice. Rather, we will need to look to a value that expresses the form of equality of respect suited to an intrinsic form of politics. In what follows, I shall put forward the republican notion of non-domination for this role.

Republicanism, Non-Domination and the 'Circumstances of Legitimacy': A 'Free Person' in a 'Free State'

The attraction of using the republican notion of freedom as non-domination as a criterion for a legitimate form of politics rests on its focus on the exercise of power. It refers to a civic condition that requires a certain sort of institutional arrangement for its realisation. Accordingly, I shall start by describing the republican notion of a 'free person' and then explore the conditions for its fulfilment in a 'free state', noting what this implies in a global context. This description offers an account of the 'circumstances of legitimacy' for a global political system, setting the stage for the assessment of different models of the EU in Chapter 3.

A Free Person: Freedom as Non-Domination

As Quentin Skinner (2008) and especially Philip Pettit (2008) have insisted, the republican notion of non-domination identifies freedom as resting on a set of conditions that go beyond those standardly identified with a 'negative' conception of freedom as freedom from interference, without invoking the controversial ethical naturalist or perfectionist reasoning typically associated with 'positive' conceptions of freedom as 'self-mastery' or the freedom to realise oneself. As Skinner has noted (1998), non-domination emphasises an understanding of negative freedom as 'freedom from mastery', in which the antonym to the free person is a slave rather than a prisoner. Whereas a prisoner's loss of freedom clearly rests on his or her being confined and interfered with by others, a slave's lack of freedom inheres in his or her status, regardless of whether he or she is actually interfered with and forced to obey a given master. Even in the absence of interference, the freedom of choice of slaves may be inhibited through being, or simply fearing being, monitored or invigilated by others who possess the right to interfere with them. As a result, slaves may strive to avoid any possibility of triggering interference from their masters by self-censorship or self-ingratiation, redirecting their choices to those preferred (or assumed to be preferred) by their masters, without being actually blocked or coerced in their choices by them.

Behind the notion of non-domination lies a picture of the autonomous agent who acts on his or her own reasons and will rather than for reasons – including the fear of coercion – arbitrarily imposed by others, be that arbitrary imposition direct or indirect (Pettit 2012: ch. 1). In this account, arbitrary means as willed by another agent or agency, without that person or body being obliged in any way to consider the reasons or interests of those persons or bodies subject to their will. As such, non-domination focuses on the way power can influence those subject to it to alter their behaviour to please or humour or simply avoid being noticed by or provoking the powerful. That does not mean that autonomous agents cannot accept any authority over them. It allows for the possibility of agents deliberating with others in ways that lead them freely to change their reasons and chose an alternative course of action through being converted to a different point of view to the one they initially held. It also allows for agents to choose to trust or delegate to another to act on their behalf if they feel there are good reasons for doing so. In both these cases, agents may themselves freely accept the authority of another, including authorising them to interfere with them – for example, by agreeing to follow a course of treatment prescribed by a suitably qualified doctor without being able to understand fully themselves the medical science underlying the proposed cure. However, agents who are manipulated or misled into accepting the reasons or following the will of others will be as dominated as those who do so from fear or inhibition. Such manipulation or misleading results from, or gives rise to, a dominating form of arbitrary power akin to, even if subtler than, that of a master over a slave.

How far this focus on domination constitutes in and of itself an alternative *conception* of freedom to that of freedom as non-interference need not concern us here. The above mentioned issues that are highlighted by the notion of domination may or may not be graspable within some sufficiently nuanced account of freedom as non-interference, as various critics have maintained (Kramer 2008, Carter 2008). The current argument merely requires the acknowledgement of their centrality for the role, functioning and legitimacy of political institutions. In other words, the crucial claim is that one should regard the realisation of a condition of non-domination as not only a key purpose of political institutions, but also one that can only be brought about through the way they function, and as intimately connected to their legitimacy.

Domination as defined above, results primarily from three circumstances: a power imbalance, dependency, and personal rule, all of which allow for a degree of arbitrariness in the way those subject to the influence of another can be treated (Lovett 2001). As earlier republicans noted (Skinner 1998), all three of these 'circumstances of domination' are inherent features of monarchical rule, which involves hierarchy and ascribed status, with all members of the kingdom 'subjects' of the monarch to serve his, or occasionally her, pleasure rather than the other way round. It is not just that these circumstances all make interference more likely and so freedom less secure. They also create domination by allowing the invigilation of the dominated by the monarch and inducing dominated behaviour, such as sycophancy, without any actual interference. They do so because personal rule encapsulates arbitrary power by placing the lives and livelihood of all subjects of a monarchy at the pleasure of the King or Queen's majesty. In parallel ways, these same circumstances can blight social relations. When, as has often been the case in the past, heads of households or employers and managers get endowed with a quasi-monarchical status vis-à-vis other family members or employees, then families and the workplace can both be dominating environments.

Avoiding these 'circumstances of domination' implies a condition of equal respect among citizens, therefore, in which each can look the other in the eye through enjoying equality of status in the making of the collective decisions that govern their lives. In this way, the removal of the 'circumstances of domination' dovetails with the establishment of the 'circumstances of legitimation'. Herein lies the logic behind the republican slogan that to be non-dominated 'free persons', individuals must be citizens of a 'free state': that is, of a polity that institutionalises a form of rule where the possibilities for domination are lacking (Skinner 2010).

A Free State: The 'Circumstances of Legitimacy'

On the republican view, a 'free state' has both internal and external conditions. They provide a response to the domestic and global 'circumstances of legitimacy' respectively, whereby political and social relations more generally can be so organised as to remove the 'circumstances of domination'. I shall explore each in turn.

Internal Non-Domination and the Domestic 'Circumstances of Legitimacy'

The accounts of both legitimacy and non-domination given above stress the normative significance of collective self-government (Rawls 1999; Macedo 2004: 103; Pettit 2010a and 2010b). The use of coercive power by a government can only be legitimate and non-dominating when it is exercised via processes and within constraints that are accepted by those subject to it, and for purposes that correspond to their needs and values. Therefore, a legitimate and non-dominating government must be representative of the views and interests of the governed. These criteria might be met in part within a non-democratic regime, such as those designated by Rawls as 'decent hierarchical peoples' (Rawls 1999: 62–70), in which benign and expert rulers govern according to a moral code subscribed to by the ruled. However, modern societies tend to be pluralist and complex, undermining the possibility of a generally agreed comprehensive conception of the good and rendering the perspective of even well-intentioned and informed rulers partial and limited. Consequently, the representativeness of such regimes can be doubted. Democracies seek to overcome these difficulties by putting in place procedures of authorisation and accountability designed to ensure governments represent the diverse views and interests of all citizens with equal respect and concern (Christiano 2010: 121–2).

Nevertheless, democratic procedures will not operate legitimately, that is in a non-dominating fashion, unless they likewise function according to norms and serve ends that can be commonly avowed by those involved (Pettit 2010b: 145–9). The criterion of 'commonly avowed' should not be understood as entailing universal consent, which would be impossible to meet (Simmons 1979), but rather the weaker notion of equal respect for the views of the governed by virtue of the existence of a plausibly democratic system that gives citizens equal participation in decision-making (Buchanan 2002). Nevertheless, to meet even this weaker condition it will not be sufficient that democratic processes merely involve the public. Rather, they must do so on a basis that can be publically acknowledged by those to whom they apply as fair and appropriate, not least in demonstrably giving equal consideration to their views and interests in framing collective policies. No matter how far such procedures may conform to abstract democratic principles in theory, their legitimacy will be impugned to the extent their operation is perceived in practice to reflect unduly the values of a subsection of the political community, such as the ruling elite, and of responding disproportionately to their sectional interests (Christiano 2008). As a result, democratic legitimacy will depend to some degree on whether those to whom democratic decisions apply relate to each other in ways that render such a public and equal process possible and appropriate (Rawls 1999: 23–5).

At a minimum, therefore, internal legitimacy depends on there being a balance rather than an imbalance of power, citizens must be mutually and reciprocally interdependent, and personal discretion under the control of those subject to it. These conditions should ensure that laws are under the equal influence and control of those subject to them, so as to render them justified and justifiable to those concerned, reflecting their commonly avowable interests. Laws that satisfy these conditions may interfere with the choices of those subject to them, restricting what they may or may not do, but in not being arbitrary, they will not dominate them. As such, they point to certain democratic arrangements being intrinsically and not just instrumentally necessary for citizens not to be dominated (Bellamy 2007; Pettit 2012).

As will be argued more fully in Chapter 3, achieving the requisite balance, reciprocity, and interdependence necessary among both rulers and ruled for democratic decision-making to be non-dominating rests on being able to align the 'regime' aspect of the state – the norms and processes that structure decision making – on the one hand, with its 'polity' aspects – the social, economic and cultural relations prevailing among the various group of individuals who together form the people or *demos* – on the other hand (Bellamy and Castiglione 2003). To the extent the one is congruent with the other, it becomes possible for a state to be so organised that its government is representative of its people. Such legitimate representative states provide citizens with civic freedom of the kind republicans associate with freedom as non-domination (Pettit 2010b: 144–5). For the regimes of such polities provide the means for their citizens to secure and advance their interests on an equal basis to each other as defined by public terms and procedures that they can share and control as a people. Citizens can ascertain that the administration and legislation conform to public norms and pursue public purposes, informing and controlling the definition of these norms and purposes as part of an on-going process of public deliberation among and between the people and their representatives. As a result, governments are constrained from governing arbitrarily – according to their own or some sub-group's views or interests. They can only employ the coercive power of the state in so far as they have been authorised and are accountable to do so on grounds that conform to the commonly avowed views and interests of the people they serve.

Thus, states have internal legitimacy to the extent they are able to represent peoples in ways that are public and equal, and in so doing create mechanisms that provide for civic freedom among citizens. Of course, these criteria are not met in full by any actually existing democratic states. No regime represents its polity entirely equally and publically – not least because peoples are rarely sufficiently homogenous for that to be possible. However, as will be explored in Chapter 6, even among quite diverse peoples, the regime can be so tailored to the composition of the polity as to promote equity and publicity among different groups to some degree, as the experience of various multinational and multicultural states indicates. Yet, as these states also illustrate, the more economic, historical and cultural divisions become aligned with territorially concentrated groups and/or the various social cleavages found within pluralist societies cease to be cross-cutting and become segmented in ways that create separate political communities, the less acceptable collective decision-making among them tends to become. Over time, one or more groups begin to question not just the regime but also the polity legitimacy of the state, demanding various special rights to protect their interests, guaranteed representation in central decision-making, and ever more devolution of power (Kymlicka 2001: 212–13). Consequently, there may be limits to how much internal polity diversity can be accommodated by a single regime without giving rise to domination, and hence the degree to which it is desirable or possible to have a cosmopolitan state, even with a highly differentiated regime, as opposed to a cosmopolitan system of states.

As we shall see in Chapter 3, and develop further throughout Part 2, especially Chapter 6, this issue poses a potential problem for those who wish the EU to become a polity (e.g. Duff 2011, Habermas 2012). Most commentators acknowledge that while the EU possesses a regime of a supranational as well as an intergovernmental nature, its transnational features are at present limited (Haltern, Meyer and Weiler 1995). Yet, these features are necessary for the development of the kind of social relations needed to form a polity capable of sustaining legitimate forms of democratic decision-making. Directly empowering a supranational regime in the absence of such polity conditions would risk making the EU an instrument of domination rather than a mechanism for reducing it. By contrast, an alternative approach is to see the EU as a regime under the direct control, and in the service of, its constituent polities, the member states. So conceived, it forms not a polity in the making but an international regime these polities have forged to maintain their internal democratic legitimacy by counteracting the possibilities of external domination, not least by each other, while avoiding creating a supranational polity that might itself pose precisely this kind of threat itself to them all. It is to the problem of external domination that I now turn.

External Non-Domination and the Global 'Circumstances of Legitimacy'

Within a system of states, for a state to be 'free' it will not be sufficient for its internal political system to be non-dominating. It must also be free from external domination by not only other states but also various public and private agencies, such as international organisations, like the WTO or the EU, and corporations or financial institutions that are located in other states or operate to some extent multi-, trans- or supra-nationally (Pettit 2010a: 77–9). Such domination may arise not only from actual direct or indirect interference, but also – and more insidiously – through the mere existence of various imbalances of power and dependencies, as in interpersonal relations.

External interference by other states – be it intended, as in the case of conquest or the threat of armed conflict, or an unintended product of various negative externalities resulting from domestic decisions – limit the capacity of governments to represent their peoples in fairly obvious ways. However, a government that must act to palliate or defend against the *potential* aggression of a hostile state is also dominated by that other state. It is inhibited in its actions and to that extent is unfree to respond to and represent the views and interests of its citizens, curtailing their freedom in the process. Likewise, if the domestic policy choices of one state effectively undermine those of another, say by one state polluting upstream from another state that has tried to reduce pollution, then the behaviour of the one reduces the presumptive options of the other in ways that involve illegitimate coercion of one people by another.

Powerful states can also dominate weaker states in numerous ways that fall short of explicit or potential interference (Pettit 2010a: 73–7). For example, they may impose inequitable and disadvantageous terms of international trade on them by exploiting various forms of economic pressure that arise from their control of important markets, their ability to manage various financial instruments, or their access to key resources, and so on. Powerful corporations can exert similar forms of pressure and influence, as when they threaten to withdraw from states with taxation or employment policies they regard as unduly reducing their profits. In such situations, governments become to a greater or lesser degree controlled by these alien powers. They feel obliged to act 'responsibly' and satisfy these various external demands lest the domestic economy suffer and be less able to supply the basic needs of the population. Yet such responsible action can lead to a failure to adequately represent the concerns of their own citizens. For example, they might overturn domestic employment laws or cut public spending in ways citizens not only did not desire but also would not have needed to do had it not been for such external demands (Mair 2011).

To avoid such external domination, states and their peoples must likewise be organised so as not to dominate each other and to regulate their interactions in non-dominating ways. At a minimum, therefore, states seeking to have their own democratic legitimacy respected have reason to acknowledge a set of international norms whereby they respect the democratic legitimacy of others by observing a duty of non-intervention (Rawls 1999: 34–5). Yet, in an increasingly inter-connected world, states are likely to interact so intensely and fre-quently that there will be ample scope for some to exert various forms of domination over others. Such domination may stop short of direct intervention but inhibit and intimidate states in ways that undercut their representative character. Interconnectedness also gen-erates problems that can only be effectively tackled through collective action between states, where again powerful states may skew common agreements in their favour without deploying outright coercion. Finally, globalisation has brought with it not simply greater interaction between states but also directly between their peoples and citizens. Not only are peoples involved in global processes of production and exchange, but also migration is altering their character, rendering them increasingly multicultural, and creating a growing problem of stateless persons and denizens, who belong to dispersed and oppressed peoples and lack citizenship.

As a result of these developments, peoples and persons have a growing interest not only in the legitimacy of democratic decision-making *within* states but also *between* them (Pettit 2010b: 151–2). On the one hand, they will wish their governments to be representative of them when negotiating with those of other states, and for the negotiations to give equal weight to each state so that the ensuing accords tackle matters of common concern in mutually beneficial ways. In other words, they will wish similar criteria of publicity and equality to operate in the international sphere as they do at the domestic. On the other hand, peoples will want their direct inter-actions with other peoples to involve mutual respect on both sides, with each respecting the domestic rules and regulations of others so long as no peoples discriminate against other peoples when it comes to trading with or travelling in a different state to their own. In other words, every state should treat all peoples as equals under domestic law, with a similar rule of non-discrimination operating for those seeking access to citizenship and prepared to undertake the same duties as already existing citizens.

One solution to this problem might be what in Chapter 1 I called 'thick' statist cosmopolitanism and the creation of a cosmopolitan form of democracy. This solution aims at dissolving the problem of securing external non-domination by creating a system satisfying the conditions of internal non-domination at the global level. This response would require the formation of a global, or, in the case of the EU, a pan-European, *demos*. By contrast, what I called cosmopolitan statism, involving state*s* in the plural, can be characterised as a form of what Kalypso Nicolaïdis (2004) has termed *demoi*-cracy. On this account, the EU involves an ever-closer union of people*s* rather than the evolving formation of a European people, and exists to serve their joint and several interests (Cheneval and Schimmelfennig 2013; Nicolaïdis 2013). On the version of this thesis adopted here (Bellamy 2013), agreements between member states at the EU level must follow the normative logic of a two-level game (Putnam 1988; Bellamy and Weale 2015): they must be democratically legitimate both to the governments that negotiate them and to the citizens that each of these governments represents. The democratic legitimacy of EU level decisions, therefore, would depend on them meeting a dual standard. These decisions must not only reflect the consent of each of the *demoi* to whom they apply but also must not undermine the capacity for those *demoi* to give or withdraw that consent. As such, this approach operates as a form of 'republican intergovernmentalism' (Bellamy 2013), since it requires the on-going democratic authorisation and accountability of EU decision-making by national governments, MEPs and the Commission by and to the citizens of the member states they represent. As we shall see in Chapters 3 and 4, the key to such an arrangement lies in states so organising their interactions that they avoid mutual domination by providing mechanisms that promote equal respect and mutually agreed on forms of equal concern between their respective peoples. The result is a republican Europe of sovereign states.

Conclusion: Non-Domination as a Criterion of Legitimacy

This chapter has argued that the design of any global or regional institutional order has to take into account the 'circumstances of legitimacy'. These circumstances can be best understood not in terms of the securing of justice or basic rights, both of which are in need of legitimation, but rather as the securing of equality of respect through the instantiation of relations of non-domination. Such an account of legitimacy places politics first in Williams' sense (Williams 2005: 3). For it is only within an institutional arrangement that makes politics possible as a fair mechanism for reaching collective decisions all can regard as legitimate, that questions can be posed, debated and resolved about justice or the supply of goods that people have non-moral reasons to regard as beneficial.

As I noted at the start of this chapter, if correct, then this analysis rules out those 'thin' statist cosmopolitan approaches that conceive states as merely instrumental to the realisation of a particular conception of global justice. It also excludes from consideration what I designated as 'thin' pure cosmopolitanism for a similar reason. For this model likewise advocates that relations between individuals be conducted simply on the basis of a preferred conception of justice. By contrast, four positions remain in contention: a form of 'thin' cosmopolitan statism that argues that states only have a minimal obligation to uphold those basic rights intrinsic to any system of politics;[1] 'thick' state cosmopolitanism, which effectively merges into a cosmopolitan state; 'thick' pure cosmopolitanism, which involves a network of post-sovereign organisations; and a 'thick' cosmopolitan statism that arguably involves elements of these other three. All four allow for the 'circumstances of legitimation', the first as located exclusively within states, the second in terms of a global or, in the case of the EU, a pan-European *demos* as the subject of a form of cosmopolitan democracy, the third and fourth by advocating democratic decision-making among diverse *demoi*, though they characterise these *demoi* and their decision-making somewhat differently. Moreover, versions of all four have been cast in republican terms. The scene is set, therefore, for a comparative assessment of them in Chapter 3.

---

[1] As I noted above, though, a 'thin' cosmopolitan statism can be regarded as ignoring the 'circumstances of legitimacy' if these basic rights are viewed as pre-political minimal standards of justice. Moreover, given there are likely to be reasonable disagreements even about 'basic' rights, it proves hard for this 'thin' position to be coherent without moving towards the 'thick' cosmopolitan statist position. I develop this argument further in the next chapter.

3 Sovereignty, Republicanism and the Democratic Legitimacy of the EU

Introduction

At the heart of the competing models of democratic legitimacy sketched at the end of Chapter 2, lie competing views of state sovereignty. Indeed, the issue of state sovereignty animates many debates about European integration more generally. On the one hand, 'thin' cosmopolitan statist critics of the EU frequently complain it erodes state sovereignty and thereby weakens the capacity of domestic electorates to control and influence how they are governed (Malcolm 1991). On the other hand, defenders of the EU often argue either, from a 'thick' statist cosmopolitan perspective, that shifting at least some sovereignty to the EU provides a means for increasing such control and influence given the global nature of many issues (Held 1995: 111–13; Morgan 2005: 142–54; Habermas 2012: 37–53); or, from a 'thick' cosmopolitan standpoint, that the weakening of state sovereignty helps promote a cosmopolitan respect for individual rights and justice (Pogge 1992: 58; MacCormick 1999: 128–9). If the first group defends the sovereignty of the member states, the second group seeks a transfer of sovereignty to the EU level, while the third group aims to go beyond any form of state sovereignty.

What follows defends a view that in key respects can be situated midway between these three more familiar positions: that of a 'thick' cosmopolitan statist view of the EU as an association of sovereign states. As I remarked in the last chapter, in mounting this defence I shall assess it against these alternatives in terms of the republican theory of non-domination (Pettit 2010a: 70–5). Obviously, sovereignty can be assessed in relation to many other values besides non-domination (Caney 2005: ch. 5). However, as we saw, non-domination provides a criterion for judging how far different institutional arrangements prove adequate to the global 'circumstances of legitimacy'. Indeed, this concern has been central to the sovereignty debate, relating as it does to the capacity for citizens to be free from alien control and influence (Laborde and Ronzoni 2015). Both sovereignty and non-domination are qualities realised through a certain configuration of political institutions (Pettit 2012: 22). Indeed, a central tradition of republican thought, to which my argument aligns itself, has associated the achievement of non-domination with sovereignty (Rousseau 1762; Kant 1797). Yet, republicans also have been wary of the potential for domination offered by certain conceptions of sovereignty (Pettit 2012: 14–15), with a number of contemporary republicans rejecting the notion entirely, often on grounds analogous to those of pure cosmopolitans (e.g. Bohman 2004a). In fact, all three of the familiar positions outlined above have been justified by various theorists on republican grounds and offered as models of the EU (e.g. respectively by Miller 2008 for the 'thin' cosmopolitan statist view; Marti 2010 and Habermas 1999: 106, 116–17, 150 for the 'thick' statist cosmopolitan view; and MacCormick 1999: ch. 9, Bohman 2004b, Besson 2006 and Ladvas and Chryssochoou 2011 for the 'thick' cosmopolitan post-statist view). As a result, exploring which configuration of sovereignty might best realise non-domination within the EU seems necessary if the implications of republicanism for not only Europe but also global governance more generally are to be clearly ascertained.

The position proposed here conceives the EU as a republican association of sovereign states that is designed to overcome the possibility for their mutual domination while providing a mechanism for their securing certain global goods and avoiding various global bads, not least through their reciprocal recognition of rights to citizenship – an aspect explored more fully in Chapter 5. As such, this position seeks to combine the respective advantages of the other three positions while escaping their disadvantages. Like the defenders of state sovereignty, I shall argue that popular sovereignty presupposes state sovereignty of a kind that has been already constituted within the member states. However, 'thin' versions of both 'pure' statism and 'cosmopolitan' statism risk ignoring the degree to which global interconnectedness can inhibit the capacity of states for self-government and creates or reinforces moral obligations of a cosmopolitan kind to uphold the right to citizenship of all individuals regardless of state borders. Like the statist cosmopolitan advocates of shifting sovereignty to regional or even global bodies, therefore, I shall contend that popular sovereignty can be enhanced rather than diminished through states cooperating within a regional organisation such as the EU. Yet, these defenders of supra-state sovereignty underestimate in their turn the normative loss incurred in dismantling already existing legal and political orders and reconstituting them to encompass a far larger and more diverse population. Even more than 'pure' state sovereigntists, they also pay insufficient attention to the dominating potential of sovereignty within states and how these might be exacerbated in a larger unit. As the cosmopolitan post-sovereigntists suggest, I shall maintain such a regional arrangement need not – and should not – be conceived as involving any transfer of state sovereignty to the EU. But it need not and should not lead to a weakening or dispersal of state sovereignty either. Cosmopolitan supporters of dispersing sovereignty among a range of functional, local and transnational bodies above and below the state overlook how effective and equitable control and influence depends on individuals forming part of a people, capable of exercising collective oversight on the basis of commonly avowable reasons over the whole range of policies and forces effecting their shared interests. Moreover, outside such arrangements it may prove hard to obtain agreement on which rights to enforce, when and how, or to mobilise support for doing so (Bellamy 2012a). Consequently, those agents and agencies seeking to uphold cosmopolitan norms risk being illegitimate and ineffective. By contrast, I shall show how a republican association of sovereign states allows citizens to regulate their external sovereignty in non-dominating ways consistent with cosmopolitan norms by creating supranational institutions under their mutual control that uphold the rights of their respective citizens to self-government.

The argument develops in two stages. Stage one defines state sovereignty and defends it on republican grounds as necessary to establish a form of politics capable of instituting relations of non-domination among citizens. The first section defines sovereignty as a political authority that possesses finality through being supreme and comprehensive. These qualities are then said to presuppose a territorially demarcated polity and a corresponding regime, both of which develop coevally with the constitution of a related people and an agent or agency enjoying the right to rule. The second section argues that sovereignty so conceived provides the context for institutionalising a form of popular sovereignty in which citizens can fairly and freely agree on public rules of justice in a non-dominating manner.

Stage two examines the possibility and justifiability of sovereignty so defined and defended once states and their peoples interact and become interconnected. In these circumstances, the external sovereignty of states has been regarded as not only promoting injustice (Caney 2005: 182; Pogge 1992: 58) but also impossible (Sassan 1996: 29; Slaughter 2005: 12), thereby undercutting internal sovereignty. Taking the EU as a response to this situation, the third section explores whether sovereignty within the EU ought to be displaced upwards to the EU level, as suprastate federalist sovereigntists argue; while the fourth section examines if sovereignty can be dispersed and divided, as post-sovereignty theorists propose. Having rejected both these proposals, stemming respectively from the 'thick' versions of statist cosmopolitanism and pure cosmopolitanism, the fifth section argues for the thick cosmopolitan statist position according to which the EU is best conceived as an international association of sovereign states and their peoples, whereby they accord each other equal concern and respect by delegating certain competences to supranational institutions that regulate their interactions while remaining under their mutual control.

Defining Sovereignty

The defining features of sovereign rule are standardly given as finality, supremacy and comprehensiveness, in which the first depends on the second and third (Hinsley 1986: 1, 26). To possess sovereign authority is to be able to decide an issue. Hence the sovereign must have the final word. As such, a sovereign must be supreme vis-à-vis alternative sources of authority and have a comprehensive jurisdiction over the activities of those under its sway. Without the separation and supremacy of political over religious, legal, economic and other forms of authority and power, political decisions will be open to challenge by rival authorities and so cannot be final. Likewise, if sovereign authority does not encompass all social interactions, it will be impossible to take into account the knock-on effects of a decision in one area for those in other areas, thereby also making the finality of any decision open to question.

Sovereignty so defined has typically been associated with a sovereign state possessing the following four features: it forms a territorially defined *polity*, with its own system of governance or *regime*, its own *ruler* comprising the agent(s) or agency(ies) forming the highest and decisive organ within the regime, and its own *people* (the *demos*) (Troper 2010: 137–9). These four features interact in a variety of ways, with sovereignty being the product of that interaction. For a ruler and a regime to be sovereign, they must be supreme with regard to the social activities of the individual members of the people residing within a sovereign polity. Sovereignty so conceived has both an *internal* and an *external* dimension. Sovereignty implies being subject to no other authority at home and the equal of other sovereigns abroad. It also involves both a *de facto* and a *de jure* condition – it designates, respectively, the capacity to rule and the right to rule over those subject to the sovereign's authority. In addition, sovereignty may be understood both *negatively*, as freedom from other sources of power and authority, and *positively*, as freedom to act in self-chosen ways. Finally, sovereignty is an attribute not only of the agent(s) or agency(ies) that rule but also of the regime, the domain and the people through and over which and whom they rule: it refers not only to the sovereignty of the rulers but also of the regime whereby their rule is implemented and legitimated and the polity and the people to which and over whom it applies (Caney 2005: 149–50).

An externally and negatively sovereign realm or polity offers the context within which the internal and positive sovereignty of a regime and a ruler can be exercised, with the *de jure* right to govern of a given regime and ruler resting on their *de facto* capacity to preserve the sovereignty of the polity. Indeed, within the developing language of sovereignty claims, the sovereignty of the polity and its members and the sovereignty of rulers – be they princes or the populace – and a given regime became inextricably connected and coeval (Sheehan 2006; Skinner 2010). The status of sovereign rulers depended on their ability 'to maintain' the sovereignty of their state, as the polity came to be termed, with such maintenance involving not only the securing of the negative, external sovereignty of the polity but also the internal exercise of positive sovereignty to promote its well-being and prosperity. In other words, the sovereign right to rule involved an obligation to preserve and foster the sovereignty of the polity, and hence of its members, externally and internally, negatively and positively.

These four elements of sovereignty form a mutually supporting package, therefore. As I shall argue in section 2, they prove necessary for a government to be duly authorised to represent a people and their polity and be accountable to them. By supporting popular sovereignty they help secure the value of non-domination among individuals who acknowledge the importance of showing each other equal concern and respect. Yet, an appropriate configuration of internal sovereignty will not be sufficient to secure non-domination if the polity and regime do not possess external sovereignty and so can be dominated from outside. Hence the need to address the plausibility and desirability of sovereignty claims in an interconnected world, and to investigate how the dimensions of polity, regime, ruler and people might be reconfigured to achieve non-domination in such circumstances – the topic of sections 3–5.

Defending Sovereignty

The definition given above is essentially Hobbesian (Hobbes 1651; Skinner 2010: 34–7). Developing its reworking by Rousseau (1762) and Kant (1797), as analysed and advocated in a number of recent studies (Stilz 2009; Ripstein 2009; Flikschuk 2010), this section defends sovereignty so defined on republican grounds as necessary to secure non-domination.

State sovereignty and free persons

As we saw in Chapter 2, the republican concern with domination involves a view of human beings as moral equals, each entitled to act on their own autonomous choices on the same basis to everyone else. Following Philip Pettit (2010a: 73–5; 2012: ch. 1), non-domination can be defined as the absence of alien, non-deliberative control. Deliberative control, whereby others seek to persuade you via reasons you can accept or not, respects one's equal status as an independent reasoner and so involves no domination. By contrast, an agent or agency exercises non-deliberative control over your choices when they influence them either directly, be it through coercive interference or, more subtly, by manipulation or deception, or indirectly, without actual interference, through your simply fearing or anticipating their capacity to interfere and inhibiting your actions as a result of invigilation or monitoring, in ways that may lead to self-censorship or self-ingratiation. On the republican account, domination of both the interfering and the inhibiting kind results from a relationship of actual or potential mastery of one agent or agency by another. It derives from a situation in which one is no longer an equal and independent chooser. Herein lies the link that a number of republicans sought to establish between non-domination and sovereignty. If domination arises from being subject to a master, then individuals will only be non-dominated to the extent they are free from mastery as a result of possessing sovereignty, which we saw by definition entails having no superior (Rousseau 1762: I.6, 7 at pp. 49–53; Kant 1797: 138–139).

Establishing a situation in which each individual possesses sovereignty poses a dilemma, as both Rousseau and Kant fully appreciated. If individuals could live entirely independently of one another, as self-sufficient units, without any interaction, then each could be sovereign over his or her choices and domain. Likewise, if all acknowledged the sovereignty of justice, then cooperation between individuals could be based on voluntary agreements that acknowledged their respective rights. However, given that social interaction proves both necessary and unavoidable, while the partiality of all individuals to their own interests and perspectives makes disagreements about justice inevitable, then – following Hobbes (1651: ch. 13) – these authors argued that the need arose for a sovereign political authority capable of determining and enforcing collectively binding rules of social conduct. Without such an authority, then – again drawing on Hobbes (1651: ch. 17) – they contended each individual ran the risk of being dominated by, or themselves dominating, every other individual they came into contact with.

In the terminology I used in the last chapter, this tradition of republicanism entirely concurred, therefore, with the view that we encounter the 'circumstances of justice' within the 'circumstances of politics'. Indeed, they took the further step of suggesting that there can be no justice outside politics. In a situation where individuals unilaterally decide whether others have infringed their rights or they have infringed the rights of others, then – unless they all happen to agree on what is right – none has a duty to respect the view of rights held by others. They also cannot rightfully impose their view of justice on anyone else without similarly denying their moral equality as an equally authoritative judge of what justice demands. Therefore, sovereign authority becomes a precondition of justice because only such an authority can deliver a decisive and common process of adjudication capable of reliably and stably establishing objective duties on all. It provides this possibility precisely through being supreme and comprehensive, and thereby offering the prospect of replacing the unilateral will and subjective judgement of particular individuals with an omnilateral will in which each decides the same thing for all (Rousseau 1762: II.6 at pp. 66–8; Kant 1797: 137–8; Stilz 2009: 38–56).

The danger with this proposal lies in such a sovereign power also offering an unrivalled prospect for domination through becoming itself the instrument of a particular will, a worry raised once more by Hobbes and his account of sovereign power, with its apparent rejection of republican fears regarding domination (Hobbes 1651: ch. 21). From a republican perspective, the fundamental challenge posed by the creation of such a sovereign authority was whether it was possible, in Rousseau's words (1762: I.6 at pp. 49–50), *to find a form of association which will defend and protect with the whole common force the person and goods of each associate, and in which each, while uniting himself with all, may still obey himself alone, and remain as free as before.* Rousseau's dilemma restates in republican terms the 'circumstances of legitimacy' encountered in Chapter 2. As is well known, Rousseau's response was that the only way to meet this challenge was by locating sovereignty in the people's democratically constructed general will (Stilz 2009: ch. 3). What follows extrapolates from that argument to offer a rationale for why a non-dominating form of democracy assumes the four dimensions of a sovereign polity, regime, rule and people outlined above.

Popular Sovereignty, State Sovereignty and Non-Domination

The attraction of a sovereign political authority rests on its providing a solution to the problem of individuals being dominated by the partial judgments and particular wills of others. Any single individual – however well intentioned and selfless – will have a partial perspective, in the sense of being inevitably limited in their ability to comprehend or even be aware of all other peoples' situations, interests and views, and likely – even unwittingly – to favour their own interests and point of view. Yet that means overcoming partiality cannot be achieved by deferring to arbitration by some self-styled impartial third party or parties. So conceived, a sovereign authority would be part of the problem rather than its solution, for it could not avoid acting arbitrarily towards those subject to it. Democracy proposes a solution to this difficulty by placing sovereign authority in an impartial mechanism that offers a public means for showing equal concern and respect to the views and interests of all citizens in determining collective policies. Such a mechanism aims to allow citizens to agree despite their disagreements by providing a way of making decisions all can accept as legitimate even when they dissent from a given decision (Christiano 2008: ch. 6).

A democratic procedure consisting of majority rule based on one person one vote formally meets this requirement in being anonymous, neutral and positively responsive (May 1952). However, such a formal mechanism offers at best a necessary but not a sufficient condition to avoid domination. If a majority vote reflects the 'will of all' rather than a 'general will', then, as Rousseau (1762: I.3 at p. 60) noted, the possibility arises of certain groups dominating others because each will have voted with the sole objective of furthering their partial interests and perspective. For example, a consistent minority could be subject to the arbitrary will of a majority if the majority's partial interests can be furthered through the exploitation of the minority and the suppression of their views. Such worries lay behind the republican hostility to factions. To avoid this possibility, a democratic process must also incentivise citizens to justify their collective decisions to each other on the basis of commonly avowable reasons that acknowledge the entitlement of all citizens to be treated with equal concern and respect. Though many policies will benefit particular groups, they must do so for general reasons that are acknowledged as applying equally to all and that promote a shareable public interest. Therefore, democratic legitimacy will depend to some degree on whether those making up the citizenry relate to each other in ways that render such an equal and public process possible and appropriate (Rawls 1999: 23–4).

Two types of relations prove especially important in defining a *demos* among whom a democratic process for collective decision-making will be legitimate. As we shall see, the four dimensions of sovereignty provide the context for the emergence of both. First, there needs to be a high degree of interdependence between the members of a community and their most important interests must be more or less equally tied up in it, and be so over a long period of time – sufficient to care about the impact of current decisions for future generations (Christiano 2010: 130–2). Interdependence stimulates crosscutting cleavages that make interest groups less factionalised, ease trade-offs and diminish the possibility of consistent winners and losers. A rough equality of stake in the overall package of collective decisions gives citizens an equal interest in ensuring the basic structures of social cooperation are fair and equitable. It frames a commitment to promoting and sustaining investment in certain public goods that are conducive to their different projects, including collective schemes of social insurance and the maintenance of fair democratic procedures for deliberating on the public good. If some have less of a stake in these collective decisions than others, then it would not be legitimate for them to have an equal say because their interest in them will be partial by definition. They will be more inclined to underfund policies supporting a common good in which they do not share and to promote policies that support their sectional interests.

Second, and relatedly, citizens need to conceive themselves as a public and be able to act as such (Miller 2009: 212). Such a self-conception gains support from a shared public culture and sphere, themselves the product of a shared history, language and customs that create a feeling of like-mindedness and the sense of participating in a collective project. A shared public culture provides a source of agreement on the kind of issues that can be raised and the values that can be appealed to, making it less likely interlocutors will view each other's points as mere personal opinions and interests that do not need to be addressed and responded to, thereby aiding compromise through focussing on common principles and priorities. A shared public sphere involving common media, discourse and language or languages allow citizens to address each other as a public and encourage politicians to do so by offering common forums through which to communicate with each other. Otherwise, the danger is that politicians could simply play different groups off each other, saying different and even contradictory things to each. Citizens too will not be forced to hear the other side. There will be no incentive to develop only commonly avowable policies and principles that address shareable values and interests or mutually acceptable compromises. Such incentives oblige those seeking special privileges, such as a religious group seeking an exemption from certain common policies or a business asking for a tax break, to frame their demand in terms of a general principle or benefit applicable to the whole community and not just them. Again, the risk is that otherwise society will become divided into discrete and insular publics, with distinct views and interests on key issues. As a result, the possibility of partial decision-making favouring only given sectorial groups increases, as does the potential for persistent minorities.

A democratic process that operates subject to these conditions proves non-dominating. As I outlined in Chapter 2, mastery of a kind that leads to domination arises from an imbalance of power, dependency and arbitrariness (Lovett 2010: 119–20). If A has more power than B, then A can reliably alter B's choices but not vice versa. In this scheme, all have an equal power in making collective decisions and none can reliably control another. If B is dependent on A, then the cost to B of defying A may be prohibitively high. However, under this arrangement all are equally subject to and have an equal stake in collective rules and goods that are under their free and equal control. As Rousseau observed, 'each, by giving himself to all, gives himself to no one' (Rousseau 1762: I.6 at pp. 50). There is mutual but not personal dependence. Finally, arbitrariness exists if A can will what B chooses according to A's partial judgment and interests, without consulting those of B. Here, though, collective rules must consult the commonly avowable judgements and interests of those subject to them.

Clearly, actually existing democratic systems operate with varying degrees of success in meeting these conditions and at best are 'nearly democratic' in the specified senses. To some degree, this variation depends on specific details of their political and social arrangements, such as the electoral system, which cannot be explored here. However, they will also be affected by the way sovereignty is arranged. Historically, state sovereignty has provided the context within which democratic mechanisms have been able to emerge within all the member states (Skinner 2010). How has state sovereignty helped give democratic decision-making these qualities?

First, as we saw, supremacy and comprehensiveness supply a precondition for all policies being made by and applying equally to all. Unless a single authority has ultimate responsibility for the totality of social relations and is under the control of all subject to them, then collective decisions will not be those of and for the collectivity. They will reflect partial interests and perspectives. Second, these attributes of sovereignty arise from a sovereign ruling agent or agency being located within a polity with its own regime and people. State building typically created all four aspects simultaneously, and in the process formed a national economic system and political culture (Rokkan 1974). These developments typically came about coercively, invariably through armed force, and were further solidified by war. Yet, as a result, citizens became part of a polity-wide scheme of social cooperation and could share a public sphere. However unjust their origins, they provide an environment within which citizens can establish justice by engaging in the collective practice of defining and upholding a fair scheme of rights.

Internal Sovereignty and the 'Mixed Constitution'

On this account, the self-determination of a sovereign people provides the 'right to have rights' (Arendt 1958: 296). Nevertheless, some contemporary republicans fear that having a single sovereign authority reduces the possibility for minority groups to contest majority decisions. They regard dividing sovereignty via a mixed constitution as favouring such contestation (Pettit 2012: 12–13, 220–5). As we shall see, similar considerations motivate advocates of a dispersal of sovereignty. However, such mechanisms risk allowing groups to avoid offering a public, commonly avowable, justification for their partial interests, for example by vetoing decisions they claim infringe their rights. Yet, to be legitimate, rights claims need to be made in a way that shows equal concern and respect towards those being asked to uphold them. Otherwise they will be based on private judgements, and not morally obligatory for other citizens. As Rousseau (1762: I.7) remarked, that would involve individuals seeking 'to enjoy the rights of a citizen without being willing to fulfil the duties of a subject'. At some point, such claims need to be made in a way that involves an impartial weighing of the rights of the community as a whole. That does not invalidate having ways to ensure minorities are not unduly overlooked and their voices get an equal hearing, merely that fairness requires that ultimately they must be considered as part of a collective scheme that treats all as free and equal.

Hobbes' (1651: ch. 29: 228) objections to 'mixt government' notwithstanding, a sovereign agency of rule need not be indivisible nor a sovereign regime unitary. Sovereign rule can be shared between different bodies with distinct roles or that must act concurrently, such as an upper and a lower house. Such divisions may help promote a balance of power between citizens. Yet, sovereign power could still lie in a single joint agency, as in the British formulation endowing sovereignty in the Queen in Parliament, signifying a concurrence of the executive and the upper and lower houses. Likewise, a sovereign polity can have a federal regime in which certain powers are devolved to sub territorial units as a matter of administrative convenience on the basis of rules and criteria decided at the federal level. Power sharing and devolution allow a regime to adapt to the diversity of a polity, such as the presence of socioeconomic and cultural differences, while still remaining sovereign. There simply needs to be procedures or mechanisms capable of resolving conflicts between different bodies that constitute a single sovereign authority. Nevertheless, the more segmental the divisions within the polity become, the more the devolution of power to sub-territorial units is likely to give rise to separate peoples within a polity. To the extent that is the case, citizens of these different units will gradually cease to regard themselves as engaged as a public in making common policies. Rather, they will increasingly wish their political representatives to share power at the federal level and represent their right as different peoples to collective self-government. Their aim will be to secure fair terms to do so alongside other peoples within the polity and even negotiate secession (Dahl 1989: 258–9). In so doing, they will move towards a republican association of sovereign states of the kind described below. In this regard, it is unsurprising that minority nations, such as Scotland and Catalonia, have believed the EU could and should facilitate their political empowerment.

External Sovereignty and Free States

The argument given above contends that a sovereign democratic authority provides the basis for non-domination among citizens, it does not stipulate how many such authorities there should be or where they ought to be located. Yet, as we saw in Chapter 2, for a sovereign state to secure the context for free persons through a non-dominating form of popular sovereignty it must be a free state, not dominated by other states, agents or agencies (Laborde and Ronzoni 2015). Many scholars believe such conditions no longer hold because global interdependence has challenged the external sovereignty of states and with it their internal sovereignty. New technologies have brought polities and their peoples closer together and rendered them more interconnected than ever before. Borders are not just more open to conventional and unconventional forms of armed aggression, with terrorist attacks penetrating the defences of even the most militarily mighty states, but also have been made progressively permeable by the globalisation of production, property ownership and finance as well as trade, and are increasingly tested by the migration of people. These global processes diminish the capacity of a sovereign polity and its regime to act as a supreme authority capable of securing the physical and economic well being of a people. A sovereign people risk being dominated and interfered with by the decisions and actions of different kinds of externally situated agents and agencies – be they other polities, wealthy financiers, multinational corporations, armed groups, or poor migrants (Pettit 2010a: 77–9). Likewise, it has become ever harder for polities to reap the benefits of any positive externalities resulting from their activities or to protect themselves from the negative externalities of the activities of other polities. For example, their clean environmental policies may benefit neighbouring states but be unable to counteract the pollution stemming from poor environmental controls of these same neighbours. At the same time, many argue that the continuing exclusions created by sovereign institutions involve unjustly dominating individuals who happen to have been born into poor or failing states and find themselves unable to leave or forced to take huge risks to do so only to end up in migrant camps.

Polities cannot tackle these problems effectively on their own. The pure statist response of a system of autarchic states is not an option. In greater or lesser ways, they need to cooperate to regulate their interactions and secure certain global public goods in ways that are equal and fair. The EU has been seen as a test ground of possible responses in this regard. As we saw, some republicans argue that it enables a shift towards a regional federal union that could resolve the problems associated with the erosion of external sovereignty, on the one hand, and unjust exclusions, on the other, by including all within a larger sovereign polity (Marti 2010). Others suggest that it allows for the dispersal of sovereignty and the move towards a post-sovereign political system that avoids the risks associated with concentrating power in any single agency (Bohman 2004b). In examining both proposals below, I shall argue that neither can sustain a form of politics capable of avoiding domination of the kind described above. As an alternative, I shall propose a republican association of sovereign states.

A Sovereign EU?: Sovereignty Displaced and Diluted

The ideal of a sovereign federal Europe predates the EU and animated some of its earliest proponents, while still remaining a goal for many (Burgess 2000). As we saw, dividing and devolving sovereignty do not in themselves undermine the possibility of a sovereign authority. Consequently, the governance structures of a federal European polity could be complex, requiring agreement between bodies representing both EU citizens and various sub-federal units, such as member states and regions, and involve a considerable degree of subsidiarity to these lower units, yet still possess sovereignty. However, unlike current arrangements, within such a federal EU, the division of competences between the levels would be decided at the EU level rather than via agreement between the member states, and the legitimacy for doing so would come from citizens directly debating and endorsing European-level policy making, even if those policies were mediated by agencies operating at various lower levels, with these also retaining competences in many areas.

A federal EU would potentially provide the polity sovereignty necessary to construct a basic political structure at the EU level. However, to be non-dominating, even a highly differentiated federal EU would also need, at least for certain purposes, to possess a European people willing and able to identify and act as a popular sovereign capable of ensuring the sovereign EU regime and its rulers operate under their equal influence and control to advance their commonly avowable interests. Section 2 defined a people in the political sense as possessing the capacity to deliberate in a public way about the public interest. As we saw, this capacity is facilitated by citizens possessing interconnected interests and a roughly equal stake in collective decisions, and sharing a public culture and sphere. Proponents of the 'no-demos' thesis contend these social and cultural conditions have so far failed to develop at the EU level (Weiler 1998a: 246; Scharpf 1999: 8–9). Social and economic divergence, on the one side, and cultural and linguistic diversity, on the other, remain robust. Even if the ideological and policy preferences of citizens are no more diverse across the EU as a whole than they are within most member states and similarly cross-cutting (Hale and Koenig-Archibugi 2016), there can still be segmental divisions between both regions with highly divergent levels of socio-economic development and different national groups who conceive themselves as distinct peoples. Such divisions already exist within many of the member states and drive calls for devolution in Scotland and Catalonia, for example. Across the EU they would be even stronger, creating an ever more conflictual cleavage between nationalists and supranationalists that could be disastrous for the EU (Bartolini 2005). After all, only 2 per cent of EU citizens view themselves as 'Europeans' pure and simple, with a mere 6 per cent regarding a European identity as more important than their national one (European Commission 2015).

As will be shown in Chapter 6, in such conditions, a high risk exists of dominating decisions deriving from unequal stakes, a lack of incentives to address issues of common concern in a public manner, and the likelihood of consistent and isolated minorities (Christiano 2010: 132–6). Such problems are exacerbated by the way the very size of the EU decreases both the representativeness of the European Parliament (EP) and the capacity and willingness of citizens to become informed about complex matters on which they can make little impact. After all, if constituencies were of equal size, then each of the 751 MEPs in the EP would represent around 675,000 voters against an average of 10,000 for every MP in a national parliament such as the UK. In fact, given the over-representation of smaller countries, most constituencies are far larger. Meanwhile, trans-European interest groups and parties, which might offer cues on EU matters to electors, barely exist except as EU-funded coalitions of national groupings within European institutions. Unsurprisingly, elections to the (EP) consist of second-order national elections (Hix and Marsh 2011), with electoral turnout steadily decreasing from the high of 61.99 per cent in 1979 to the low of 42.61 per cent in 2014 despite as steady an increase in the powers of the EP. Little wonder that decision-making at the EU level is perceived and criticised as monopolised by unaccountable elites.

It can be countered that large, socially and culturally diverse democracies exist, such as India. However, as I noted, such cases of state-building occurred through war and were accompanied by extensive and invariably coercive processes of nation-building – in India's case two centuries of armed occupation and colonial rule. Today, such processes would be deemed unacceptably illiberal and dominating. Indeed, those member states that employed them in the past to incorporate other political nations are now experiencing a resurgence of minority nationalist demands for greater political autonomy. Consequently, the legitimacy of EU-level decision-making depends to a high degree on there being multiple checks and balances for the different peoples of the member states, with most decisions within the EU requiring a consensus or a super-majority of states and citizens (Moravcsik 2002). Yet such multiple veto points not only reduce effectiveness and efficiency but also can impair the equity of decisions by favouring the status quo and vested interests (Scharpf 1988). They may be justified to preserve the equal entitlement to self-government of the various EU's peoples but not as mechanisms for collective decision-making among a European people. In the former case, it will suffice to seek only Pareto improvements between the member states beyond securing to each a minimum level of socio-economic well-being sufficient to sustain a capacity for self-government. In the latter case, it would be important for individuals to seek a common framework of social and civil entitlements, and in this case counter-majoritarian checks and balances could lead to deficiencies and inequalities in provision if their origins lie in a lack of collective solidarity and identification (Bellamy 2010).

Sensitive to these issues, some advocates of a federal EU suggest EU bodies should only decide those limited matters that require European solutions, so that current polities will retain most of their functions, albeit constrained by a supranational framework that regulates their interactions and promotes EU public goods (Habermas 2012: 38–41). This dual federal scenario, where federal and state units are responsible for different policy areas, differs from the unitary federal arrangement explored above, where states would possess powers that are devolved downwards from the centre and enforce federal policies. It does not conceive the participating polities as part of an overarching sovereign European polity. Rather, states would pool certain sovereign powers at the EU level in areas that lie beyond what each could handle individually.

The crux of his proposal is that individuals possess a dual citizenship as citizens of their member state and of the Union (Habermas 2012: 29). An argument explored more fully in Chapters 4 and 5, the key point to stress here is that individuals would still need to form a EU people and their representation be relatively diluted, with all the attendant difficulties noted above. However, Habermas suggests the reduced scope of policy-making he envisages could be achieved among a people only united by the thinner bond of 'constitutional patriotism' as the basis of a common 'post-national' European citizenship (Habermas 1999: 153, 159, 161). As I detail further in Chapter 5, this argument proves unconvincing. True, the abstract rights that figure in the European Convention of Human Rights and the EU Charter of Rights are shared by all the member states. Yet, most are embraced by democracies worldwide – after all, they are largely acknowledged as universal. That different peoples have these rights in common, though, does not mean they should automatically believe it legitimate to deliberate about them as a common people and be subject to a common sovereign authority for their interpretation and implementation. For all the aforementioned reasons, they may believe these tasks will be better achieved within a polity where the preconditions for impartial collective decision-making pertain and that can more appropriately realise the fundamental right to self-determination.

Creating an EU polity and regime in the hope it might generate the conditions for a European people proves not only impractical without an unacceptable degree of domination but also unjustifiable and unnecessary. Unjustifiable, because it rests on a mistaken domestic analogy that assumes the citizens of member states can be likened to individuals who lie outside any constituted sovereign political order. However, citizens are already constituted as peoples within a sovereign polity, which are capable of offering them valuable ways of living that possess moral worth. Nor are these states to be regarded as relating to each other in the manner of individuals in the state of nature. As juridical orders, they can act as moral agents with regard to each other, as the development of international law indicates. Unnecessary, because the required task is not so much to offer individuals a basic political structure at the EU level capable of securing justice for them in a legitimate manner, as to ensure the existing structures of the different member states prove mutually supportive rather than oppressive, and can cooperate in non-dominating ways that enable their citizens to live on free and equal terms with each other. I return to both these points in the fifth section below. Before doing so, however, I wish to explore the arguments of those who reject sovereignty altogether.

A Post-Sovereign Europe?: Sovereignty Divided, Discrete, Dispersed and Dissolved

Post-sovereigntists also view state sovereignty as practically and normatively untenable in a globalising world but regard the displacement of sovereignty upwards to a federal EU or even a world state as equally indefensible, in part for parallel reasons to those given above. Instead, they propose the vertical dispersal of sovereign authority both above and below the state, with the result that individuals would be 'citizens of, and govern themselves through, a number of units of varying sizes, without any one political unit being dominant and thus occupying the traditional role of the state. And their political allegiance and loyalties should be widely dispersed over these units: neighbourhood, town, county, province, state, region, and world at large' (Pogge 1992: 58). Once again, the EU gets presented as an opportunity and a model. Its alleged multilevel governance structures are said to allow citizens to participate in a variety of different sub-state, state, trans-state and supra-state political organisations and bodies, forming in each case a member of a different *demos*. These bodies are not necessarily hierarchically organised and depend often on voluntary compliance and consensual agreement between the various parties involved – be it in standard-setting bodies such as the Open Method of Coordination (OMC), the comitology processes for devising EU regulations, or the ordinary legislative procedure of the EU that requires agreement between the EP and the Council of the European Union, thereby involving an agreement between the representatives of states and of citizens in bodies that themselves generally operate by broad consensus. As a result, through membership of the EU the member states are losing sovereignty without transferring to any other body within the EU itself (MacCormick 1999: 126).

The descriptive accuracy of this picture of the EU is deeply controversial (Morgan 2005: 120–4). Even if accurate, though, its normative coherence remains questionable. Republicans have taken up the post-sovereignty thesis and related it to the republican theory of the mixed constitution (MacCormick 1999: ch. 9; Bellamy 2003 – a position I now reject; Bohman 2004a: 348–9; 2004b; Besson, 2006; Ladvas and Chryssochoou 2011). They take inspiration from what Pettit (2012: 12) has called the Italian-Atlantic tradition of republican thought rather than the Continental tradition of Kant and Rousseau defended in the second section above (Bohman 2005: 299). Just as the authors of *The Federalist* argued that a large and diverse republic rendered republican liberty more secure than in small republics (Hamilton et al. ['Publius'] 1778, 10: 44–6), not least when combined with the separation of powers, on the one side, and a territorial division of powers, on the other, so these cosmopolitan republicans consider an even more radical horizontal as well as vertical dispersal of sovereign authority as favouring safeguards against domination rather than otherwise (Bohman 2005: 300). They concede that a single EU (or ultimately global) *demos* overlooks the divergent impacts of, and interest in, common policies of different groups of people across the EU, despite their being interconnected to various degrees (Bohman 2005: 339). As a result, they argue one should conceive the EU as consisting of different *demoi*. However, they contend these *demoi* are not simply or primarily the peoples of the different member states, but increasingly the members of various subnational, and especially transnational associations of different kinds – not only regions and cities, but also CSOs and interest groups – that are functionally rather than territorially organised (Bohman 2005: 298).

Like earlier republicans, they conceive the key risk in democratic politics as factionalism, with the problem no longer that of one part of the *demos* dominating the other but of different *demoi* dominating each other. Whereas the Rousseauvian solution had been to create a coherent public among whom collective decision-making would be possible, they adapt the Madisonian reasoning to advocate the dispersal of sovereign power so that different *demoi* may each check and balance each other. However, the republican post-sovereigntists dispute the need for either supremacy or comprehensiveness. Instead, they argue that decisions must be shared among, and challengeable by, a range of different power centres and *demoi*. Moreover, decisions will necessarily be discrete, operating in specific areas and relating only to those people(s) with an equal interest in it. The focus in this account is as much on the democratic qualities of deliberation and contestation as on those of authorisation and accountability in order to secure responsiveness. The aim is to reduce the capacity for any one *demos* to dominate others through having to contend with multiple levels of power and authority (Bohman 2004b; 2005: 306). Yet sovereignty is not necessarily incompatible with this goal. Indeed, it may be necessary to its achievement.

Though sovereignty implies a degree of unity among the people and their system of governance, the second section indicated how it need not involve homogeneity or uniformity. The regime advocated by Publius was purposely that of a sovereign *United* States. And though they proposed a strong separation of powers and a bicameral legislature, each power has finality in its own domain and operates at the federal level, while a *Supreme* Court oversees the legal system, emerging as the body capable of resolving disputes between the federal and state governments regarding their competences. In other words, a prime rationale behind dividing power so that different groups could check and balance each other was to nudge them away from pursuing purely sectional interests towards public deliberation and negotiation on the public interest. However, this was only achieved to the extent the federal system was itself both comprehensive and supreme, forcing citizens, albeit mainly indirectly through their representatives, to converge as a collectivity on a common decision. Notoriously, the US system of government has failed to operate as Publius hoped it would. Far from diminishing the factionalism of local and sectional interests, the USA has long been characterised by pork-barrel politics at both the local and the federal level. Yet, in many respects, this feature results from an excess of checks and balances that weakens the capacity for the people as a whole to exercise sovereignty (see Dahl 2001). When a regime enjoys supremacy and comprehensiveness within a given polity, it can function as a community of communities for its members. The polity-wide regime both obliges and enables local and other discrete communities to take into account the effects of their decisions on non-members as well as other aspects of their members' lives, providing a mechanism through which those involved can negotiate these relations in an equitable and public manner as a people possessing multiple memberships. These mechanisms also allow members to leave a given sub community and join others should they so choose.

In the absence of any such comprehensive mechanisms, the dispersal of sovereignty among a multiplicity of discrete regimes would risk degenerating into a chaos of conflicting and partial polities, each self-reflexive and incomplete. No incentives to give equal concern and respect to all citizens necessarily exist in an entirely dispersed and non-hierarchical system (Miller 2008: 141–7). They would only be likely to arise if interconnectedness was so symmetrical that individuals belonged to crosscutting groups. But if the divisions are segmented and asymmetrical, as cosmopolitan republicans concede is likely, then the rich and powerful may ignore or dominate the poor and powerless. In the absence of any basic political structure through which they might impartially establish mutually acceptable just relations, individuals would be divided in themselves and from each other (Thompson 1999). Of course, some critics of state sovereignty claim that the relations between states within an interconnected world operate in precisely this chaotic and partial fashion (Slaughter 2004: 186). The issue is to see if this situation can be avoided.

A Republican Europe of Sovereign States? Sovereignty Delegated and Domesticated

It was argued above that for a popularly sovereign polity to incorporate under a supranational or transnational sovereign authority, even of a partial character, would be self-contradictory and a denial of the moral values the existing systems instantiate for their members. Yet, it would likewise be a contradiction in terms – both morally and for self-interested reasons – for such popularly sovereign polities not to accept an obligation to respect and uphold the moral equality of other popularly sovereign states or the rights of those subjects and individuals denied citizenship of such bodies to enjoy that status. To do so would involve a failure to accept the moral status and obligations of sovereign authority as the means through which we can achieve justice in a manner consistent with non-domination.

The third proposal, therefore, takes as its starting point that a supranational political structure must uphold: (1) that individuals can live as free and equal citizens of popularly sovereign polities; (2) that these popularly sovereign polities can be free and equal with regard to each other; and (3) that to achieve (1) and (2) involves not just non-interference but also, given they interact and are interdependent in many ways, ensuring that the regulations governing their interactions and mutual dependency treat the polities involved with equal concern and respect (Pettit 2010a; 2010b). The three elements are linked. Only if (1) is met will polities be likely to make agreements of the kind specified under (3) and so secure (2). They suggest a double form of delegation, whereby citizens exercising popular sovereignty at the domestic level delegate their respective representatives to make agreements with each other at the inter-polity level, including delegating and devolving authority upwards to appropriate regulatory bodies, so long as these remain under their joint and equal control.

This double delegatory process means that such associations can be regarded as the product of a form of two-level game that can be termed 'republican' intergovernmentalism (Bellamy and Weale 2015; Bellamy 2013). In other words, politicians within such an association must show each other equal concern and respect as the authorised and accountable representatives of their citizens, aware that any agreement among themselves must also be capable of being agreed to among their respective peoples. The net result of this double delegation is to preserve both popular and polity sovereignty of the contracting states to any international agreement, including one – like the EU – which involves the creation of supranational institutions. The upward delegation and devolution of power to the supranational level works in this respect in a parallel fashion to its downward counterparts at the domestic level. In both cases, the sovereign authority of the people remains in the last analysis final, supreme and comprehensive with respective to themselves (Troper 2010). Yet they obtain the facility – albeit mediated through their representatives – to cooperate with other peoples so as to support their mutual capacity for non-dominated rule. In this way, polities and their peoples preserve their internal sovereignty by agreeing on mutually agreeable institutions and laws for the regulation of their external sovereignty – including the movement of citizens between their respective states (Cohen 2012: 317–18, 322).

The resulting arrangement can be termed an inter-national association of popularly sovereign national polities, albeit one that leads to the creation of common supranational institutions. To a degree, such arrangements can be likened to a form of federation of states that does not involve sovereignty at the supranational level while modifying the exercise of sovereignty at the member state level (Kant 1797; Cohen 2012: ch. 2). However, from the perspective outlined here, certain proponents of this view go too far in considering that state sovereignty itself has been undermined by this arrangement (Forsyth 1981: 7, 207). Its very purpose and legitimacy depends on that not being the case. By contrast to Habermas's two-level Federation, we need not regard the EU as an independent constituted order with a direct relation to citizens, in which EU institutions make laws that the Court of Justice of the EU then applies in a hierarchical, top-down manner, as the product of a self-standing, superior legal order. Habermas's attempt to constitutionalise the EU misunderstands its rationale (Weiler 2001: 66, 68–70). Rather, as post-sovereigntists note, it is an order that states and their peoples have given and implement themselves not to supplant their sovereignty but to regulate its exercise with regard to each other.

Such an association seeks to promote, and be compatible with, the possibility for all individuals to live in representative states that possess democratic systems where collective decisions are made in ways that show them equal respect and concern through being under their equal, public control. Four criteria guide this arrangement. First, it presupposes a commitment to the values of representative democracy, and their equal enjoyment by all the associated peoples. Without this commitment, the association risks giving a spurious legitimacy to the domination of the citizens of its member states by their political rulers. It may also allow one or more member states to dominate the citizens of another or more member states by imposing terms and conditions of membership upon them that they could not be expected to democratically endorse. Second, if the legitimacy of popularly sovereign polities stems from them offering reasonably effective, public mechanisms for the identification and equal advancement of the interests of their citizens, then the legitimacy of supra-national organisations stems from them doing likewise through being in their turn under the shared and equal control of the signatory polities acting as the representatives of their respective peoples. In other words, 'output' legitimacy must always depend on an appropriate 'input' legitimacy from the constituent peoples of the association. Third, citizens of different peoples ought not to be discriminated against in their interactions on the basis of their nationality. The mutual concern and respect that operates among sovereign polities ought to apply to the citizens of those polities in moving and trading between them, so long as this proves consistent with the capacity of the citizens of each state to shape their domestic policies in diverse but mutually respectful ways. This criterion follows from the fact that underlying the contract among peoples is a contract among their respective citizens to recognise each other (Bellamy and Lacey 2018). Finally, membership of such international systems should be voluntary and allow for 'opt-outs' and exit clauses. Not all polities will have an equal stake in collective arrangements on a given issue, and many will not have equal bargaining power. Voluntary arrangements allow sovereign polities to tailor their commitments to the interests of their populations and ideally to negotiate the terms of their adherence accordingly.

Part 2 will argue that many of the EU's current structures could – with some adjustments – and should be assimilated to such an association (Bellamy 2013; Chevenal and Schimmelfennig 2013), which better cor-responds to the aims of the main state actors involved in their creation than the aspirations of the so-called founding fathers (Milward 1992). Chapter 4 explores why and how the representative structures of the EU can be aligned with the first and second criteria outlined above, while Chapter 5 relates Union citizenship to the third and Chapter 6 indicates ways the integration process and the EU's legal order might accommo-date the fourth of these criteria.

As we shall see, the EU's associational character is evident in the way intergovernmental arrangements remain crucial in deciding the scope of the EU. After all, the goals of the EU are defined by the Treaties, which require unanimity to be agreed and where national governments naturally take the lead. Although the European Council has no legislative functions (again, contra Habermas 2012: 44), it has become an increasingly key actor that 'defines the general political directions and priorities' of the Union (TEU 2012: 15.1). Meanwhile, as Chapter 4 details, this inter-governmentalism has taken a republican turn through the increased powers accorded national parliaments that enable them to influence and control the negotiation positions of their Ministers and align them to domestic electoral preferences (Kröger and Bellamy 2016). True, the powers of the EP have grown. Yet, even it can be regarded as representing the EU *demoi* more than its *demos*. Constituencies are allocated on a national basis employing degressive proportionality, thereby allowing each member state to be represented by a range of parties, with European parties essentially parliamentary coalitions of national parties. Such a structure involves states delegating power upwards rather than downwards, but, as with downward delegations within a sovereign polity, involve these states still keeping these competences under their joint and equal influence and control. Moreover, the normative legitimacy of such a supranational, delegated authority involves its policies according equal concern and respect to each of the contracting states as popularly sovereign polities and so being capable of obtaining the long-term endorsement of their peoples.

Such an interpretation of the EU has a firm basis in its political and constitutional structures. For example, Article 4.2 of the Treaty on European Union (2012) expressly states:

The Union shall respect the equality of Member States before the Treaties as well as their national identities, inherent in their fundamental structures, political and constitutional, inclusive of regional and local self-government. It shall respect their essential State functions, including ensuring the territorial integrity of the State, maintaining law and order and safeguarding national security.

In a similar vein, the revised Article 5.2 TEU now insists on 'the principle of conferral', emphasising that 'the Union shall act *only* within the limits of the competences conferred upon it by the Member States in the Treaties to attain the objectives set out therein'. As the German Federal Constitutional Court noted in its Lisbon Judgment (2009), this principle upholds the member states as 'the primary political area of their respective polities', with the EU only having 'secondary responsibility for the tasks conferred on it'. In other words, on this account the EU operates as a delegated authority under the equal control of the domestic political systems of its constituent states – a position that Part 2 will argue is best articulated in terms of the 'republican intergovernmental' perspective introduced here.

Conclusion: Republican Intergovernmentalism

The EU is currently subject to three apparently opposed political demands: calls for a return of sovereign powers to the member states; advocacy of the transfer of sovereign power upwards to the EU level; and support for a dispersal of sovereign power across multiple levels and different kinds of *demoi*, including minority national groups within member states desiring ever more devolved power. Each of these demands reflects a different evaluation of sovereignty and its role in ensuring the conditions of democratic legitimacy, which can be related in certain key aspects to a republican argument for non-domination. I have suggested all are right in some respects and wrong in others, and proposed an alternative vision of the EU (and of the international order more generally) as an international republican association of sovereign states that draws on all three. Such an association has as its constituent parts sovereign states that provide the context for popular internal sovereignty. Yet, they create external supranational institutions with certain federal-seeming features with the capacity to enable their mutual regulation of their external sovereignty given global interconnectedness. However, this supranational order is in itself not sovereign over them. As a result, it is not itself a source of domination but rather a mechanism for the member states to avoid the possibility of any one of them dominating the others. In this way, it answers to the demand to provide a response to the pressures on external sovereignty in an interconnected world, on the one hand, and the potential injustice perpetrated by a sovereign authority on those who are excluded from membership, on the other, without giving up on internal state authority as the context for a popular sovereign regime capable of sustaining a non-dominating legal and political order for its citizens.

Part 2 of this book sketches in more detail the implications of this model for how we can and should understand the institutional structures of the EU with regard to democratic decision-making at the EU level (Chapter 4); the value and nature of Union citizenship (Chapter 5); and the possibilities for states to adopt different policies, belong to different decision-making structures, and be subject to different European laws (Chapter 6). It seeks to show that conceiving the EU through the cosmopolitan statist perspective offered by a 'republican intergovernmentalism' provides a more functionally effective and normatively appealing account than either a predominantly statist, liberal intergovernmental view, or a largely cosmopolitan, neo-functionalist and federal position.

Part 2

A Republican EU of Sovereign States: Republican Intergovernmentalism, Demoicracy and Non-Domination

4 Representing the Peoples of Europe: Addressing the Demoicratic Disconnect

Introduction

Chapter 3 argued that the democratic legitimacy of a republican association of democratic states involves meeting a dual standard of representativeness. This standard was defined by the first two of the four criteria outlined at the end of that chapter. The first criterion for such an association requires that the governments of the associated states must represent their citizens in ways that show them equal concern and respect, and both acknowledge and be acknowledged by the other states as so doing, while the second criterion insists the collective decisions reached between these governments at the international level must be under the shared and equal control of the peoples of these states, albeit indirectly via their duly elected representatives. This chapter explores what satisfying this dual standard entails, both normatively and institutionally, through a critical analysis of the democratic decision-making structures of the EU.

Probably no normative question regarding the EU has aroused greater attention than that of its alleged democratic deficit. However, from the perspective adopted here, the standard ways of understanding this debate prove misconceived because they fail to consider the effects of the integration process on democratic decision-making at the national level. With a few honourable exceptions (e.g. Schmidt 2006), policy-makers and academics have generally understood the democratic deficit of the EU in terms of the weak, or absence of, direct democratic accountability of central EU institutions to EU citizens. As a result, they have typically assessed the democratic prospects of the EU in terms of the practicality and acceptability of strengthening the powers of the EP as the one directly elected body (Rittberger 2005, 2014), and relating EP elections more closely to the selection of the Commission, which in turn would acquire the status and powers of an elected EU executive. However, this way of envisioning the debate confuses arguments regarding more or less democracy at the EU level with arguments for more or less political integration of a federalising kind. For those advocating strengthening the EP have usually done so, at least in part, as a means for democratically legitimating and, they believe, making more likely, steps towards a more federal political union (e.g. Hix 2008). Unsurprisingly, therefore, the most powerful criticisms of this approach have come from liberal intergovernmentalists (Moravcsik 2002; 2008), who have argued that the multiple checks and balances of the EU's political system, and the control exercised by member state governments in particular, render the EU almost too democratic as it is, and certainly make redundant any shift towards a more centralised federal EU possessing a direct democratic mandate from EU citizens.

The flaw with both sides of this standard debate lies in their common failure to address – indeed, they tend to provoke – the criticisms raised by those who view EU integration as inherently democratically illegitimate on account of its detracting from democracy at the domestic level by taking decision-making away from national legislatures. For these critics, the problem with the EU lies in its promoting a domestic democratic deficit. Proponents of the first, federally inclined argument, usually see the 'no EU demos' thesis (Weiler 1995: 225) as the main criticism to address, a problem they regard as more apparent than real. They note that a similar left-right cleavage exists across the EU and claim that empowering the EP further would promote a commensurate shift of interest and allegiance to the EU level among EU citizens (Hix 2008). Yet, the trouble with their proposal lies less with the difficulties of creating an EU demos *per se* and more with the presence of already existing national and sub national demoi. There is no reason to believe that citizens would (or, as has been argued in Part 1, should) follow this neo-functionalist logic and feel the empowerment of an EU demos compensates for the disempowerment of a national demos, especially if the former is responsible for the latter. Indeed, as we shall see, much of the evidence suggests the opposite. Likewise, supporters of the second, liberal intergovernmental, argument, overlook the way decision-making among governments at the EU level has empowered national executives and disempowered national parliaments and electorates, given EU affairs rarely figure as central issues in domestic elections (Maurer and Wessels 2001). Both a neo-functionalist federal EU and a liberal intergovernmentalist EU could be interpreted as involving an association of democratic states, albeit the former more centralised and hierarchically organised, with greater authority at the supranational level, and the latter more international in character. However, both fail to meet the two associational criteria for democratic legitimacy outlined above.

By contrast, this book has pronounced 'a plague on both your houses' by rejecting each of these perspectives. Instead of conceiving European integration as replacing national democracy, and so, by implication, undermining it; I have suggested that we should understand the EU as playing a necessary role in fostering it within the context of an interdependent world. So the challenge is a different one – it involves finding ways whereby the various national demoi can at one and the same time control their representatives at the EU level while acknowledging a duty to show equal concern and respect towards other demoi and to avoid dominating them. To fulfil this dual requirement involves ensuring representation at the EU level possesses a certain moral quality – one I shall associate below with the notion of 'civicity'. I shall argue that this quality is not only currently missing from, but also unachievable by, either federal representation within the EP and Commission, or liberal intergovernmental forms of representation within the European Council and the Council of Ministers. Instead, I shall argue we need to adopt a *demoi*-cratic approach of a kind I will associate with a 'republican intergovernmentalism' that, in Kalypso Nicolaïdis' felicitous phrase, conceives the EU as a 'Union of peoples who govern together, but not as one' (Nicolaïdis 2013: 351).

This demoicratic approach suggests that the key democratic failing of the EU lies less with a *deficit* of democracy at the EU level *per se*, and more with the presence of a democratic *disconnect* between EU decision-making and the democratic processes of the different demoi within each of the member states (Lindseth 2010: 234). From this point of view, the crux lies in ensuring that the different peoples of the EU can exercise a degree of equal influence and control over their governmental representatives when negotiating in the European Council and the Council of the European Union, as well as their MEPs within the EP, with these latter representing not a European demos through transnational parties, but the demoi of different member states via their *national* parties. At the same time, though, the act of governing together must be such as to oblige both these different demoi and their elected representatives to show equal concern and respect to each other's democratic processes, so as to avoid one or more peoples dominating any others.

As I noted in Chapters 2 and 3, these requirements follow from the normative demands of a two-level game, whereby governments must not only agree amongst each other but also have the agreement of those who they represent (Savage and Weale 2009). The rest of this chapter tackles this issue. I shall suggest that neither a federalist-inspired empowering of the EP as a directly elected representative of a putative EU demos, on the one hand, nor liberal intergovernmental bargaining, on the other, can provide an adequate response to the democratic deficit precisely because they serve simply to deepen the democratic disconnect. Without a robust connection to national demoi, they promote a quality of democracy that cannot escape being deficient in terms of representing those on whose behalf they claim to speak and act. By contrast, as I noted above, I shall argue for a form of what I have called republican intergovernmentalism (Bellamy 2013), within which national parliaments and parties play a crucial role. This structure seeks to encourage the different demoi to recognise their mutual obligations to preserve the capacity of the associated peoples for representative democracy by promoting common policies in ways that not only avoid, but also serve to protect against, the domination of one people by another.

The EU's Three Channels of Representation

The key difficulty within the current arrangement lies in the tensions between the three main channels of representation within the EU. Title II Article 10 of the Post-Lisbon Consolidated Treaty of the European Union (TEU) declared the Union to embody the principles of representative democracy and identified three channels whereby European citizens are represented in the EU's political system. First, directly via elections to the European Parliament (EP); second, indirectly via their Heads of State or Government in the European Council and in the Council by their Government; and third, in domestic elections that hold these last democratically accountable to National Parliaments (NPs) or to the citizens of the various member state demoi. One potential difficulty with this arrangement involves a possible tension between the representation of individual Union citizens; of states, via their governments; and of national peoples, respectively. No clear distinction exists between when and for what purposes member state citizens are to be represented either as Europeans, or by their elected state governments, or as citizens of national demoi, or of the connections between the three (see Kröger and Friedrich 2013; Bolleyer and Reh 2012, though they concentrate only on the tension between the first two channels). Consequently, EP decisions can be at odds with European Council decisions and both EP and Council conflict with the decisions of national peoples, whether these latter are expressed directly in referenda or indirectly via their representatives in national parliaments. In what follows, I shall argue that not only do these three channels represent different subjects, but also that each channel involves a different type of representation and form of democracy, that constructs a different and conflicting conception of the EU.

Such differences can be productive. For example, bicameral systems often employ different electoral systems and constituencies for each of the chambers, the idea being to bring different voices into the democratic dialogue with short-term and long-term, national and regional, majority and minority interests balanced against each other. Though systems of compound representation can be criticised for multiplying veto points and creating inefficiencies (Scharpf 1988), they are generally motivated by a desire to prevent the capture of government policy by sectional interests and to promote a concern with the public interest (Hamilton et al. [1778] 2003). However, at present no such logic can be attributed to the EU political system because these three channels are not related to each other in a systematic and coherent manner. Instead, they offer incompatible images of the relations between individuals, state governments, and peoples in Europe.

Each channel not only invokes different subjects of the process of EU integration but also constructs a different account of the European public interest these subjects might converge upon and of how they might do so. To use the terminology introduced in Chapter 1, if the first aspires to represent a putative European demos by appealing to an emergent 'thick' statist cosmopolitanism; the second involves a 'thin' cosmopolitan statism; while the third, offering as we shall see the potential for a 'thick' cosmopolitan statism, has hitherto barely figured in EU decision-making at all. The first draws on a neo-functionalist logic to suggest that the democratic deficit of the EU can be eliminated by shifting political authority to the EU level along with an appropriate form of pan-European democracy (Risse 2005). By contrast, the second relies on a liberal intergovernmentalist logic to deny the existence of any democratic deficit on the grounds that the integration process remains under the control of the elected representatives of the member states (Moravcsik 2002). Meanwhile, I shall argue that the third offers the possibility of a 'republican intergovernmentalism' that reconnects these other two to the domestic democratic processes of the different peoples of the member states.

Developing the work of Pitkin (1967) and Pettit (2005) on political representation, I will argue that the first two approaches both involve an elite perspective that ignores the democratic disconnect with the electorates of the various national demoi. Adapting Pitkin's discussion of representativeness (1967: 69, 71, 75–82), the first can be characterised in terms of MEPs and the Commission 'standing as' an emergent European demos, on behalf of whom they claim to 'act as' trustees and to deliberate on a presumed European 'common good'. The second sees national executives 'standing for' their respective states, which they claim to 'act for' as putative delegates by adopting reasons of state to arrive at policies reflecting the mutual self-interest of the member states. Yet, while both sets of actors claim to be acting 'as' or 'for' those they in some symbolic sense can stand 'as' or 'for' and represent, neither has been fully authorised to do so nor is held accountable for what they do given that EP elections tend to be second order, while EU affairs rarely figure in domestic elections, or, if they do, seldom prove decisive. As a result, the 'democratic disconnect' persists, provoking a hitherto 'permissive consensus' among the member state electorates with regard to the elite process of integration, to turn into a 'constraining dissensus' as the EU moves into ever more salient issues and shifts EU decision-making into mainstream mass politics (Hooge and Marks 2009). At the same time, they not only suffer from a problem of democratic legitimacy but also have contrasting and often contradictory conceptions of the EU and the public interest it exists to promote, leading to conflicting policy proposals.

In the rest of this chapter, I shall argue that these two main representative channels of the EU currently misrepresent the 'public' of Europe both in their conception of that public – as either a European people or simply a collection of states – and in the type of representation they employ and the form of politics it leads to. The resulting problems seem epitomised by current attempts to resolve the Euro crisis, where the proposed measures have failed either to promote a supposed European interest sufficient to allow credit transfers between member states, or to satisfy national interests as these are perceived by domestic electorates. A parallel problem afflicts the response to the migration crisis, where a similar divide exists between a hypothetical European and the various national interests. The upshot has been policies widely criticised as suboptimal. I shall contend the solution lies in the European peoples being represented in a way that allows for greater interaction between them in the collective decision making of the EU. In line with the TEU's meta democratic principle of 'equality', a form of representation is required that pays 'equal attention' to citizens as citizens of a Union of peoples rather than as either members of a putative European people or merely nationals of a member state. In sum, we need to promote a workable form of European 'demoi-cracy' (Nicolaïdis 2004) rather than either a European 'demos-cracy' or an 'executive federalism' (Habermas 2012: 6–7) where either the EU or some member states can dominate all or other member states.

The argument proceeds as follows. I shall start by distinguishing three forms of representative democracy and three related conceptions of political community. If the first form of democracy is 'thick', concerned with the intrinsic promotion of a supposed common good, and the second is 'thin', orientated towards an instrumental protection of individual rights and interests, the third seeks to combine these two in ways that have become characteristic of most working liberal democracies. These three forms of democracy reflect three different political ontologies – what, following Philip Pettit (2005), I shall term solidarism, singularism and civicity – which conceive the relations between the members of a political community and the appropriate modes of representing them in contrasting ways. I shall contend that the capacity to promote public policies that give mutual recognition to the rights of individuals can only be found in the interactional form of representation characteristic of a civicity. Turning to the EU, I shall argue that the supranational, international and national channels of representation within the EU currently correspond respectively to the three forms of representative democracy and political community delineated above. However, the social conditions are lacking for the solidarist account invoked by the EP and the Commission to represent the collective interests of a European people; while the singularist account that legitimises bargaining between the member states prevents their governments moving beyond policies that can be portrayed as Pareto optimal. A final section proposes that if European issues could be introduced into the national channel of representation that might in its turn modify the other two channels sufficiently to move them closer to the form of representative democracy typical of a civicity. The result would be a European demoicracy, in which political representatives at all three levels would be socially and politically authorised and accountable for policies that show equal concern and respect to the different peoples of Europe. Such policies involve less than the common good of a European people but more than the mutual self-interest of the member states. Figure 4.1 below summarises the argument, noting how the various theories complement each other to support a particular channel and mode of democratic representation within the EU.

Political Ontology	Solidarism	Singualism	Civicity
Model of Democracy	Thick Democracy	Thin Democracy	Thick-Thin Democracy
Mode of Representation – standing as/for and acting as/for	Trustees 'stand as' and 'act as' an EU demos – participatory deliberation to achieve hypothetical EU common good	Delegates – 'stand for' and 'act for' states – protective – bargaining, to achieve the mutual interest of member states	'Relational' representation – a product of authorisation and accountability – means can stand and act 'as' and 'for' through negotiation and compromise on shared interests
View of Global Justice	Thick Statist Cosmopolitanism	Thin Cosmopolitan Statism	Thick Cosmopolitan Statism

(cont.)

Political Ontology	Solidarism	Singualism	Civicity
Theory of EU Integration	Neo-functionalism	Liberal intergovern- mentalism	Republican intergovernmentalism
Channel of Representation	EP/Commission	European Council	National Parliaments influencing EP/EC and Council

Figure 4.1: Three Types of Political Ontology, Models of Democracy and Modes of Representation

Three Models of Representative Democracy

The Nature of Political Representation

In formal terms, representation involves someone taking the place of some-one else through a process involving both the authorisation of the representative *by* the represented, and the accountability of the representative *to* the represented (Pitkin 1967: 42–3, 55–9, 232–6). Authorisation concerns the procedures by which people transfer a lesser or greater amount of their power to either act or decide to other political and/or legal 'persons' or institutions. Accountability deals with the ways by which the represented can exercise a lesser or greater degree of control over what their representatives do in their name. These two moments reflect the initial and the final stage of the representative relationship respectively, and are central to the legitimacy of democratic representation.

How political agents enact this formal relationship substantively also matters. On Pitkin's account, a representative may 'stand for' or 'act for' those they represent (Pitkin 1967: 61, 113). The first involves descriptive or symbolic representation, as in a portrait or logo, and hence a degree of identification between representative and represented. The second can be as a trustee or a delegate. Historically, substantive disputes about *how* representatives represent have centred on the trustee–delegate dichotomy, though a whole spectrum of possible relationships exists between the two (Pitkin 1967: 115–39). However, despite its limitations (Saward 2010), this dichotomy captures an important dilemma confronting democratic representation. As Pitkin noted, representation involves a paradox whereby it makes 'present' those who are 'absent'. As such, it involves a relationship of relative independence between the representative and the represented (Pitkin 1967: 209). If the legitimacy of representatives tends to rest on their having a mandate of some kind, and so being in certain respects delegates, the activity of representation tends to involve their being able to act in some ways independently, as trustees.

In what follows below, I shall develop Pitkin's analysis to note that all forms of representation involve symbolic elements, and that the extent and nature of the social relationship assumed to exist between representatives and those they represent by the processes employed for their selection conditions how far and in what ways representatives seek to bridge the gap between trusteeship and delegation. In other words, the manner in which representatives act 'as' or 'for' their principals depends to a large degree on how they stand 'as' or 'for' them. Note, the presumed social relationship may or may not exist – indeed, below I shall suggest that in the case of the EP it does not. Rather, different forms of representation rest on a claim about the existence of a certain type of relationship that is mirrored in the way the political system operates.

I shall suggest that to the extent representatives have a presumed social relationship with those they represent that is premised on shared values and interests, they can 'stand as' them and be trusted to 'act as' them, as trustees. That may seem at odds with the *locus classicus* of democratic representation as trusteeship, Burke's Speech to the Electors of Bristol of 1774. Yet, his claim to be able to deliberate on his voters' behalf turned on the assumption that, properly speaking, the interests of the electors of Bristol formed part of the national interest. Parliament's job was to represent the whole nation rather than its parts, and this was possible and legitimate because these parts were organically related in a way that was discoverable through deliberation among representatives and their conscientious exercise of reason. Despite any appearances of divergent opinions or concerns, therefore, representatives could be trusted because they shared a common interest in pursuing a collective good, both with each other and their constituents. However, if individuals are conceived as having not only distinct but also diverse and potentially conflicting interests and can reasonably adopt a plurality of reasons, then these grounds for trusting representatives no longer apply. After all, they too may have interests and reasons of their own that differ from those of their constituents. Consequently, they will need to be formally delegated to 'stand for' and 'act for' the represented. Such delegates need to act under instructions in a way that trustees do not, and require to be checked and controlled by those they represent.

Three Democratic Ontologies

How citizens are represented in the democratic system – as trustees or delegates – reflects different political ontologies, or view 'of the relationships and structure in virtue of which individuals in a polity constitute a people, a nation, and a state' (Pettit 2005: 157), and leads to different ways of conceiving the political process. These differences determine in turn the view of the public interest that representatives will seek to construct, and the political and social legitimacy they have to do so. Drawing on the trustee–delegate distinction and their respective social underpinnings, I shall identify below three broad conceptions of democracy – what I call 'thick', 'thin' and 'thick-thin' – which respectively rest on an assumed 'strong', 'weak' or mixed 'strong-weak' social relationship between representatives and represented. Each involves a different understanding of how representatives may stand as and for citizens that corresponds to a different 'political ontology' that, following Pettit (2005), I term 'political solidarism', 'political singularity' and 'civicity'. While the first makes possible representation as 'trusteeship', as defined above, the second requires 'delegation', and the third enables what I shall call a 'relational' form of representation. As we shall see, both the 'thick' and 'thin' models of democracy lead representatives to pursue a limited understanding of the public interest that, in the one case, subsumes the individual into the collective interest and, in the other, the collective into the individual interest. By contrast, the relational, interactive form of representation typical of the thick-thin model balances the two.

Democratic politics encompasses two main tasks: the positive task of facilitating the equal participation of citizens in the construction of the public interest, and the negative task of protecting the interests of the ruled from being dominated and manipulated by their rulers via their control of the state apparatus. Both the participatory and the protective tasks figure in most theories of democracy. However, different conceptions of the democratic process tend to read either the second through first or *vice versa* (Macpherson 1977).

Thicker conceptions of democracy emphasise deliberation. Democracy serves an intrinsic purpose whereby the political community can discover and sustain the common good. This theory places great epistemic weight on public deliberation and the possibility of achieving a reasoned consensus (Habermas 1984, 1987; Bohman 1996). It aims at generating a general will, which has moral priority over the particular wills of individuals. As a result, the second, protective, task of democratic politics is conceived in terms of the first, participatory, task. The public interest is construed in positive terms, as the product of citizens identifying with each other and the polity.

'Thick' democracy presupposes an organic unity among the demos, and a natural conception of the common good. This unity of interests can be represented in descriptive and symbolic ways that can be characterised as 'standing as'. Consequently, representatives can be trusted to 'act as' the represented by virtue of certain personal characteristics that allow them either symbolically or descriptively to express the commonality of interests of those they represent. The governing body, be it an elected parliament or an unelected council, gains its authority by reproducing internally the same kind of unity (of the nation, for instance) that allegedly characterises the political body at large. Democratic representation reflects a unity of interests that already exists before the political process is in place and which deliberation among representatives merely seeks to clarify and express.

This understanding of democracy presupposes an ontology of 'political solidarism'. Citizens are conceived as part of a corporate body, whose standing, interests and judgements is both separate and independent from them: they are 'incorporated' into the body politic, which can then act in their collective name. A conception of political relations found today in legal notions of corporate personality, it characterises theories of democracy that seek to identify the common good with the will of the people conceived as a collective agent. This view assumes citizens and their representatives possess a sympathetic identification with each other and an underlying agreement on ethical principles. They regard themselves as forming a stable collective unit with common goals.

By contrast, thinner conceptions of democracy emphasise the protection of private rights to liberty and the aggregation of separate individual interests. Democracy serves an instrumental purpose. The ruled seek to maximise the exercise of their private rights – either by protecting them or combining with fellow citizens who have similar or convergent interests – and to minimise the capacity of others – especially the rulers and the state – to interfere with them. Thus, the positive, participatory, task of democratic politics is conceived largely in terms of the negative, protective, task. The public interest is construed as the product of a system that maximises the possibility of each affected agent to block those interferences with their individual rights they deem unnecessary (Madison in *Federalist* n. 10 in Hamilton, A., Madison, J., and Jay, J. (2003 [1778]) provides the *locus classicus* of this approach).

The thin conception's understanding of representation oscillates between privileging either a substantive sense of accountability or the formal processes of authorisation. On the one side, it focuses on the capacity of representatives to deliver certain policies or objectives, while denying that authorisation implies a real transfer of power. On the other side, it stresses the constraints imposed by the authorisation of representatives, but has a limited view of the process of accountability. Adapting

Pitkin (1967: 139), the one interprets the role of representatives as 'acting for' in the generic sense of acting 'in the interest of'; while the other conceives representatives as 'substitutes' who 'stand for' the represented and act 'under instructions'.

Elitist versions of this thin conception, such as Schumpeter's (1947), deny that the democratic selection process is properly representative. Leaders recruit their electors through charisma or the policy package they offer rather than being authorised by them as their representatives. Schumpeter refuses any possibility of a transfer of authority. In Adam Przeworski's words, 'Our institutions are representative. Citizens do not govern' (2010: 15). The representative's responsibilities and responsiveness to the represented is no more than a technical mechanism through which the electors express satisfaction or dissatisfaction with the way in which they have been governed or expect to be governed. Yet, the process of accountability gives liberal elites an incentive 'to act in the interest of' a broad section of the electorate. By contrast, on the substitution and mandate views, the rulers are authorised to represent the interests of the ruled. When acting as substitutes, representatives employ their own judgements as to how the interests of those they represent might best be pursued. Their role is to maximise a return to their diverse supporters. Authorisation gives them the right to do so until it is withdrawn. When mandated, representatives are authorised to act 'under instructions' from the represented, who are conceived as forming a discreet interest group with a shared view on how it should be promoted. However, whether the stress is on accountability or authorisation, the conception of the public interest that issues from these thin views consists of Pareto optimal improvements or the lowest common denominator. On the elite view, this arises from competing elites striving to win a majority through aggregating individual interests and appealing to as broad a constituency as possible. On the substitution view, it results from substitutes seeking a return for the diverse interests of their backers. On the mandate view, it stems from the delegates of different interests seeking to block any collective decision that might not advantage their principals.

The ontology underlying this account of representation is 'political singularism'. Formal processes of accountability and authorisation are vital because people are assumed to be so distinct that no representative can 'stand as' another. Originating in the natural rights tradition, claims against governments and others are grounded in rights that inhere in individuals by virtue of their humanity rather than their social status. Political society is simply an aggregate of separate individuals with no politically significant relationship to each other apart from their various mutual contractual agreements. They enter these agreements solely to protect their rights and further their interests. Democracy consists of selecting politicians able to pursue these tasks and removing those who fail through incompetence or corruption.

Each of these two conceptions of democracy has advantages and related disadvantages. The thick conception supports public goods but at the expense of potentially overlooking the pluralism of modern societies. Consequently, social and cultural diversity may be undervalued, with certain private rights overridden and cultural and other minorities marginalised. By contrast, the thin conception emphasises individual rights but at the expense of so multiplying veto points that it proves hard to move beyond the *status quo*. Given that power and resources are unequally distributed in society, this arrangement may entrench and potentially enhance existing privileges and inequities. It also risks failing to provide adequately for the public goods on which many rights depend – from the police and legal system to welfare, health and education. Most working democracies involve mechanisms that balance the two models by making democracy thick enough to promote the public good, but sufficiently thin to allow for the protection of individual and group rights.

This thick-thin model of democracy is sustained by a rather different, relational, view of representation. Neither the thick nor the thin views consider democratic representation as a dynamic and interactive *relationship* between the represented and their representatives. In the thick view, representatives act 'as' the represented by virtue of certain supposed intrinsic similarities. In the thin view, representatives act 'for' the represented either like the executive of a public company charged with maximising the returns to shareholders, or by virtue of a mandate. In both these cases, representatives claim to act on the alleged revealed preferences of their principals. However, a relational view interprets the relationship between representatives and the represented in more dynamic terms. As I noted, representatives are both dependent on the represented, who authorise them and hold them to account, and independent actors in their own right. Such independence not only results from them having to make decisions to meet unanticipated circumstances between elections but also from their being able to persuade voters and recruit a following during them. In Iris Young's words, the moments of authorisation and accountability involve 'a cycle of anticipation and recollection between constituents and representative' (2000: 129), in which both sides of the representation relationship are engaged in mutually constructing what and who is represented, how and by whom.

A thick-thin conception of democracy has this relational dynamic at its core. The process of representation forces citizens to dialogue with each other and obliges them to portray their various rights claims and individual interests in public terms in ways that can relate to those of others. Representatives neither appeal to the passive assent of the unreflective, naked preferences of citizens, nor merely reproduce their particular sectional interests, or the alleged pre-political interests of a collective body. Rather, the incentives are such that they need to employ public reasons that can be avowed and shared by a broad cross-section of the citizenry. Such public reasoning leads citizens to reflect upon their interests in ways that help construct shared interests (Sunstein 1991). As Bernard Manin (1997: 196) has noticed, contrary to Schumpeter's view, the competitive party system has tended to play just this role in facilitating the emergence of a popular general will within elections by making politicians construct programmes of government with broad enough appeal to attract the median voter.

The relational reading of the representative process conceives the public interest as constructed via an on-going dialogue between the particular interests of citizens. This dialogue occurs both vertically, between the represented and their representatives, and horizontally, among representatives themselves or various sections of the public. In this way, it combines both the intrinsic democratic qualities of 'thick' democracy, with its focus on the common good, and the instrumental qualities of 'thin' democracy, with its emphasis on protecting individual rights and furthering particular interests, so as to construct shared interests that balance both considerations.

This form of democratic representation assumes a political ontology akin to what Pettit calls a 'civicity' (2005: 167). This ontology involves aspects of the other two views. Like political solidarism, citizens within a 'civicity' regard themselves as forming a people with certain common interests and values. However, like political singularism, they also have distinct interests, make divergent rights claims and so differ over many public policies. Citizens combine both perspectives by seeking to resolve their disagreements and differences in public terms that can be seen as plausibly, if for some contentiously, as treating them with equal concern and respect. For example, if a government within a civicity offers a given group a tax break, be it the very poor or the very rich, they will be expected to at least make a show of defending this measure as both equitable and contributing to the welfare of the rest of society. They cannot simply insist that this group is entitled to this money as a privilege and regardless of its effects on others. The measure must treat others in society with equal concern and respect by giving equal weight to their rights and interests, and their views regarding them. Of course, how far the proposal does meet these criteria will be disputed by many, but the fact of free and fair elections forces the government to dialogue with citizens and justify its position to them.

The Preconditions of a Civicity

To work, the members of a civicity must be linked by the two types of social relations identified in Chapter 3 as essential to democratic legitimacy. These consisted of a self-conception as a public associated with a common public culture and sphere, on the one side, and interdependence and shared interests deriving from being part of a common scheme of social cooperation, on the other. These two types of social relations support respectively the 'thick' and 'thin' modes of democracy, and enable their interaction.

As I remarked in Chapter 3, the first type of social relation involves what J.S. Mill referred to as 'common sympathies' among members of a political community (Mill 1972 [1861]: ch. 16; Rawls 1999: 23–4). We can to some extent detach the logic underpinning this idea from Mill's historical and sociological speculations as to its origins in a shared history and political culture of a kind associated with a common nationality. The argument is that if citizens and their governments are to pursue common rather than sectional interests, they must regard themselves as having certain obligations towards each other as members of the same political community, including a duty to adopt certain common modes of public reasoning (Miller 2009, 212–13; Rawls 1997). For example, a religious or ethnic group will be more inclined to seek rules that oppose discrimination against all groups, rather than to employ government power to suppress groups different to theirs, where solidarity exists between groups, so that they see themselves as part of the same political community, and if they are capable of sharing certain public principles that extend beyond the convictions of their own particular group, such as a commitment to a given understanding of toleration. The sense of being part of a public committed to public reasoning gets further reinforced if there is sufficient public communication between groups for them to share a public sphere within which genuine public debate is possible (Miller 2009: 212). This condition allows different sections of the political community to communicate with each other, and enhances transparency and encourages the responsiveness of governments to publically justifiable interests alone. As I observed, a public sphere of the requisite sort involves shared cultural instruments, such as a common media – newspapers, blogs, television and radio programmes – that address and are accessible by all, not least because they are in a common language or languages all those involved can understand. Such instruments help the various groups within a society to inform and respond to each other and make it harder for governments to play them off against one another or to pander to one group at the expense of another.

As I also noted, the second type of social relation reinforces the first and involves the conditions pluralist theorists of democracy associate with what they call polyarchy (Dahl 1998: 90). These theorists note how the ability of the citizens of today's complex and diverse societies to make fair and equal collective decisions together depends on their varying and often conflicting interests and ideals being to some degree cross-cutting. That is, individuals whose interests and ideals diverge in some areas must converge in others, so that they belong to a variety of different groups composed of different sections of the community rather than being segmented into a single group. Collective decision-making on the basis of an equal vote can only be justified when the persons and groups concerned have important issues in common and possess a roughly equal stake in the overall set of these decisions, if not each and every one of them. Otherwise, the danger arises of a permanent majority and discreet and isolated minorities (Christiano 2010: 130–2). Cross-cutting cleavages within a common scheme of social cooperation replace the tyranny of rule by a majority or powerful minority with the non-dominating rule of changing coalitions of minorities. In such a social context, citizens and those who represent them have incentives to seek fair outcomes that show people's varied interests and ideals equal concern and respect. Such social relations also foster reciprocity and compromise and facilitate convergence on shared interests and values (Bellamy 1999: ch. 5).

The presence of both these types of relations creates a demos in which citizens regard the democratic system as offering a public and fair mechanism for the equal consideration and promotion of their values and interests (Christiano 2010). The weaker these conditions are, the more culturally and socially segmented a society, the greater the likelihood that the political community will be unable to support a civicity. In these circumstances, democratic politics risks dividing between appeals to a false solidarism and reassertions of a self-regarding singularism (Dahl 1998: 114–17). As the next section illustrates, this risk proves all too present within the EU. On the one hand, certain EU elites have called for a European solidarity based on the common good of an imagined EU demos that the national demoi have mostly viewed with scepticism, opening them up to counter appeals to an equally spurious will of the national demos by populist political entrepreneurs who exploit dissatisfaction with this elite consensus (Müller 2016; Kriesi 2016). On the other hand, national governments have attempted to counteract the impact of both types of solidaristic appeal by adopting an individualist and protective stance typical of singularism. Either way, the prospect of domination ensues.

The next section draws on the foregoing analysis to explore more fully how the absence of the two conditions capable of fostering a civicity at the EU level has produced this turn to solidarism and singularism. I shall begin by relating the supranational and intergovernmental channels of representation outlined in the TEU to the two conceptions of representative democracy associated above with solidarism and singularism respectively. If the first, supranational, channel aspires to emulate the 'thick' solidarist model; the second, intergovernmental, channel operates according to the 'thin' singularist model. I shall argue that while the intergovernmental channel possesses a stronger social basis and greater political legitimacy than the supranational channel, it suffers from the generic risk of 'thin' democracy of potentially producing inequitable and suboptimal solutions to collective problems. A subsequent section will then explore whether the EU can overcome this dilemma by developing the qualities of a civicity. The attempt to do so through post-national models of democracy that aim at addressing the democratic deficit at the supranational level prove flawed and unlikely to succeed. Instead, I shall suggest that a more promising approach is to address the EU's democratic disconnect by enhancing the influence of the third, domestic, channel. The claim will be that reconnecting the democratic systems of the member states to the EU in this way opens the possibility of so modifying the other two channels that the EU's political system can function as a thick-thin model of European demoicracy, capable of formulating shared European policies that treat the peoples of Europe with equal concern and respect.

Representing the EU: Between Supranational Cosmopolitan Solidarism and Intergovernmental Statist Singularism

This section critically examines the supranational and intergovernmental channels of representation, noting how they suffer from the respective problems of the 'thick' and 'thin' forms of representation associated with the political ontologies of 'solidarism' and 'singularism'. Both channels involve elites who claim to stand 'as' or 'for' their corresponding constituencies and who can consequently act either as cosmopolitan-inclined trustees of an EU demos, in the first case, or for their member states in the guise of statist delegates, in the second.

Supranational Cosmopolitan Solidarism

The supranational channel operates mainly through the EP and, more indirectly, the Commission. As a common channel for representing the whole European citizenry, the EP potentially offers a European-wide perspective. Yet, European elections continue to be second-order and dictated by domestic issues (Hix and Marsh 2011), while the activities of civil society organisations remain similarly tied to the national context, even among the few interest groups possessing the incentives and resources to become more Europeanised (Beyers and Kerremans 2007; Kröger 2016). MEPs represent national parties but typically are chosen from countrywide lists and have weak links to voters within any given constituency. This is true of all 96 German MEPs, for example. Consequently, they are largely unauthorised and unaccountable as promoters of pan-European concerns (Scharpf 2017: 329 n. 82). As a result, they can engage in EU-level deliberations without having to sustain their electoral base. Rather, they appeal to an ontology of solidarism and claim that, as a collective body, the EP stands and can act 'as' a putative European people. For example, though analysts of the EP generally acknowledge the weakness of the formal legitimacy provided by the electoral process, many counter that it nonetheless reflects the broad distribution of ideological positions found across the EU (Hix 2008). As such, it can reflect the common concerns of Europeans despite having no clear mandate to 'act for' them or even the capacity to mobilize European public opinion and provide the catalyst for forming a European public interest on either specific or general issues.

As I have noted in earlier chapters and shall detail below, no European *demos* with the requisite solidarist qualities of strong mutual identification, agreement on principles and shared collective interests exists. However, these qualities do characterise the majority of political actors within EU institutions (Shore 2000). Indeed, this underlying concurrence of views and backgrounds facilitates the highly consensual decision-making typical of the EU policy process. EU policy makers generally justify articulating such apparently unfounded solidarist assumptions on two related grounds. First, they maintain that the EU tackles largely technical and organisational matters that are issues of 'good' governance (Shore 2011: 291–3). EU polices are deemed to provide public goods most rational actors would regard as beneficial to any view of life, such as the resolution of coordination problems, better and cheaper utilities, or a clean environment. Such policies can be assumed to reflect the collective interest of European citizens, while their efficient and effective delivery is largely a matter of expertise (European Commission 2001: 3–8). Second, as a consequence, the means chosen for providing these goods requires a technocratic rather than popular consensus, such as can be achieved through mechanisms such as the Open Method of Coordination (OMC), which become exemplars of 'thick' deliberative democracy (European Commission 2007). Since the Commission drafts policy proposals, the role of the EP within this system, even under co-decision, is to legitimate rather than legislate (Burns et al, 2000). Opposition to the EU is regarded as resulting from ignorance and misinformation. Measures purporting to promote democracy and participation invariably turn out to be what is euphemistically called 'public diplomacy' and 'information actions' aimed at forging a European demos among 'opinion multipliers' and 'young Europeans' (Shore 2004).

The Euro crisis has shattered this vision of solidarist 'organic' democratic governance (Chalmers et al. 2016). Far from giving rise to a European public space in which common solutions might be deliberated, the crisis has raised the profile of European issues in national public spaces in ways that are increasingly critical of the EU (Börzel 2016). Moreover, the main actors in responding to the crisis have been the member state governments, whose electoral room for manoeuvre has been correspondingly restricted, with the EP in particular largely sidelined. As a result, the cosmopolitan solidarism of supranational institutions finds itself increasingly constrained by, and in conflict with, the quite different representational logic of intergovernmental institutions.

Intergovernmental Statist Singularism

Within the intergovernmental channel, the forms of representation and decision-making conform to the 'thin' democratic model appropriate to the political ontology of singularism. National governments and their ministers operate largely as authorised substitutes and very occasionally as mandated delegates of domestic interests, though with limited electoral accountability for what they do at the EU level given the low salience of Europe in domestic elections. The assumption is that their judgements can be relied on to maximise the interests of their citizens. True, those judgements can only be challenged by defeat in either a parliamentary vote or a referendum, so that only a significant miscalculation of public opinion is likely to be successfully contested. Yet, as primarily domestic politicians, their main incentives lie in promoting national rather than European interests. To a large extent, the national governments 'act for' their principals in the manner of the executive of a joint stock company relative to its share holders – acting on their own judgement to maximise

the several interests of those they serve without assuming a collective
interest other than as private investors in a common enterprise.

The political singularism of the intergovernmental channel severely
constrains the political solidarism projected by the supranational
channel, making it difficult for European institutions to escape
national controls (Moravcsik 2008: 334). EU legislation requires
a far higher degree of consensus than in any national political system.
A proposal from the majority of the Commission must secure consensual support from national leaders within the European Council to
be placed on the agenda, a formal 2/3 majority – but in practice
a consensus – of weighted member state votes in the Council of
Ministers, a series of absolute majorities within the EP and the assent
and active support of the different national administrations, legal
systems and parliaments responsible for its implementation. Treaty
changes require unanimity between the national governments and
ratification by NPs and in an increasing number of cases national
referenda as well.

These constraints mean that EU governance mainly provides
a mechanism for a singularist type of representation, whereby the
various member state governments seek mutually advantageous bar-
gains that maximise the interests of their respective states. Yet it also
suffers from the limitations and drawbacks typical of such arrangements. First, because agreement is so difficult, it has a *status quo* bias.
It proves hard to reform or drop policies that have outlived their
usefulness or failed, or to respond to crises or fast-changing situations.
The high consensus requirements not only make European solutions
to common policies difficult to agree on, but also can inhibit experi-
mentation and innovation at both the national and the European level
to improve or adapt those policies once they are agreed. Second, the
logic of collective action among a large and heterogeneous group of
states that are not subject to a central coercive power, as in a federal
system, leads to the under-provision of collective goods, as the smaller
or poorer seek to free ride on the larger or wealthier and the larger or
wealthier seek to minimise the degree to which they subsidise the
smaller or poorer (Majone 2016: 220). Third such inflexibility and
inefficiency applies even more to the independent institutions – to
a degree the Commission and especially the European Central Bank
(ECB) and the Court of Justice of the European Union (CJEU) – that
monitor particular policies outside the political process. These bodies
risk either applying uniform rules dogmatically to very different situations, or attempting to address such variations and cope with novel
circumstances by exercising discretion in ways that may depart from

what was intended by the contracting parties. Either way, if their power and competencies have a basis in the Treaties, as is the case with the ECB's remit to maintain price stability at all costs, say, or the CJEU's power to interpret EU law, then it will be near impossible to reverse or effectively challenge their decisions.

The assumption has been that the EU provides solutions to Prisoner's Dilemmas, where a collective agreement is in everybody's interest but there are temptations to free ride or disagreements over the most appropriate solution (Scharpf 2009: 183–4). In both cases, Pareto improvements can be expected. Thus, in areas such as environmental protection or deregulation, that only prove generally beneficial if all adopt them, but that powerful interests at the national level can effectively lobby to block, the EU has operated as an effective self-binding mechanism for tying the member states into mutually beneficial policies. However, the more the EU extends into policy areas where no such win-win solutions exist because of variations between the member states, the more contentious action by the EU will be.

Between Solidarism and Singularism

The central dilemma of the EU emerges at this point. European elites embraced a neo-functionalist logic, whereby integration was viewed both as producing endogenous 'spill-overs' into ever more sectors and bringing in its wake greater political unity and solidarity (Haas 1958). Mobilising pan-European democratic support for integrationist measures was thought unnecessary. A permissive consensus legitimated elites 'standing as' European citizens until such time as the benefits of integration had forged an active consensus among a European people. However, as Chapter 6 details, an ever-closer economic and legal union has proceeded against a background of ever-greater political and social heterogeneity, not least because of enlargement. Consequently, greater integration has tended to reinforce rather than undermine the EU's political and social ontology of singularism. As we saw, those EU bodies, such as the EP, the Commission, the CJEU or the ECB, which have a role as promoters of common European interests that in principle might balance the singularist ontology with a solidarist one, have a limited capacity to do so. Structural funds apart, the EU bodies do not have the competence to make significant direct transfers between different member states or groups of people. Their policies are regulatory, and biased towards enhancing a single market from which all private actors – be they states or individuals – are presumed to benefit.

Thus, the ECB cannot engage in an effective rescue of the debtor states without violating the no-bail-out clause, Article 125(1), of the Lisbon Treaty. To act in this and other ways would require a Treaty change that would likely attract a German veto, given that Germany would be called upon to underwrite such measures. Since the German government represents its citizens in EU affairs according to the ontology of singularity, their loan must be guaranteed in the simplest manner through decreased spending by the recipient states. Likewise, the Court of Justice has the remit of promoting the four freedoms. As I explore in Chapter 5, many have regarded the introduction of Union citizenship and the new European Charter of Fundamental Rights as marking a move away from the market bias of the EU (e.g. Kostakopoulou 2008). Integration through law would no longer simply be integration into a single free market. But, as I will show, the Court has little ability to act otherwise. For example, though it has declared that 'a certain degree of financial solidarity' now exists between the member states (*Grzelczyk*, para 31), the limits to that solidarity have been all too evident in the initial responses to the Euro crisis. The Court can only liberalise and deregulate, it cannot create new European-wide social and economic policy regimes. As decisions such as *Laval* and *Luxembourg*, on the one hand, and *Swartz* and *Watts*, on the other, indicate, the rights of citizens at the Union level are the rights of private individuals to produce, trade or consume but with no correlative duty to contribute to public goods or provide for social welfare. These are member state responsibilities. Yet, by conceiving the EU as a whole as simply a collection of rights-bearing individuals along the lines of the ontology of singularity, the Court effectively undermines their ability to meet these obligations. The social solidarity of the requisite kind proves entirely alien to this perspective (Scharpf 2009: 190–8).

Towards an EU Civicity?

Is it possible to overcome this impasse? Is it either desirable or feasible to shift the EU towards an ontology of civicity capable of sustaining a more relational form of representation? Those liberal intergovernmentalists who contest the desirability of enhancing EU democracy have hitherto done so by arguing that the current system of 'thin' democracy suffices for the functions the EU performs (Moravcsik 2008; Majone 2001), and arguably already goes further than is normatively mandated from a thin cosmopolitan statist position (Miller 2008). A judgement already contestable following the Single European Act (Follesdal and Hix 2006), even its proponents grant that the debt crisis of the Euro zone has revealed the limits of the current system of governance (Majone 2012; Moravcsik 2012). The effects of decisions by the ECB or politicians and bureaucrats in Brussels are apparent not just to experts or special interest groups, but also to all citizens through their impact on savings, mortgages and public services.

The problem is whether a sufficient basis for an ontology of civicity exists for this proposal to be feasible. Two possibilities exist. The first is to develop such an ontology at the EU level by creating an EU demos. The second is to develop it among the various demoi and their representatives in the context of EU affairs. I shall examine each of them in turn below. Before doing so, however, some consideration should be given to Habermas's recent suggestion of an apparent third possibility that combines these two (2012: 28–37; 2015: 554 n. 22). His proposal rests on the simultaneous representation of individuals as citizens of the EU and of a member state. So conceived, citizens are presumed to possess a dual identity and to be capable of voting accordingly, depending on whether they are involved in European or national elections (Habermas 2012: 37). Yet, even supposing citizens could sustain such a split personality (for criticism of the schizophrenic character of Habermas's conception of dual citizenship, see Cheneval and Nicolaïdis 2016), this proposal retains the current twofold structure criticised in the last section, and the tensions between a 'thick' solidarist democracy among representatives of a putative 'EU demos', on the one hand, and a 'thin' singularist democracy among representatives of member states, on the other. Habermas simply transfers this tension into the minds of citizens themselves, by noting that the electors of both sets of representatives are the same people.

Habermas's argument could only resolve this tension if, as Euro federalists traditionally claim could be the case, one conceives the second, member state affiliation, as nested within the first, EU affiliation. In this case, his argument would collapse into the first possibility given above (see Patberg 2017). However, as I shall detail below, *prima facie* this first possibility seems doubtful. Instead, I shall defend the second possibility and argue that we can only endow EU politics with the qualities of a 'civicity' by viewing it in terms of the representation of demoi and reconnecting politicians to the peoples of the EU.

An EU Demos-cracy?

As we saw, a civicity depends on cross-cutting values and interests and a shared public sphere. The problem with the first possibility lies in part in the absence of these features at the EU level. While there is evidence that similar political cleavages can be found within each of the member states, the EU encompasses considerable cultural and social divisions of a segmental kind that correspond broadly to national cleavages between the various member states, and lacks the necessary common public culture for a viable European demos. For example, if one takes views on abortion as an indicator of social values more generally, then the difference between Poland, which only permits abortion if the life of the mother is in danger, when pregnancy results from rape or incest or, though this may be repealed, in the case of foetal abnormalities, and Sweden, which allows abortion on demand, is immense. Social divisions between the member states are as great. Per capita income in Denmark is getting on for five times that of Lithuania – almost three times the difference between Delaware and Mississippi, respectively the richest and poorest states of the USA.[1] Meanwhile, despite the spread of English as the *lingua franca* of the educated classes, news and other media remain firmly national and regional in focus and only Europeanised to a limited extent that mainly benefits government elites (Koopmans 2007). As I noted in Chapter 3, empirical evidence suggests a European identity to be marginal and fragmentary (White 2011).

Advocates of a fully fledged post-national EU parliamentary democracy contend these difficulties can be overcome. First, they counter that Europeans share basic constitutional values (Habermas 2001). After all, every member state is a signatory of the European Convention of Human Rights, with the EU itself likely to accede soon. Yet, these rights have been configured differently in each country to reflect domestic democratic preferences regarding welfare, privacy, religion and so on, often in incompatible ways (Bolleyer and Reh 2012: 476–8). Second, they argue that a transnational civil society is emerging, which currently lacks representation within national systems. Yet, the evidence for this development is meagre. Only 12 million EU citizens reside in another member state to that of their nationality – 2 per cent of the EU population, mainly from professional backgrounds – and even this group is only modestly denationalised in outlook and identity (Favell 2008). Likewise, membership of pan-European civil society organisations is very low – most depend for their funding on EU grants and offer at best 'proxy' representation of assumed interests (Warleigh 2001, Kröger 2016), while European parties have failed to emerge in electoral as opposed to parliamentary terms – even following the introduction of the *Spitzenkandidaten* in the 2014 election (Christiansen 2016). As was noted above, a profound democratic disconnect already exists between many MEPs and those they claim to represent. Habermas's (2015: 548) and similar proposals for self-styled

---

[1] Figures from GDP/capita world bank data http://databank.worldbank.org/ddp/home.do?Step=12&id=4&CNO=2.

European parties to present pan-European lists would only increase this disconnection by extending the distance between European politicians and their electoral base (Scharpf 2017: 329 n. 82).

Of course, segmental divisions exist in the member states too, many of which contain minority national and other groups. However, as I again remarked in Chapter 3, the main pressures across Europe to resolve this problem are not to shift power upwards, to the European level, but for ever greater devolution of political, legal and economic powers downwards to linguistic, ethnic and religious minorities. Consequently, Europe is becoming more rather than less segmented. Contrary to post-nationalist arguments, an abstract commitment to similar liberal democratic values has not of itself generated a willingness or capacity to deliberate on them in common (Kymlicka 2001, especially chs 11 and 17). Indeed, as I show in Chapter 6, such segmental divisions provide a normative basis within democratic theory for rejecting a uniform system of political representation incorporating majority rule. For they make structural majorities and persistent minorities likely. Those member states characterised by similar divisions, such as Belgium, have avoided conflicts and the possibility of disintegration by adopting forms of 'consensus' or 'consociational' democracy (Lijphart 1977). As a number of commentators have observed, the current political system of the EU can be likened to such arrangements and share much of their rationale (Costa and Magnette 2003; Scharpf 2015: 394–5).

So long as the demoi of the EU remain overwhelmingly national and/or, at least in some member states, subnational, the danger of seeking to create an EU demos is that it will result in consistent minorities and majorities split along national lines. In such circumstances, an explicit move towards a demos-cracy would provoke political conflict in which disagreements over policy would spill over into constitutional contestation and galvanise anti-EU opposition among those groups who might feel their national socio-economic interests and cultural values are being overridden by majorities in the EP (Bartolini 2006: 35). In fact, the accompaniment of the deepening and increasing politicisation of integration post-Maastricht with the rise of populist parties across the EU that exploit just this rhetoric offers ample testimony of this dynamic (Hooghe and Marks 2009).

As a result, the most plausible models of supranational democracy continue either to invoke an elite-based ontology of solidarism that largely circumvents democracy, or to involve a complex system of multilevel compound representation that remains rooted in the ontology of singularity. Thus, James Bohman concedes that his proposed shift from national to transnational democracy involves a change in forms that 'may sometimes seem like *less* democracy' (Bohman 2007: 21). Indeed, when he refers to the deliberative aspects of this new form it invariably involves agents that have neither formal authorisation from, nor accountability to, any given demoi, such as those allegedly promoted by the Open Method of Coordination (Bohman 2007: 85–6). However, such instruments lack the relative independence and reciprocal influence that we saw are essential to representative democracy within a civicity (Kröger 2007). Likewise, suggestions for a supranational system involving multiple demoi (e.g. Lavdas and Chryssochoou 2011; Fabbrini 2010) end up multiplying veto points, with all the drawbacks of gridlock, entrenching inequalities, and under providing public goods that I explored earlier (Miller 2008).

Despite their flaws, some version of these latter models, which build on national more than transnational demoi, nevertheless offer the most realistic avenue for the democratisation of the EU given the segmental divisions noted above. However, as with the consociational and consensus democratic systems that form their domestic analogues, the challenge is to see how far such structures can be moved away from the centrifugal logic of the ontology of singularism, in which in the absence of win-win options the tendency is to seek separate rather than integrated forms of governance, and to promote instead the centripetal logic of the ontology of civicity (Lacey 2017). It is to this task that I now turn.

An EU Demoicracy?

The second possibility involves attempting this shift from singularism to civicity by treating the national demoi of the member states as the basic building blocks and deliberative contexts of a demoicratic association of European states (Christiano 2010). As I remarked in Chapter 3, such an association takes the democratic peoples of Europe as its starting point, and seeks to promote an ever-closer Union between them based on principles of political equality and mutual respect. As I observed at the start of this chapter, the democratic legitimacy of such a Union rests on its meeting a double standard of representativeness that combines two criteria (Pettit 2010b). According to the first criterion, governments should represent their citizens in ways that treat them as individuals with equal concern and respect and treat other governments as representatives of their respective peoples with equal concern and respect. According to the second criterion, intergovernmental decisions should be made in ways that are under the shared and equal control of governments as representatives of their respective peoples. Each entails the other. Meeting the first criterion forms a logical precondition for satisfying the second, which assumes that governments recognise each other as being authorised by and accountable to their citizens. Yet, in an interconnected world, this first criterion can only be met in its turn if the second is also satisfied, otherwise decisions at the EU level will undercut democracy at the member state level. Drawing on the analysis above, we can now add the additional requirement that representation at both levels must be promotive of civicity. Again, the claim will be that each level supports the other in doing so. I shall argue below that an EU civicity can emerge if we domesticate European politics, on the one side, by giving domestic electorates a sense of influence over decisions at the EU level that renders European decision-making responsive to the domestic concerns of the various demoi, and Europeanise domestic politics, on the other side, by making national electorates and their representatives feel responsible for EU decisions and the impact of their domestic decisions on their European associates. Taken together, I shall contend these two processes foster a 'normalised' form of European policy-making characterised by left-right rather than pro-/ anti-EU divisions, and orientated towards achieving a shared conception of the public interest that reflects not only the equal influence and control of the various member state demoi, but also their mutual respect and concern.

Formally speaking, both of the representative criteria could be said to be met by the EU as currently constituted within the Post-Lisbon Consolidated Treaty of the European Union (TEU 2012). Thus, the first criterion, involving a commitment to the values of representative democracy by all the member states as a precondition for membership, is evident in the preamble and Article 2. The preamble confirms the Union's 'attachment to the principles of liberty, democracy and respect for human rights', while Article 2 notes how these values are 'common to the member states'. The contracting parties also affirm that the deepening of 'the solidarity between their peoples' has to be balanced by 'respecting their history, their culture and their traditions', while the process of 'an ever closer union among the peoples of Europe' has to be one 'in which decisions are taken as closely as possible to the citizen in accordance with the principle of subsidiarity'. Indeed, as was noted at the end of Chapter 3, Article 4.2 explicitly requires the Union to 'respect the equality of member states before the Treaties as well as their national identities, inherent in their fundamental structures, political and constitutional, inclusive of regional and local self-government' and portrays the Union as based in a principle of 'sincere cooperation' and 'mutual respect'. Thus, the commitment to democratic values goes hand in hand with respect for the ways the various peoples of the member states may have configured these differently, and that as far as possible decisions ought to be taken by each of these peoples according to their own democratic procedures.

Likewise, the second criterion, whereby an international association should be under the shared and equal control of the signatory states in order to ensure the public and equal advancement of the interests of their respective peoples, emerges from the account of the Union's political system in Title II. This commits the Union to being itself organised in accordance with democratic principles and the equality of citizens, with Article 10 explicitly grounding its functioning in representative democracy. As I observed at the start of the chapter, this Article identifies three channels whereby European citizens are represented in the EU's political system: directly via elections to the European Parliament (EP), indirectly via their Heads of State or Government in the European Council (EC) or in the Council by their Government, and in domestic elections which hold these last democratically accountable to National Parliaments (NPs) or to citizens. However, we have already examined the first two channels and seen how in acting according to an ontology of solidarism and singularism respectively, they fail adequately to meet this second criterion. I now want to suggest both can be modified by the third channel towards an ontology of civicity, while preserving the EU as essentially demoicratic in character.

Lisbon resulted in NPs being mentioned in the main text of the Treaty for the first time. Article 12 assigns them a negative and a positive role, described below, with the first offering a 'thin' corrective to the solidarism of the EP and the second a 'thick' corrective to the 'singularity' of governments. At the same time, I shall argue both roles have the effect of reconnecting EU policy making to the domestic democracy of the various demoi by both bringing EU politics 'home' and 'normalising' it, institutionalising along the way a 'republican' intergovernmentalism. I shall explore each role in turn.

The negative role relates to the powers NPs possess to police subsidiarity. The Treaty introduced an 'Early Warning Mechanism' (EWM) that assigns national legislatures the right to scrutinize proposed EU decisions and initiatives for compliance with the principles of subsidiarity and proportionality. If a third of national parliamentary bodies offer a 'reasoned opinion' objecting to a given measure, they trigger the so-called 'yellow card', whereby the Commission must reconsider its proposal. Furthermore, NPs can have a collective legislative influence in that a majority of them may force, by way of a so-called 'orange card', an early vote on an EU legislative proposal in the Council and the EP. They are also now involved in the evaluation of measures taken within the area of freedom, security and justice (Articles 70, 85, 88 TEU), may block Treaty changes under the simplified revision procedures (Article 48 TEU) and must be informed of new applications to join the EU (Article

49 TEU). Though this power remains weak due to the high threshold requirement, it does legitimise criticism of the EU for overreaching its competencies. For example, it supplies a democratic grounding for Scharpf's proposal (2009: 199–200) that the European Council be able to challenge Court of Justice interpretations of primary and secondary European law that overstep the intent of the Treaties, as has arguably been the case in a number of decisions relating to free movement and Union citizenship. It offers a 'thin' civic check on the 'thick' solidarist aspirations of EU institutions, forcing them to give equal respect and concern to the democratic preferences of the peoples of Europe.

The positive role arises from NPs receiving EU legislative proposals and having had to create European Affairs Committees to scrutinise them and the decisions made by ministers, though important national differences remain as to how powerful these are (Karlas 2012; Winzen 2012, 2013). They may also send reasoned opinions to the Commission independently of the yellow and orange card procedures and so engage in an informal political dialogue (Jančić 2012). National politicians currently lack the same legitimacy to act flexibly and to construct the public interest at the European level that they possess at the domestic level. The domestic politics of the member states is only very indirectly linked to the EU system of governance. No dynamic relationship exists between representatives and those they represent when it comes to European issues. Worse, their decisions regarding Europe are increasingly perceived as undermining the established democratic practices within the member states (Mair 2011). Enhancing the influence of parliaments in the European sphere may help foster an interactive relationship between the national demoi and their respective governments over EU policy-making, thickening the thin democracy of the intergovernmental channel. It may thereby enhance the capacity for ministers and governments to act 'as' the agents of the national *demos*, empowering them to operate more proactively than hitherto, without losing the trust of their citizens.

These measures provide a more relational foundation for political representation at the EU level, while bridging the democratic disconnect by domesticating and normalising EU policy making in ways consistent with a republican intergovernmentalism (Kröger and Bellamy 2016). On the one hand, they domesticate EU politics by 'taming' it and 'bringing it home' in ways that ground the first criterion. Not only is EU policy making to some degree tamed by NPs through their subsidiarity checking powers, but also the obligation to scrutinise both EU legislative proposals and the decisions of ministers brings EU politics home by giving domestic politicians an interest in EU policy-making that was hitherto absent. As a result, the decisions of governments and their ministers in the

European Council and the Council are more likely to be representative of their peoples rather than of a putative state interest.

At the same time, due weight is given to the second criterion. NPs cannot employ their subsidiarity control as a national veto. They need to collaborate with other NPs to block measures or get their reasoned opinions listened to, a possibility facilitated through cooperation in COSAC (the French acronym for the 'Conference of Community and European Affairs Committees of Parliaments of the European Union'), which is entitled 'to submit any contribution' it deems appropriate to the EP, the Council and the Commission, and the way all NPs now have representation in Brussels (Cooper 2013; Sprungk 2013). Inter-parliamentary bodies have also developed in those areas where EU institutions and actors operate at the borders of their sphere of competences and possess a degree of executive discretion: namely, Financial and Monetary Policy and Common Security and Defence Policy. Such bodies not only provide mechanisms for NPs to retain their power to scrutinise executive action in areas where national governments have delegated their authority to EU officials, but also offer incentives for national parliamentarians to discover commonalities and form alliances with their counterparts across the EU (Cooper 2016). Likewise among governments, decision-making in the European Council is invariably taken by consensus, which nominally at least respects the norm of giving equal weighting to each member state. The situation in the various configurations of the Council is more complicated, but similar reasoning prevails. Even though qualified majority voting (QMV) is formally the default for decision-making, in practice it operates through consensus wherever possible. Moreover, the double-majority rule for QMV introduced from 1 November 2014, involving 55 per cent of member states representing at least 65 per cent of the EU population, is designed to ensure that decisions must balance the interests of large and small states by preventing the former imposing a decision on the latter and vice versa.

Nevertheless, it might still be feared that these changes move as much, if not more, in the direction of an ontology of singularity than of civicity. To move in the latter direction, the involvement of NPs must offer incentives both to Europeanise domestic politics and, in the process, to normalise EU politics. Two features of the way the predominately pro-EU centre parties currently debate EU affairs serve to promote the democratic disconnect. First, there is a pronounced lack of congruence between these parties and their voters on EU affairs. Like elites more generally, the main governing parties hold more positive views of the integration process than those who elect them (Hooghe and Marks 2009: 11, 19). Second, and relatedly, there has been a disinclination to politicise EU affairs along the main ideological cleavages (Mair 2011; Puntscher Riekmann and Wydra 2013; Bellamy and Kröger 2014; Wendler 2014). Indeed, this consensus has been institutionalised within the EP by the fact that decisions there are largely governed by a grand coalition between the two main party families – the European People's Party, bringing together the Christian Democrats and Conservatives of the Centre Right (with the recent and conspicuous exception of the British Conservative Party), and the Progressive Alliance of Socialists and Democrats, comprising the main Centre Left parties. As a result, voters seeking to contest policies at the EU level get driven to supporting Eurosceptic parties, with the main political cleavage being between pro- and anti-integration, with identity issues predominating, rather than between left and right wing policies. To the extent such ideological divisions do emerge, they tend to be portrayed as pragmatic and technical disagreements for fear of appearing to call the EU itself into question.

Again, involving domestic political actors directly in EU policy making has the potential to overcome such de-politicisation and to bring it within the scope of 'normal', left-right, ideological cleavages. The very process of bringing EU politics home in the two senses described above offers a means to undercut the fear that the integration process necessarily involves a shift of democratic sovereignty away from the member states. It also poses the main parties with a clear choice. Either they must find a way of politicising EU policy in left-right terms at the EU level; or they must retain sufficient autonomy at the national level for such contestation to be meaningful in the domestic context. Almost all domestic politicians have a greater interest in the latter than the former, but so do the vast majority of their constituents. However, taking the latter route does not mean withdrawal from the process of EU integration, as the supporters of Brexit clearly believed. Rather, it involves shifting the view of the EU away from which rules best promote the four freedoms that lie at the heart of the single market, to what EU policies are needed to allow the different member states to prosper in the various ways they may democratically choose (Rodrik 2011). In an interconnected world, that cannot be achieved outside a Union that allows for multilateral negotiation on the terms of their mutual interactions. However, such terms need not be entirely uniform – a point to which I return in Chapter 6. Moreover, debate can arise over the degree to which these rules may shift the advantage towards pro-market or pro-welfare measures, both at the national and the EU level – the two may be connected. As a result, the EU becomes recognised as playing a crucial and justified part in framing what can be achieved at the EU level. At the same time, it becomes harder for predominantly right wing political entrepreneurs to mobilise feelings of national identity around opposition to both the EU and globalisation, given that the EU becomes recognised as a means for supporting that identity by controlling global processes.

One mechanism for achieving this move towards a more 'normal' and 'domesticated' politicisation might be through allowing a more positive Parliamentary Legislative Initiative (PLI) or 'green' card to balance the negative 'yellow' card process of the Early Warning Procedure. Advocated in general terms by the House of Lords and supported by COSAC,[2] Sandra Kröger and I have proposed elsewhere that a PLI be triggered by at least a 1/3 of the MPs in a minimum of a 1/4 of all the NPs in the EU (Kröger and Bellamy 2016: 146–8). The total number of NPs would be calculated by counting each chamber in bicameral systems as 1 and weighting the NPs of unicameral systems as 2. In the case of the threshold being reached, the Commission would be obliged to put forward a legislative proposal to be considered by the normal legislative procedure. This threshold is set deliberately below requiring a majority of MPs in 50 per cent of all NPs in order to stimulate debate in part by empowering opposition parties as much as those in government. The *demoi*-cratic legitimacy of any measure would still be guaranteed by the normal legislative process requiring a super majority in the Council and the EP for any proposal to be enacted. Being entitled to influence EU affairs positively rather than merely in a reactive way, through subsidiarity checks, allows mainstream parties to avoid simply debating mere technical and pragmatic considerations of a 'responsible' rather than a 'responsive' character, or being forced into opposing the demands for less integration on the anti-systemic grounds deployed by the Eurosceptic parties. Instead, they may seize the initiative to promote a policy measure which accords with their general ideology. Parties in government can push their executives towards adopting proposals that go beyond the compromises they may feel obliged to make as members of an EU level 'grand coalition'. Such moves could aid their bargaining power by revealing a ground swell of domestic support for particular measures. More importantly, the comparatively low threshold of a 1/3 of MPs is designed to allow opposition parties also to promote such initiatives and thereby to put forward alternative EU policies to the government. That not only empowers the opposition to develop EU policies of their own but provides an additional incentive for government parties to also defend their position on ideological grounds. Meanwhile, the need to cooperate with other

[2] HoL EU Committee, 9th Report Session 2013–14, The Role of National Parliaments in the EU, 24 March 2014, pp. 19–20; Questionnaire for the 23rd Bi-annual Report of COSAC, 23 February 2015, Section 2.

NPs under the PLI will work against parties acting purely opportunisti-cally or operating in the manner of Eurosceptic parties to protect a narrowly conceived national self-interest.

On the surface, the EP offers a less obvious fit with this demoicratic arrangement. The wording of Article 10 suggests the existence of a European demos in stating that European citizens are represented directly in the EP. However, Union citizenship derives from being a national of a member state and is 'additional to national citizenship and shall not replace it' (Art 9 TEU), a characteristic I shall defend in the next chapter. As I remarked in Chapter 3, the derivative and additional character of this status is reflected in the way seats are allocated within the EP by member state rather than simply by population, employing the principle of 'degressive proportionality', with a minimum threshold of 6 seats for the smallest MS and a maximum of 96 for the largest (Art 14.2 TEU). The official rationality behind this arrangement has been to ensure that the range of political opinion found in even the less populous mem-ber states gets represented. Indeed, European parties do not mobilise a pan-European electorate, but are rather groupings of national parties within the Parliament. As the German Federal Constitutional Court noted in its Lisbon Judgment (2BvE 2/08: para. 286), the EP's allocation formula is testimony to the absence of a European demos and the need adequately to represent each of the European demoi. Therefore, the EP can also be conceived as an institutional embodiment of European demoicracy. Again, giving domestic political parties more of an interest in EU affairs by enforcing their role through NPs will hopefully have the effect of ensuring that MEPs maintain a closer relation to MPs.

Involving NPs and national parties in the representative structures of the EU can improve the democratic legitimacy of decisions that are not Pareto optimal, but have the wider European interest in view; while enhancing the scrutiny of national governments and subjecting them to greater accountability when they engage in the definition of what the European interest entails. They create the basis for a European civicity, whereby national demoi may construct shared interests in ways charac-terised by equal respect and concern.

Conclusion

This chapter has argued that the EU is caught between a weak form of 'thick' representative democracy at the supranational level, based on an ontology of solidarity, and a strong form of 'thin' representative democ-racy among the member states, based on an ontology of singularity. Strengthening the former is implausible, but leaves the EU unable to articulate a European interest that goes beyond the mutual interests of the member states. I have proposed overcoming this impasse by making member state representatives more authorised and accountable on EU affairs via an improved dialogue with their NPs. In this way, the EU political system might develop the resources of an ontology of civicity within and between its component demoi. It remains to explore the implications of this arrangement for Union citizenship and the differentiation of EU policy-making and law in Chapters 5 and 6 respectively.

5 Union Citizenship: Supra- and Post-National, Transnational or International?

Introduction

Chapters 3 and 4 have suggested that the EU is best conceived not as some kind of super state or a form of organisation that takes us beyond the state form but rather as an association of sovereign states. This argument might be thought to be at odds with the very idea of Union citizenship, given that historically citizenship has been conceptually linked to an individual's status as a full member of a polity, thereby suggesting the EU must have some polity-like attributes of a statist or post-state kind. Yet in the case of Union citizenship, this status derives from being a full member of one of the member states. Moreover, for the most part, the entitlements accruing from Union citizenship do not involve goods supplied by the Union itself so much as non-discrimination on the basis of nationality in accessing goods provided by other member states (TFEU 2012 Articles 18, 20). In what follows, I shall defend these features of Union citizenship as following from the third criterion of a republican association of sovereign states outlined at the close of Chapter 3, whereby the citizens of the associated peoples and their governments ought not to discriminate against each other in their interactions. They exemplify a cosmopolitan statism, in which citizens of different democratic states have international rights and duties to treat the citizens of other states with equal concern and respect, not least when they move between states. Those who seek to transform Union citizenship into something either more akin to state citizenship or as a means for going beyond the state form altogether, fail to appreciate its genuinely innovative qualities and normative value.

Many people, prominent academics and policy makers among them, believe the current subordination of Union to member state citizenship will be, and ought to be, ultimately reversed. They regard the current position as at best transitory at worst incoherent and anomalous. For supporters of this view, the status of Union citizenship has aroused expectations and disappointment in equal measure ever since its establishment in the Treaty of Maastricht (Weiner 1998; O'Leary 1996).

In line with the conception of the EU as involving either the displacement of sovereignty to the European level or a shift to post-sovereignty, various legal and political commentators and actors, not least the Court of Justice, have welcomed this status as dissolving a world of borders and exclusions that they regard as making citizenship, in Joseph Carens's memorable phrase, 'the modern equivalent of feudal privilege' (Carens 1987: 252). As such, Union citizenship symbolises what they see as the 'transformative' potential of the EU (e.g. Kostakopoulou 2007: 623; Kochenov 2013: 97). Through the association with citizenship, they hope to move the integration process away from a focus on creating a single market and the associated economic rights of the free movement of labour, capital, goods and services (Article 26 TFEU), and towards an emphasis on the social, civil and political rights of a citizen of a transformed Union, as laid out in the Charter of Fundamental Rights of the European Union (2000).[1] Those who conceive this transformation in terms of the displacement of at least some sovereignty to the EU level treat this shift in terms of the creation of a supra- or post-national civic allegiance for individuals in Europe (e.g. Habermas 1992: 1), with the representation of states through intergovernmental arrangements giving way to the direct representation of Union citizens within a more powerful European Parliament able to initiate legislation. Post-sovereignty theorists go further. They contend that this new status signifies an even more profound transformation away from the traditional view of citizenship as membership of a given, territorially located, polity. It offers a reconceptualisation of citizenship as a transnational and global status that transcends all borders (Kostakopoulou 2007: 642–6). It arises simply from the recognition of all individuals as rights-bearers, entitled to equal concern and respect wherever they choose or happen to reside (Balibar 2004).

From these perspectives, the reality of EU citizenship has appeared misconceived and disappointing from the start. Not only do the entitlements of Union citizenship get triggered by cross-border activity linked to the exercise of the four economic freedoms at the heart of market integration, but also – as I noted – they remain inextricably tied to, and constrained by, possession of citizenship of a member state (see the criticism in Kochenov 2009: 169). By contrast, this chapter endorses this reality against the aspirational rhetoric of many theorists of EU citizenship. That is not to deny that Union citizenship has added an important dimension to national citizenship within the member states. However, against the

---

[1] The Charter became binding on EU institutions and member states in their implementation of EU law and policies with the coming into force of the Lisbon Treaty in 2009 (Article 6 TEU).

reasoning of the Court of Justice, such justified changes need not be linked to a supranational or transnational teleology, whereby 'citizenship of the Union is destined to be the fundamental status of nationals of the member states'. A formula first used in *Grzelczyk* [2001], para 31, it has been ritually repeated in all but the most recent subsequent citizenship cases involving a potential clash between the entitlements of Union citizens and the rights or benefits that member states seek to reserve to national citizens. Yet, it goes against the real purpose and spirit of Union citizenship that lies in offering a normative and practical defence of the fundamental status of national citizenship in an interconnected world. In this regard, the value of Union citizenship consists in its enabling the mutual concern and respect that operates among sovereign polities to apply to the citizens of those polities in moving and trading between them.

As will be argued below, the advocates of the transformative views of EU citizenship overlook what Rainer Bauböck has called 'the circumstances of citizenship and democracy' (Bauböck 2015: 5). These circumstances cut across the circumstances of justice and politics explored in earlier chapters. They concern the already existing system of bounded polities, each with their practices of citizenship and democracy. As we saw in Chapter 1, the need for principles of justice and politics arise respectively from the presence of moderate scarcity, on the one hand, and moral disagreement about the most suitable distribution of limited resources and the most appropriate public goods to maintain, on the other. In a parallel fashion, the need for principles of civic inclusion and exclusion derives from the existence of a plurality of bounded polities within which citizens can settle their disagreements about justice and the common good through free and equal democratic processes.

Building on Bauböck's argument for 'stakeholder citizenship' (Bauböck 2007), I shall contend that advocates of either a scaling up of citizenship to the supranational level, or a dispersed and unbounded form of transnational citizenship, confuse three separate issues. First, there is the issue of entitlement to be part of a bounded civic practice of collective decision-making; second, there is the issue of the impact of such decisions on those who are excluded from making them; and third, and following from these two, there is the issue of free movement between different bounded polities. The supranational conception holds that the second and third issue can only be addressed by responding to the first in a way that is as inclusive of as many individuals as possible. Yet, even if feasible, that approach puts at risk the pluralism provided, and in part defended, by the existence of different civic communities. The transnational conception seeks to dissolve all three issues by unbounding citizenship from membership of any one community. Yet, the entitlements of citizenship derive from the very existence of such communities and the willingness of their members to collaborate in generating them. I shall seek to avoid these problems by conceiving Union citizenship as what I shall term an 'inter-national' status that complements national citizenship at the member state level in a way that allows all three issues to be addressed to a sufficient degree while respecting the circumstances of citizenship.[2]

The rest of this chapter develops this argument. The first section outlines the main features of Union citizenship, noting how many of the aspirational accounts overlook the truly significant aspects of what already exists. The second section provides a normative case for civic membership of the political community as found at the member state level. The third section then critically examines arguments for scaling it up to the EU level, while the fourth section disputes the coherence of arguments for the dissolution of any such membership though the disaggregation of citizenship rights and their disembedding from the different circumstances of citizenship found within the member states. The fifth section then makes the case for seeing Union citizenship as a supplement to national citizenship. I shall argue that it addresses the problems related to the exclusions and externalities of domestic citizenship, without requiring the creation of a form of membership of an equivalent kind at the EU level. According to this analysis, the current situation ought not to be viewed as transitory: Union citizenship necessarily depends on national citizenship, with the two playing different but complementary roles. The sixth section then turns to the implications of this account for third-country nationals and the challenge posed by the migration crisis.

The Rights of Union Citizenship

So many normative discussions of Union citizenship are aspirational in character that they often provide misleading guides to what Union

---

[2] As noted in the Introduction, I use 'transnational' and 'international' citizenship here as terms of art, and employ them in slightly different ways to their usage in some of the related academic literature. By 'transnational' I mean a right to the goods associated with citizenship in whatever state an individual happens to move, rather than to denote an ongoing connection between emigrants and their state of origin that extends the reach of national citizenship beyond a state's borders, as is common usage in the migration literature. By 'international' I mean a status, such as I conceive Union citizenship to be, that relates to the relations between the national citizens of different states, creating a right to non-domination and to equal concern and respect for the citizens of the different associated states. It encompasses the common meaning of the term in international law as recognition of the right of states to determine the rights and duties of their citizens, but also entails rights and duties that follow from the agreements made between states to ensure the mutual recognition and non-domination by them of each other's citizens.

citizenship as it actually exists entails, overlooking in the process the virtues of this status as currently constituted. Since I intend to defend this actually existing status in what follows, a preliminary brief overview of the rights associated with Union citizenship seems in order.

The key rights of Union citizenship, as enumerated in Article 20 (2) TFEU and expanded elsewhere in the Treaties, are:

(a) the right to move and reside freely within the territory of the member states;

(b) the right to vote and to stand as candidates in elections to the European Parliament and in municipal elections in their member state of residence, under the same conditions as nationals of that state;

(c) the right to enjoy, in the territory of a third country in which the member state of which they are nationals is not represented, the protection of the diplomatic and consular authorities of any member state on the same conditions as the nationals of that state;

(d) the right to petition the European Parliament, to apply to the European Ombudsman, and to address the institutions and advisory bodies of the Union in any of the Treaty languages and to obtain a reply in the same language.

Five points are worth stressing (Nic Shuibhne 2015a). First, not only are these rights restricted to citizens of a member state, but also the Treaties have become ever more insistent that 'Citizenship of the Union shall be additional to national citizenship and shall not replace it' (Article 9 TEU, Article 20 (1) TFEU). Second, the rights of Union citizenship are fulfilled for the most part by the member states rather than the EU itself, the exceptions being the rights to vote for and petition the EP and to apply to the European Ombudsman concerning possible procedural improprieties in the functioning and decision-making of the EU institutions. Third, the other rights stem from free movement within and, with regard to diplomatic representation, outside the EU. As we shall see, the right to move and reside is closely linked to the single market in the jurisprudence of the Court of Justice and the four key market freedoms of the movement of goods, services, capital and labour across the EU (Article 26 TEU). Fourth, and relatedly, the rights of Union citizenship are framed by the articles prohibiting discrimination on grounds of nationality (Article 18 TFEU), and for combating discrimination on the basis of 'sex, racial or ethnic origin, religion or belief, disability, age or sexual orientation' (Articles 10, 19 TFEU). Finally, Union citizenship rights are not absolute, but 'shall be exercised in accordance with the conditions and limits defined in the Treaties and by the measures adopted thereunder' (Article 20 (2) TFEU). By and large, these limiting conditions seek to protect the capacity of the member states to deliver social protection and public goods to their citizens and maintain the link between the circumstances of citizenship, on the one hand, and the rights of citizens *qua* stakeholders, on the other. For example, they include derogations to the right to move and reside on the basis of 'public policy, public security or public health' (Articles 45 and 52 TFEU, and see *Uecker* 1997), and make the right of residence for periods of longer than three months dependent on having employment in the host member state, or having 'sufficient resources for themselves and their family members not to become a burden on the social assistance system', or to those who have 'comprehensive sickness insurance cover' (Article 7 Directive 2004/38), with that right being retained only 'as long as they do not become an unreasonable burden' (Article 14 (1) Directive 2004/38).

Through the linkage of Union citizenship to free movement and non-discrimination within the single market, the core of EU citizenship has come to consist of free access on a par with national citizens to engage in economic activity within and with another member state, and, for EU citizens resident in another member state, to enjoy the same services and benefits it provides to its citizens, subject to the limits enumerated above (Everson 1995; Nic Shuibhne 2010). It is only activated through a citizen moving to another member state or engaging in cross border EU trade. In most respects, therefore, Union citizenship ought not to be conceived as if it was offering citizenship of a quasi-EU polity in the manner we shall see is proposed by Habermas (1999: 124–7) and other advocates of a supranational Union citizenship, thereby making all citizens of the member states dual national and EU citizens. Rather, it operates more like the transnational conception of Union citizenship in allowing Union citizens to move more or less freely around the EU and to exercise the four fundamental freedoms anywhere in the Union without discrimination on grounds of nationality. Yet, as I shall argue below, Union citizenship remains necessarily and rightly constrained by the need to respect the integrity of the various national systems of citizenship, within which most people remain. Despite the hyperbolic language of *Grzelczyk* (especially paras 3 and 44), it must perforce supplement rather than supplant national citizenship in the manner of what I call 'international citizenship'.

The following sections defend this view as not only a descriptively plausible account of the status quo but also as normatively attractive. I start by noting the achievements of democratic citizenship within nation states. For all their manifest shortcomings, such political systems remain the most effective mechanisms so far for rendering governments accountable to citizens in ways that encourage the pursuit of policies that treat them with equal concern and respect. To avoid throwing the baby out with the bathwater, attempts to address the failings of national citizenship regimes need to preserve their achievements or offer viable substitutes for them. The comparative advantage of the international conception lies in its offering a more credible and coherent prospect of achieving this balance than either the supra- or trans-national conceptions.

National Citizenship: The Dimensions and Circumstances of Citizenship

Citizenship at the member state level developed through the linked processes of state-building, the emergence of commercial and industrial society, and nation-making – all three being driven forward by war (Rokkan 1974; Marshall 1950). Differing social and political circumstances – both structural and contingent – meant their historical phasing and configurations varied considerably between states (Bellamy 2004: 15–17). However, in diverse ways, these three processes served respectively to create a sovereign authority presiding over a given territory and possessing a monopoly of military, police and legal-administrative power; to promote the partial breakdown of traditional social hierarchies and the creation of an equitable system of justice and the public infrastructure associated with the market; and to produce linguistic standardisation, a workforce educated to basic standards of literacy and numeracy, and the mobilisation of affective bonds between citizens themselves, on the one hand, and between them and their state, on the other (Gellner 1983).

Citizenship in this context acquired what have become its three defining dimensions of belonging, rights and participation (Carens 2000: ch. 7). First, citizenship involved belonging to the national community. That need not imply that nationality *per se* provides the normative basis of our political obligations to a particular state, as liberal nationalists typically claim (Miller 1995; Tamir 1993; Kymlicka 1989; Canovan 1998). As was argued in Chapter 2, such duties can be derived from a state simply providing a necessary mechanism for a historically situated group of people to establish the preconditions for a system of freedom and equality between them (Stilz 2009). Nevertheless, as a matter of social psychology, national identity has served to reinforce a common civic consciousness and allegiance to the state and one's fellow citizens (Miller 1995: ch. 3). In particular, national systems of education created a public language and inducted citizens into the nation's political culture.

Second, lack of ascribed status led individuals to being treated as equals, possessing certain rights by virtue of their humanity – including the right to be treated equally before the law. Their involvement as actors in markets also gave them equal rights to pursue their interests by buying and selling goods, services and labour (Pocock 1995). Meanwhile, citizens looked to the state to provide social and economic rights as part of its regulatory function and demanded political rights to secure equal access and recognition within its decision-making and organisational structures (Marshall 1950).

Finally, citizenship involved the capacity, entitlement and obligation to participate as a full and equal member within the economy and the polity (Barbalet 1988). For example, the right to vote was standardly tied to the ownership of property, payment of taxes, military service and the undertaking of such public duties as sitting on juries. Similarly, social and economic rights were linked to the duty and ability to work and to contribute to national schemes of social insurance. Those persons deemed socially irresponsible, a label applied at various times and places to lunatics, children, criminals, women, the propertyless and the indigent, either were ineligible for or forfeited most citizenship rights.

These three dimensions have proved mutually reinforcing, creating a condition of civic equality in the making and upholding of the laws and policies associated with the liberal democratic, welfare states that emerged in Europe between the late nineteenth and the mid-twentieth centuries. Citizenship became in this way the 'right to have rights' (Arendt 1958: 296), extending the entitlements and resulting obligations of the citizens of member states way beyond the basic rights owed to humanity in general. As Chapter 2 indicated, it is through belonging to a sovereign political community, where one lives in a condition of civic equality with others, that it becomes possible to participate in determining the collective rules and structures on which one's rights depend. Outside such collective arrangements, an individual may claim certain rights but, given these claims are open to reasonable disagreement, with all persons partial to their own point of view, no obligation exists on the part of others to uphold them. However, individuals are morally obliged to support a democratically authorised and accountable political authority that offers a mechanism for them to make their claims on an equal basis to everyone else, and to uphold those rights that can be collectively agreed upon in a manner consistent with a condition of non-domination (Waldron 1999: ch. 11; Bellamy 2001, 2007: ch. 4). Through belonging to and participating in a polity that instantiates such processes, citizens' rights get shaped and legitimised (Bellamy 2012a).

If a shared history of social cooperation leads to a certain way of doing things that supports a shared identity among participants and gives them a sense of ownership and attachment to their collective arrangements, their identity and collective arrangements get shaped in turn by subsequent democratic decision-making, thereby gradually giving both belonging and rights their civic character and rendering them more inclusive and egalitarian. Participation and belonging thereby form a virtuous circle that together foster the feelings of solidarity and trust between citizens required to generate a commitment to promote on an equitable basis the public structures and goods – such as a well-functioning legal system – on which their rights depend (Bellamy 2008c: 12–17).

Solidarity leads citizens to feel certain obligations towards their fellows, while trust gives them faith that others will reciprocate in fulfilling them (Offe 2000: 67–8). Without such sentiments, citizens will be tempted to either free ride or defect from collective arrangements out of fear that others are already doing so. This temptation will be especially strong in the case of those goods of a quasi-public nature in the technical sense, such as education or health care. A sense of commonality both facilitates and is buttressed by cooperation, diminishing these tendencies to distrust and disengage. Those who believe they share common values and interests, including a common language and customs, will be more inclined (and find it easier) to interact. Moreover, regular and open-ended interaction between repeat players reduces the incentives for free riding and defection, and builds confidence in the possibility of collaboration. It helps engender the bonds of reciprocity needed to produce benefits that are diffuse and public rather than direct and purely personal.

Citizenship so conceived reflects what Rainer Bauböck (2007) terms the 'stakeholder' conception. On this account, the claim to being a citizen of a given sovereign political community belongs to those who regard their freedom and rights as inherently linked to the collective self-government and flourishing of this polity over time. This argument links citizenship rights to the performance of civic duties and a commitment to the political community and its members, including to future generations. On this view, inclusion in the citizenry or demos depends on participation in the production and shaping of the collective goods on which the rights of citizens depend and of the obligations entailed by membership of a community.[3]

---

[3] As will become clear later on, there is some overlap with Sangiovanni's (2013) account of reciprocity. However, Sangiovanni contends that because simply obeying the law helps sustain and reproduce it, that would be enough to make a long-term resident the equivalent of a stakeholder. Yet, that passive position could lead to the reproduction of inadequate or unjust as well as good laws. On my reading, which is also more demanding than Bauböck's, stakeholders have to be citizens so they can be involved in actively making and challenging the law.

As I remarked earlier, national citizenship raises three distinct but related problematic issues. First, how does one come to be included as a citizen of a given polity in the first place? Is not birth an arbitrary criterion that unjustly advantages those born into citizenship of wealthier polities over citizens of poorer polities? Second, what about the impact of the collective decisions of a given community of citizens on those who are excluded from citizenship of that polity? Should non-citizens not be involved in decisions that affect them, however indirectly? Moreover, are not both these issues especially relevant in the case of non-citizen residents who live under the laws of the community? Are they not entitled to shift from being subjects to becoming citizens? Third, what about those who wish to leave or to enter a political community – should they not have the right to freely move between states? Yet, in so doing, do they not have obligations to ensure the sustainability of the system of states between which they move and on which the fulfilment of the entitlements they wish to claim depends?

These are big issues, each worthy of a book-length treatment in its own right. In what follows, I shall restrict myself to critically examining those arguments that have figured in the literature on Union citizenship and to indicating how this status can be understood as offering a defensible response to each of them. These issues have become particularly salient in an inter-dependent world, with enhanced migration – often of people fleeing abject poverty and/or oppression – being particularly pertinent to the first and third issues, and the negative externalities of decisions by rich countries on poorer countries being central to the second issue. They can be framed as matters of rights and justice. Yet that poses a dilemma if, as was maintained in Chapter 1, such matters lie within the circumstances of politics and the only context for a political, and non-dominating, determination of them is the very democratic states whose exclusionary policies are in certain respects productive of them in the first place. It is for that reason that some writers have argued that we need to see national citizenship as nested within a more encompassing Union citizenship, while others have considered cutting citizenship adrift from any strong attachment to a given political community altogether. The following two sections critically examine each of these proposals respectively.

Scaling Up the Circumstances of Citizenship: Union Citizenship as Supra- and Post-National

The first proposal seeks to address the arbitrary exclusion of individuals from a given citizen body by either nesting national citizenship within, or replacing it by, European citizenship. However, advocates of this position accept that this functional change will only provide the basis for a republican form of democratic citizenship if accompanied by some form of civic bond between EU citizens. Such a bond legitimises their considering themselves as a collectivity, entitled to decide together on their shared rights and duties and obligated to abide by these common decisions. Without some such pan-European bond, the demos may remain segmented into a number of discrete and insular cultural groups largely mirroring current national divisions, of a kind that often bedevil multicultural and multinational polities, raising the possibility of persistent minorities (Christiano 2010: 133–5).

As we saw in Chapter 1, this argument has elicited two different responses from supporters of a more politically integrated EU: the supranational and the postnational conceptions of Union citizenship. The first response adapts the arguments of liberal nationalists (e.g. Miller 1995), who contend that liberal norms, such as rights, cannot in and of themselves attach individuals to a given political community. They accept such loyalties derive from other sources, notably a shared, collective identity of an ethnic or cultural kind, although they believe they can nonetheless sustain liberal relations among co-citizens. For this group, Union citizenship must go hand in hand with the development of an EU identity on the model liberal nationalists associate with national identities and which they claim functional integration is gradually bringing about (Bruter 2005; Risse 2010). By contrast, the second response argues for the sufficiency of a postnational EU identity (Habermas 1992; 1999: ch. 4), that can be associated simply with a commitment to the constitutional rights and values common to European democracies as found in the European Convention on Human Rights (ECHR) and the Charter of Fundamental Rights of the European Union of 2000. Both arguments prove problematic (Bellamy 2008b).

Supranational Citizenship

The policy of European citizenship was initially conceived as part of a package of symbolic measures to promote the identification of the citizens of member states with both the Union and each other. It went along with the introduction of a European passport, anthem and flag (Adonnino 1985; 1988). Although European integration was bringing European states closer together in certain core policy areas, it was perceived that this process had not brought with it a commensurate increase in the attachment of their citizens either to EU institutions as a legitimate locus of decision-making, or to each other as the basis of pan-European solidarity. The creation of a common status of citizens of the Union was hoped to support the development of suitable practices of identification with both Europe and fellow Europeans. The aspiration was to create a form of over-arching European identity that could operate at the EU level and within which the various national identities operating at the level of the different member states might be nested (Shore 2000; 2004).

Such a European identity has been seen by its advocates as essential to the governability of the EU, and a key component of the formation of a European demos. The importance of this strategy lies behind the attempts to track its development empirically through regular Eurobarometer opinion polls asking respondents about their degree of identification with Europe and as Europeans relative to their attachment to their member state and co-nationals. As I noted in Chapter 2, the evidence for such identification remains weak, with considerable variation across countries and social groups (Fligstein 2008). Qualitative research reinforces this finding by suggesting an emotional attachment to Europe is rare (White J 2011), even among the highly mobile elites, who if anything tend to free themselves from all such ties (Favell 2008). Likewise, in border regions, where different nationalities interact regularly, the tendency is to construct a shared local identity as a border region involving distinctive national identities rather than to conceive their interactions as productive of a pan-European space (Meinhof 2004). At best, European citizens have a 'banal', and somewhat fragile, identification with the EU as an instrumentally useful supplement to their different national identities (Cram 2009), to which they have a much stronger emotional attachment. EU identity tends to be parasitic on national identity, a point well represented by the European currency in which national images with a historical resonance within each member state are juxtaposed with either a map of the EU or an abstract 'imagined' bridge signifying Europe (McNamara 2015: 16–17).

These findings are not surprising. National identities were forged through war as well as history and education, and the removal of such coercive pressures has resulted not only in their fracturing with the resurgence of minority nationalisms in many member states, but also in their being challenged by many immigrant groups. A European identity that aims at promoting similarity in view point and allegiances seems ill suited to the pluralism encouraged by increasingly complex, liberal societies (Bellamy 1999: ch. 8). Moreover, attempts to do so are likely to promote the centrifugal tendencies associated with analogous projects in multinational states such as Belgium, Spain and Canada (Lacey 2017: 12). The attempt to construct a European identity of a postnational kind seems both more promising and less objectionable, therefore.

Postnational Citizenship

This thesis has been advocated most prominently by Jürgen Habermas, who argues that a European citizenship can be grounded in a 'constitutional patriotism' derived from the 'universalist principles of constitutional democracy' to which all the national citizenships of the member states can be related (Habermas 1996: 499–500). Habermas's reasoning has its origins in the Kantian argument for sovereignty as necessary to and mandated by the need to establish relations of justice among citizens that was introduced in Chapter 2. However, as we shall see, to move from this argument to advocacy of European citizenship requires a number of departures from the Kantian view that involve surreptitiously appealing to some form of pan-European national identity of the kind rejected above.

Habermas contends that there is no inherent conceptual relationship between nationalism and citizenship. He concedes that historically nation states have provided the context for the emergence of democratic citizenship, with national sentiments supporting a collective intentionality and a commitment to the common good among citizens of a kind necessary for a workable and justifiable form of popular sovereignty (Habermas 1996: 495, 499; 1999: 113). However, he believes that the role played by nationalism and existing states in this development has been contingent. The conceptual basis for a civic association of free and equal persons consists of a shared commitment to liberal principles of rights (Habermas 1996: 495). Where and among whom these are culturally anchored thereby becomes an open question – there is no intrinsic link with any particular state or nation. As a result, no theoretical block stands in the way of the formation of 'a future Federal Republic of European States' in which 'the *same* legal principles', as interpreted by '*different* national traditions and histories' might 'be appropriated from a vantage point relativized by the perspectives of other traditions' and 'brought into a transnational, West European constitutional culture' (Habermas 1996: 500). Though this European constitutional culture can be differentiated from '*national* traditions in art and literature, historiography, philosophy, and so on' (Habermas 1996: 507), it nonetheless 'does require that every citizen be socialised into a common political culture' (Habermas 1996: 500). As such, 'a European constitutionalism would have to grow together from various nationally specific interpretations of the same universalist principles of law' (Habermas 1996: 507).

His advocacy of this step stems from the largely functional reasons documented in Chapter 1: namely, his belief that the democratic challenge of controlling a globalising economy requires the citizens of the member states 'to develop a new political self-consciousness commensurate with the role of Europe in the world of the twenty-first century' (Habermas 1996: 507; 1999: 120–4). Yet, as we saw in Chapters 1 and 2, that functional necessity proves indeterminate, with opinions reasonably differing as to the appropriate response along a line from free cooperation to a global union. At best, Habermas has suggested that *if* a more politically united Europe was desired, then the presence of multiple national identities and the absence of a European cultural identity need not be insurmountable hurdles to bringing it about, at least in principle. However, that hurdle remains quite high, and not as distinct from a degree of identification as Europeans as he maintains.

Habermas suggests that the citizens of the different nation states of Europe can arrive at 'a common *political* culture' without merging the linguistic, religious and historical elements of their different national cultures, citing Switzerland as an example of how that can be possible (see too Lacey 2014). Yet, even if the political component can be distinguished from the other, cultural, elements of nationalism, it need not make the task of arriving at 'a common political culture' any easier. After all, the Swiss have a common political history and traditions that have arisen over time and which they retain (Steinberg 2015). Moreover, their 'common political culture' differs in key respects from that of most of the other member states, with its emphasis on direct democracy, a citizen militia, cantonal government and strong consociational institutions. It is also facilitated by widespread multilingualism and cross-cutting cleavages across the main linguistic and religious divisions, thereby preventing the predominance of any linguistic or religious group. Meanwhile, there is considerable devolution in many administrative areas, with periodic demands for more, along with a suspicion of central government. In sum, the Swiss model seems to depend on circumstances and cultural traditions that do not pertain in the EU, and even if they did would make it a far 'thinner' federation than Habermas envisages. Indeed, the Swiss analogy seems belied by the very fact that Switzerland itself has yet to become a member of the EU.

The member states could be said to endorse a broadly similar range of liberal democratic rights, as their adherence to the ECHR indicates. However, that adherence does not constitute in and of itself a 'common political culture', as the European Court of Human Right's (ECtHR) doctrine of the 'margin of appreciation' and its increased deployment of subsidiarity indicate. Indeed, the structure and organisation of the Court remains firmly inter- rather than supra-national, and intergovernmental rather than federal (Bellamy 2014). Domestic governments, legislatures and courts remain the legitimate interpreters of Convention rights for most of their citizens and to a large degree are recognised as such by the ECtHR, which cannot strike down domestic legislation and ultimately has to work with domestic agencies to give effect to its judgments. As we shall see in Chapter 6, to a lesser degree, Europe's Court of Justice can be viewed in similar terms.

The origins and justification for this diversity of views regarding commonly held constitutional principles derives from the point made in Chapters 1 and 2 concerning their being subject to reasonable disagreement. As a result, it was argued that the circumstances of justice must be addressed within the circumstances of politics. Given that the member states have established their own political and juridical orders for resolving these disagreements, such diversity cannot be expected to give way to a consensus over and above the acknowledgement that certain basic interests deserve to be treated with equal concern and respect in any collective decision. As Habermas observes, even within the member states there is not so much a consensus on how such principles need to be interpreted as 'a common *horizon* of interpretation' (Habermas 1999: 225). Yet, that suggests it is not the presence of such a 'common horizon' that gives rise to a 'common political culture', but rather loyalty to a historically defined common political culture that renders this horizon possible (Habermas 1999: 118; Laborde 2002). After all, the constitutions of the member states not only differ along many dimensions (Finer 1995) but also have been defined within the vernacular of domestic politics rather than some constitutional Esperanto.

To bolster his attempts to base a Europe-wide republican citizenship on constitutional patriotism, Habermas ends up relying on either vague aspiration and assertion or a weak form of the European identity argument at variance with his claim to endorse a postnational view. On the one hand, he suggests that European citizens need merely be united by 'an inter-subjectively shared context of possible mutual understanding' (Habermas 1999: 159), combined with what he asserts as the urgent need to make that possibility a reality. On the other hand, he appeals to 'a common cultural background and the shared historical experience of having happily overcome nationalism' (Habermas 1999: 161). The former seems so vague as to apply potentially to anyone anywhere, while the latter assertion of the overcoming of nationalism unhappily seems wildly optimistic. Meanwhile, his appeal to a common culture veers between an overly inclusive claim that Europe is not the United States of America in being opposed to the death penalty and less neo-liberal in its economic and foreign policy (Habermas 2001: 20–1), a position shared with most other liberal democracies world-wide, and an overly exclusive view of Europe that treats the UK and Scandinavia as deviant and barely mentions Central and Eastern Europe (Habermas 2001: 25).

As I remarked in Chapter 2, the problems Habermas encounters with his postnational argument for a Union citizenship arise from the fact that the Kantian justice based duty to create a political unity capable of allowing individuals to determine freely and equally what justice and rights are for them already has been met within the member states. To that extent, we can regard all states as providing their citizens with a form of constitutional patriotism related to a common political culture. Some commentators suggest that one can extrapolate from the Kantian natural duty argument, requiring we make political terms with those in immediate proximity to us so as to establish relations of justice among those with whom we inevitably interact (Waldron 1993), to argue that in a world where we have become proximate to and interact, albeit indirectly, with unknown individuals across the world, a functional case exists to rearrange borders and establish political relations at a regional and ultimately a global level (Ingram 1996). However, as we saw in Chapter 2, the normative and empirical question posed in circumstances where civic unions already exist is not that of how their citizens might form into a different, and more encompassing, union of a similar type. Rather, it is the issue of how each of these civic unions relate to each other. As Habermas appears to realise, at least some of the time, the constitutional patriotism of these various civic unions has been overlaid by a distinctive national political culture reflecting the historical experiences and collective decisions of those who belong to them. As a result, a regional union will have a different character to a national union. It will be a union of unions rather than of citizens *per se*. As in European citizenship, the relationship of the citizens of the different states to each other will be mediated through their national citizenship.

It might be objected that this analysis ignores the potential of the right of every Union citizen to vote for the EP. After all, supranationalists standardly argue that it will be through participation in pan-European elections for a common legislature that individuals will come to identify as a European citizenry. They contend most Europeans feel a relatively weak degree of identification as a European citizen compared to their sense of national citizenship only because the EU civic space remains weak. If the latter was reinforced by further empowering the EP and encouraging the emergence of trans-European parties, then the former would become proportionately stronger. I have criticised this line of reasoning in Chapters 3 and 4 for exaggerating the capacity of political institutions to change behaviour and attitudes. Such speculations appear inconsistent with the resilience of minority nationalism within many of the member states. Yet, assuming such a change could occur, would it be commendable? As I've commented at a number of points, I believe not. Reducing the number and diversity of civic regimes comes at a cost in terms of diminishing the plurality of forms of social life that can flourish. In this regard, the transnational concept of European citizenship appears to fare much better since it is premised precisely on the freedom of European citizens to choose between different citizenship regimes. Yet, as we shall see, this account risks jeopardising the very existence of a civic community capable of securing rights.

Disaggregating the Circumstances of Citizenship: Union Citizenship as Transnational

As I noted, Union citizenship is linked expressly to 'free movement' (Article 20 (2) TFEU). Some commentators believe that this linkage implies the partial or even total dissolution of an attachment to any state in particular and the gradual erosion of the line between citizenship rights and human rights (Soysal 1994). Developing this line of argument, Seyla Benhabib contends that EU citizenship has come to 'disaggregate' citizenship rights, separating out the three 'ideal' components delineated above of belonging, or what she terms 'collective identity'; participation, or, in her terminology, the 'privileges of political membership'; and 'social rights and benefits' (Benhabib 2002: 454). In particular, it has led certain political and social rights to be 'deterritorialised' by allowing citizens of member states to settle anywhere in the Union; take up jobs in their chosen countries; access certain benefits there, albeit subject to various conditions; and to vote and stand in local and European elections wherever they reside within the EU (Benhabib 2002: 448, 454, 456, 459; 2004: 153–5; 2008: 46–7). As she notes, paradoxically – at least from a cosmopolitan point of view – these processes within the EU have often – though not uniformly – gone hand in hand with a tightening of exclusionary measures on non-EU 'third country' nationals, not only through stricter immigrations controls – that remain the preserve of each individual member state – but also by virtue of even long-term residents being excluded from participation and many rights precisely on the basis of their not 'belonging'.

In this section I want to focus on the issue that, in my view, rightly worries Benhabib, but that I shall contend neither she, nor others who adopt this perspective, ever satisfactorily resolves – indeed, many fail even to recognise it as a problem: namely, the tension between 'disaggregated' citizenship and democratic citizenship (Benhabib 2002: 462–3). Habermas wants to develop a postnational form of Union citizenship at the EU level in part to ensure the embedding of individual EU-level rights within a functioning pan-European democratic system that allows for their collective definition. I noted in the section on national citizenship how such embedding creates a link between the private enjoyment of rights by citizens and their civic duties to support the public structures and goods necessary for their establishment and exercise. The 'disaggregation' and 'deterriorialisation' of rights threaten this linkage in problematic ways. As will be argued in the next section, the anchoring of Union within national citizenship was intended precisely to avoid such threats. However, this anchorage has come under increasing challenge from the teleological reasoning of the European Court of Justice in a number of citizenship cases, leading many legal scholars to conceive European citizenship as a rights-based status that has become justifiably cut loose from any concomitant state-based duties (Kostakopoulou 2008; Kochenov 2014; and for a critique Bellamy 2015). These scholars celebrate this conception of European citizenship as emancipating individuals from the shackles of belonging and participation in a national political community. As Floris de Witte enthuses:

Freedom of movement allows Europe's citizens to move for love, work, family, language, social or cultural reasons, or simply to be somewhere 'else'. It is about liberating the individual from the possibilities, opportunities, prejudices, cultural and social norms or conventions (or even weather) that exists in their 'own' country, and about making available realizations of life in other states that might much more closely fit with the individual's own preferences. To turn this around, it also means limiting the capacity of states to force the individual to live her life in a particular fashion. (de Witte 2016)

The analysis below disputes this view. Such rhetoric overstates the reality of Court of Justice rulings and implies an ultimately incoherent form of philosophical anarchism.

Freedom of Movement and the Judicial Construction of Transnational Citizenship

In a series of judgments, the Court of Justice has argued that Union citizenship offers a Treaty-based, directly effective right of its own, which undercuts many of the limitations member states sought to build into the relevant directives (notably Directive 2004/38/EC). While these decisions have had certain liberating effects, such as those highlighted by de Witte, their main effect has been to flesh out a form of market citizenship at the EU level that potentially conflicts with political and social citizenship at the member state level (Everson 1995). Thus, in a series of cases the

Court has increasingly argued that the restrictions protecting national citizenship have to be applied in a 'proportional' manner (*Baumbast* 2002) that do not deprive Union citizens of a right to move and reside that exists independently of their pursuit of any economic activity (*Chen* 2004), thereby creating new rights for non-workers (*Sala* 1998; *Trojani* 2004), students (*Grzelczk* 2001), and job-seekers (*Collins* 2004), weakening public interest derogations that excluded non-nationals from certain public service jobs (*Marina Mercante Espanola* 2003), and altering what could be considered a 'wholly internal' matter (*Avello* 2003; *Chen* 2004; *Rottmann* 2010; *Zambrano* 2011, although see *McCarthy* 2011 which arguably reasserts the internal rule). In a parallel move, the Court has also questioned the previous understanding that the state provision of healthcare and education are not 'services' in the commercial sense of Articles 49, 50 EC, but legitimately correspond to the democratically decided collective preferences of the citizens of each of the member states, reflecting national financial priorities and other public interest considerations (e.g. *Commission v. Austria* 2005; *Humbel* 1988). As such, these services had not been subject to the prohibition on restrictions of the freedom to provide services. However, decisions such as *Schwarz* (2007), *Kohll* (1998), *Geraets-Smits* (2001), *Müller-Fauré* (2003), and *Watts* (2005) have undermined this reasoning by allowing individuals to escape national processes of rationing these goods by shopping for alternatives elsewhere in the Union. *Grzelczyk* (2001) held that 'a certain degree of financial solidarity' now existed between the member states. Yet, though the Euro crisis suggests that such solidarity is decidedly limited, the Court has consistently refused to consider national fiscal concerns as justifying restrictions on the exercise of European liberties – even treating national rules against tax avoidance as violations of the freedom to move capital (Schön 2015). Finally, there have been a series of judgments that have prioritised EU level economic freedoms over member state level social rights (*Viking* 2008; *Laval* 2008; *Rüffert* 2008; *Luxembourg* 2008). In these cases, the Court has attempted to impose a uniform, minimum standard of wage legislation that overrides local collective bargaining agreements, thereby hindering the exercise of union rights.

In various ways, these decisions uncouple the rights of individuals freely to pursue their personal goals and interests on an equal basis to others either from economic participation within and a contribution to, or membership of and identification with, the polity in which one resides (Scharpf 2009: 191–8). Consequently, many citizenship rights, including access to important social and economic benefits, have been disassociated not just from political citizenship, but also from what we have seen have become the standard prerequisites for obtaining the same: namely, an economic stake in the fortunes of the state, membership and a degree of identification with it, and political participation in shaping and sustaining the goods that it provides its citizens. It is this process that has produced what Benhabib calls the disaggregation of citizenship (Benhabib 2008: 46–7), whereby the synthesis of civic with civil and commercial liberties achieved within the nation state has been pulled apart as the second and third have become detached from the first. Instead, modern civil and commercial liberties have become the trigger of themselves for access to certain civic liberties (Bellamy 2012b): notably, the ability to vote and stand in local and European elections when residing in another member state, and admission to social benefits that hitherto have been both privileges of political citizenship and part of their foundation.

Although an advocate of 'another cosmopolitanism', Benhabib's transnational position shares the general cosmopolitan endorsement of these judgments as being in line with their critique of the moral arbitrariness of borders, and the exclusionary nature of state-centred citizenship (Carens 1987; Nussbaum 1996). Even though many, if not all, these rights apply only to EU nationals rather than all non-citizens resident within a member state, and to that extent are unsatisfactory, cosmopolitans are apt to regard any deterritorialising and denationalising of citizenship as a step in the right direction. However, as was noted in Chapter 1, there is a split within the cosmopolitan camp over what universal obligations we owe to all humans, and the mechanisms that might be necessary to uphold them. Libertarians see the individual liberties associated with free movement in largely negative terms, as merely necessitating the removal of barriers that interfere with free exchanges between individuals (Kukathas 2003: 572). On this view, there is little need for Union citizenship as a social or political status – it is sufficient to uphold the four freedoms as inherent aspects of a 'common market', avoiding welfare and political rights as creating potential distortions with its free operation, while supporting the possibility of economic migration from poor to rich countries as consistent with a genuinely free market in labour. By contrast, more socially minded cosmopolitans have argued that rich countries also have more positive obligations towards the poor (e.g. Beitz 1990: 150–3; Pogge 2008). Theorists differ as to how far these extend, but most contend some redistribution is warranted given that the wealth of the rich depends in part on their having exploited the resources of the poor and deployed their superior bargaining position to gain favourable terms of trade.

The quandary confronting social liberals, though, is that the institutional capacity for securing the libertarian, market-reinforcing view of a deterritorialised and denationalised conception of Union citizenship proves far greater than that for implementing the market-correcting view they favour. As Fritz Scharpf has noted (1999: 54–8; see too Grimm 2016: ch. 14), ever since *Cassis de Dijon* (1979) the Court of Justice has effectively constitutionalised free competition within the EU, overriding the political judgement of national legislatures on the reasonableness of their environmental, health and safety, and other regulations whenever it felt they lacked an adequate public-interest defence. The opening up of the full range of public services to competition, so that Union citizens may choose from a range of providers, is simply an extension of this logic. Yet, this possibility potentially undermines the social contract within each of the member states without establishing any at the EU level (Scharpf 2009: 198; Sangiovanni 2013: 225–6). For example, the decision in *Watts* (2005) simply enables those citizens who are sufficiently mobile and proactive to seek a given health treatment in another member state to jump the waiting lists and other restrictions that national services employ to prioritise the spending of limited resources among different kinds of health care (Newdick 2006). As such, it certainly enhances the liberty of those citizens able to take advantage of this option. But, given that national budgets are not infinitely elastic, their doing so may be at the expense of the health or other social needs of many of their fellow citizens. Moreover, these other individuals are not in a position to contest such Court decisions through the political system. Instead, their collective civic liberty has been undercut by this extension of an essentially commercial liberty.

Benhabib appears to acknowledge this dilemma in seeking to distinguish the 'human rights' claims made by refugees, asylum seekers and migrant workers from the deregulatory legal framework promoted by global capitalism – what she calls the *lex mercatoria* (Benhabib 2007: 22, 33). Yet, this theoretical argument overlooks how, in practice, the language of the first has often been deployed to legitimise the second. Like others (Caporoso and Tarrow 2008; Kostakopoulou 2008; Kochenov 2011), she has seen the Court's extension of rights to free movement and to non-discrimination on the basis of nationality to those outside the labour market as marking a move away from a market bias to one based in rights. She argues they reflect a cosmopolitan duty of 'hospitality' that, in time, ought to enable migrants from poor countries to gain access to the social rights of wealthier states (Benhabib 2008: 22–3, 36). However, in many respects, the Court has simply deployed the language of human rights to further extend its market logic. By portraying the negative rights associated with market-reinforcing liberties as extensions of humanitarian duties not to interfere unduly or exploit others and to uphold basic rights, it has been able to overcome all democratic objections on the part of the member states. These have not been examples of 'democratic iterations' as Benhabib claims (2007: 33), but rather a means to trump national exercises of self-determination (Scharpf 2009: 193).

Can Rights Be Disaggregated from the 'Circumstances of Citizenship'

The difficulties of extending positive rights on the basis of free movement are both normative and practical. Normatively, we incur such obligations to our fellow citizens through being associated with them within a given political system that possesses the capacity to determine and compel obedience to the rules governing our social and economic interactions with each other. Through the exercise of our civic liberty, we are co-responsible for these rules, and so have a mutual obligation to ensure they operate in as equitable and impartial manner as possible (Bellamy 2012a). Practically, we also help sustain them through our economic activity and taxes. However, if we can claim these rights without incurring the related obligations, say by forcing my fellow citizens to pay for a service in another country that, as a result of collective decisions in which I could and probably did participate, is unavailable or less available to me in my country of full citizenship, then this social and political compact is undone.

A justified response to the issues posed by the circumstances of citizenship cannot be one that undermines the conditions of citizenship itself. For these conditions prove necessary for the very exercise of the rights those who champion a deterritorialised and disaggregated form of Union citizenship based on free movement seek to promote. A pure, rights-only and duty-free form of European citizenship amounts to a form of self-contradictory free riding (Bellamy 2015). To be able to claim a right without relying on the forbearance or virtue of others requires that it can be enforced even when these others oppose or simply neglect to uphold it. In other words, it requires that others can be obliged to recognise that right. As a result, rights emerge as dependent on politics and a political obligation to a given political community in two related senses.

First, the very existence of rights depends upon individuals being equally subordinate to the laws of a common political authority capable of defining and upholding their rights in a uniform way. Otherwise, which rights they have, when they apply and what they entail will be matters of the differing private judgements of others – we may claim rights but will remain dependent on the consideration and benevolence of others for their recognition and enforcement. In such a situation, individuals will always be prone to injustice and domination by those more powerful than them and to committing, either intentionally or inadvertently, injustice and dominating others in their turn. Some neo-liberals of an anarchist persuasion have denied such arguments and claimed that markets emerge through conventions and are capable of operating without any need for a state (Friedman 2014). Yet, as critics of this position – including many libertarians (e.g. Hayek 1960) – note, the operation of markets requires the establishment of property rights and freedom of contract, which are only likely to be secured in an impartial and authoritative way by a state capable of enforcing duties. Not only would a pure free market, without any political assignment of rights and duties, be liable to being unjust, it would be largely unworkable as well. As a result, a duty to belong to and support some form of political community becomes an obligation of justice because such an arrangement is constitutive of the very possibility of a just scheme of rights. As I observed in Chapter 3, this argument has Hobbesian and, in the version being employed here, Kantian roots (Stilz 2009: 53–6). Outside a political community, rights not only will not be upheld but also would not even exist, because there will be constant disagreement as to which rights we have (Honoré 1993). Their assignment by courts, as the ideologues of the Court of Justice propose, will be entirely arbitrary – a form of what Natolino Irti has called juridical nihilism (Irti 2005).

Of course, though a coercive political authority might be a condition of justice, that does not mean that any given political authority is just. The second political aspect of rights emerges here. If justice is itself controversial, we cannot appeal to it as an independent standard for adjudicating on the legitimacy of the various political arrangements that serve to instantiate it. Rather, we will need some form of political mechanism for claiming and defining our rights in a free and equal way against and with others (Bellamy 2007). Here we return to the need for democratic mechanisms that are necessarily embedded in the particular states of which individuals are citizens.

The 'circumstances of citizenship' – the existing world of bounded polities within which issues of political membership arise (Bauböck 2015) – enter at this point as unavoidable. Union citizenship cannot be conceived as an alternative to these circumstances, as both supranational and transnational forms of European citizenship propose – the one by absorbing different national citizenship regimes within a more encompassing Union citizenship, the other by dissolving all such regimes. Rather, we need to see Union citizenship as a supplement to these regimes that overcomes some of the problems of the arbitrary exclusion of individuals from a given citizen body and of the potential domination of one body of citizens by the decision-making of another body of citizens. As the next section shows, Union citizenship responds to the arbitrariness of exclusion and the potential for domination of one body of citizens by another by allowing free movement across borders in ways that are compatible with a system of democratic welfare states. Yet, that means we must pay as much attention to avoiding the arbitrary inclusion of free movers within the decision-making and benefits of their host state as overcoming their arbitrary exclusion (Bellamy and Lacey 2018: 1411).

Between the Circumstances of Citizenship: Union Citizenship as International Citizenship

Union citizenship offers the potential to address the three problematic issues noted above by allowing free movement between member states while giving all citizens of the member states a direct, via the EP, and indirect, via their elected governments, say in the shaping of the supra- and trans-national framework regulating interstate relations. As I shall argue below, the best reading of this policy sees it as allowing member states to collaborate in showing and upholding equal concern and respect for their separate citizenship regimes, including when citizens move between them or even outside the EU.

The first two subsections sketch the argument by way of a stylised example. The first subsection argues that the right to freedom of movement provides a valid response to the potential domination of being arbitrarily assigned to one state rather than another. However, the logic behind this right rests on there being a plurality of suitably free states to choose between. Moreover, these states could not be sustained simply on the basis of the free choices or consent of their citizens but entail certain *prima facie* obligations on the part of those who are born into them to participate in supporting the structures on which their rights – and those of any who might choose to settle among them – depend. Contrary to the transnational view, therefore, the rights of even free moving citizens cannot be detached from their duties to particular states. Rather, such citizens have a duty to support the political and social systems of both their home and their host state, although an option to change their civic allegiance from one to the other should be available and possibly even compulsory. The second subsection turns to the implications of this argument for citizenship within an association of states. As argued in Chapters 2 and 3, I contend that forming such an association is necessary if states and their citizens are to avoid dominating or being dominated. However, I dispute the supra- and post-national argument that we should view the citizens of such an association as constituting a demos, with a specifically associational political identity, who should control the terms of the association and its governance directly. Rather than viewing the member states as being nested within the association, I defend conceiving the association as nested within and under the control of the member states and their citizens. Hence, democratic citizenship within an association must respect the logic of a two-level game, with associational decision-making subordinate to, and controlled by, member-state citizenship. That also subordinates the rights individuals possess qua citizens of the association to their duties as citizens of member states and their obligations towards the citizens of other member states. The third subsection then moves from theory to practice to defend and extend the current balance between Union and national citizenship in the sphere of welfare and political rights as reflecting such mutual concern and respect between member state citizens.

Communities of Choice and Civic Communities: How Freedom of Movement Depends Upon and Supplements the 'Circumstances of Citizenship'

All member states of the EU have to meet a sufficient threshold for the protection of civil, social and political rights to count as constitutional democracies. Moreover, as we saw in Chapter 2, and elaborated further in Chapters 3 and 4, one rationale for membership of the EU is to ensure that the decisions of one or more member state(s) do not impair and so dominate the democratic processes of others. Consequently, all the member states aspire to be at least minimally non-dominating of their own and each other's citizens. Yet that cannot be achieved simply through respecting each other's democratic decision-making. Although membership of some state might be viewed as inevitable and so not *per se* dominating (Pettit 2012: 161–2), being constrained to be a member of a *particular* state can be dominating – particularly if that state offers fewer opportunities than others one might wish to move to (Costa 2016). Border controls involve interference and coercion (Carens 1987), while their presence may inhibit the autonomous choices of individuals to move to another state for work, family, leisure or other reasons (Abizadeh 2008). After all, the different member states have adopted different forms and degrees of democracy and rights protection, so the arrangements of another state may be more attractive to certain individuals or offer them better protection than those of their own. Economic opportunities may also be greater in one country rather than another, or a different country simply more appealing to live in – be it because of better weather, a lower cost of living, a more appealing life-style and so on.

On what I shall call the 'choice' account of political membership, the only way to ensure non-domination is to allow individuals to freely choose their state. As we saw, transnational theorists of Union citizenship tend to adopt something akin to this view. However, I shall contend that this account only proves plausible in the context of what I shall call the 'civic' account of political membership, which provides a *prima facie* obligation to support the polity into which we are born (Stilz 2009). As a result, we can best see Union citizenship as supplementing the civic account rather than replacing it. As I shall argue, Union citizenship provides a non-discriminatory mechanism that helps render national citizenship non-dominating, by facilitating free movement between the different citizenship regimes of the member states, while being non-dominating in its turn, through being subject to laws (and limitations) that have been democratically agreed to by the elected representatives of the contracting states as being in the collective interests of their citizens.

The choice account stresses the importance of our being able to choose which political community we belong to. This need not imply a denial of the need for any political authority at all, as some have suggested (e.g. Kochenov 2014: 494, 495). Most cosmopolitans of a philosophical anarchist hue accept that a political authority of at least a minimal kind might be needed, while some even acknowledge that a more extensive state would be acceptable (Simmons 2001: chs 1 and 6). Either way, they argue its legitimacy depends on its being freely chosen by those subject to it (Kochenov 2014: 496–7). On this account, choosing a political community can be likened to an amateur singer choosing between choirs. Like the securing of individual civil, social and political rights, singing choral music is something that can only be achieved by being part of a collective organisation established for that purpose. If I am a big Bach fan, I will be inclined to choose the Bach rather than the Mozart choir, and if I have an above average voice I might prefer the choir I feel is strongest over the one nearest to where I live. Yet, having made these choices, I incur certain obligations – to attend practices, to follow the agreed tempo, not to sing fortissimo when my part is supposed to be piano, to stay the course and not to pull out before the final performance because I have got bored, and so forth. In other words, I acquire in this way a set of duties relating to membership of a particular choir.

A. J. Simmons, a key advocate of the 'choice' account, has conceded that where we can choose whether or not to be members of a given community that produces certain collective goods, such as the collective good of a certain pattern of rights relating to a given account of justice, then we would have something like a Rawlsian 'fair play' obligation to contribute to the political community and obey its laws. As he notes,

Nozick's famous critique of Rawls's (1964) 'fair play' argument for political obligation does not apply in such cases (Simmons 2001: ch. 1). If I have chosen to belong to a certain community, then I acquire duties to cooperate in that community's coercive maintenance of a unitary scheme of rights by obeying the law, paying taxes and so on. For advocates of the choice account, when individuals can choose whether they belong to a libertarian or a social democratic polity, say, then that alone provides the most effective (and necessary) incentive for all polities to enshrine a reasonable conception of justice (Kochenov 2014: 497).

This position would be perfectly compatible with a conception of Union citizenship as freeing European citizens from obligations to any member state in particular by allowing them free movement to choose between these states. So conceived, Union citizenship would not be free of all political duties, though, but involve something akin to what Rawls called 'a natural duty to uphold just institutions' (Rawls 1971: 333–42): that is, a recognition that all the member states reflect reasonable conceptions of justice that EU citizens should respect. Some such general duty lies behind those limits to EU citizenship rights, that, as I noted above, the Court of Justice has occasionally challenged (e.g. in *Schwarz* 2007; *Kohll* 1998; *Geraets* 2001; *Müller-Fauré* 2003; and *Watts* 2006). Yet, as we saw, these limitations amount to an obligation not to undermine the fiscal capacity of each member state to provide the public services democratically decided upon by its citizens, including by limiting access to health and social security to those who have worked and contributed for a minimum period, to restrict voting in national elections to those willing to commit more permanently to membership by naturalising and so on. Indeed, the rationale for the EU not being a duty-free zone in the literal sense of EU citizens not being able to purchase goods free of duty when travelling between member states, could be related to a general obligation to maintain the fiscal viability of member states by preventing citizens simply shopping around at whim to the extent that no stable political communities would be possible Arguably, the Court of Justice has come to close to overlooking this obligation not only by not allowing the fiscal viability of public services such as health and education to be a consideration in restricting access to them, as in the Cases cited above (Scharpf 2009: 173), but also, as I noted, by treating national rules against tax avoidance as violations of free capital movement (on which see Ganghof and Genschel 2008a). After all, the philosophical anarchist account also suggests it would be inadvisable that the EU displaced the member states to become itself a political community capable of exacting duties. For that would necessarily prevent citizens from choosing between the member states.

The coherence of the choice account of Union citizenship, therefore, rests on citizens retaining obligations towards, and membership of, one of the member states. What Union citizenship adds is a presumption that to the extent we can freely move between these states, then our obligations towards them are chosen and so legitimate. However, the most obvious difficulty with this account is that most individuals are sedentary and therefore exercise no choice – unless, somewhat implausibly, their staying put is interpreted as a form of tacit consent. Indeed, the choice account relies on this being the case. For the stable citizenship regimes of the member states create the choices the free moving Union citizens choose between.

The civic account enters here. On this account, a political authority may be legitimate even for those who have not moved or chosen their civic status but have rather acquired citizenship through birth. This account rests on the political authority being under the free and equal democratic control of those subject to it, in the manner outlined in Chapter 2 – a development that we saw in the first section above largely framed the evolution of citizenship within the member states. The civic account is sometimes given a libertarian reading as suggesting that political authority is thereby subjected to the consent of citizens, and hence comes close to being something they have chosen. Yet, as the philosophical anarchist R.P. Wolff established some years ago, it is practically impossible for even the most direct form of democracy to provide a satisfactory method for citizens to consent (Wolff 1970). A more realistic view suggests that we have an obligation to participate with others in collectively determining on a free and equal basis the system of rights under which we happen to live (Buchanan 2002).

Contra the philosophical anarchists, we can have rights-based obligations to participate in collective processes even when we have not chosen to do so (Stilz 2009: ch. 7). If I am wandering along a beach and come across a group of people who have formed a chain to pull in a fishing vessel that has got into trouble on the sea, then, assuming I am sufficiently fit to participate and those on the boat will plainly be in grave danger without this help, I am morally obliged to do my bit in this collective endeavour to save the lives of these fishermen. Analogously, it can be argued that, given rights require a political authority through which they can be claimed and secured, I have an obligation to support and participate in those institutions that regulate the majority of my interactions with others to ensure that their rights are duly recognised and to do so in the way that most effectively leads to their being treated equitably. Individuals may not have chosen their political community, yet that does not mean they have no obligations towards it. Rather, they are like the beach stroller above who has a natural duty of justice to help save the fishermen or, in this case, to support a judicial authority necessary to uphold rights.

In this respect, being born into a given political community can be likened to finding oneself already a member of the local Bach choir, the members depending on you to do your bit in bringing about the collective performance that is a fair and equitable system of laws. That need not tie you forever to a given community any more than one must remain a member of a given choir. However, it constrains your freedom to flit from one to another at whim without any obligations whatsoever, as some advocates of transnational citizenship appear to advocate. (e.g. Kochenov 2014: 497–8). It suggests that, in moving to another state, one either retains one's civic membership of one's original state, such as paying taxes, while still having the natural duty to uphold the just institutions of the state one visits, or one gives up one's previous civic obligations and acquires another set to one's new state. As a result, the choice and civic accounts are not incompatible, rather the choice account is parasitic on the civic account.

Citizenship and Democracy within an Association of Civic Communities

What are the implications of the civic account for citizenship within an association of civic communities, particularly the relationship between the community and the associational level? Imagine the choirs of my original example operate democratically, choosing what to perform, who will conduct, and how often they practise by free and fair deliberation among their members followed by a majority vote. Their freely made collective decisions might have mutually adverse effects. If all the choirs decided to perform the same works on the same day and rehearsed at the same time every week, it probably would be disadvantageous to all of them. It would reduce the potential audiences for their performances and possibly their members, say in a situation where two parents wished to join choirs that rehearsed on different nights so as to share child care. It might lead to choirs with more resources seeking to reduce the likelihood of audiences going to the poorer choirs, say by offering a free wine reception after the performance. They might also pay their choirs to get the best singers.

As a result, self-interest and fairness suggests that some coordination between the choirs would be mutually warranted if their collective decisions were not to undercut each other in various ways. Indeed, as I noted in Chapter 2, a certain moral consistency suggests this should be a matter of concern for the richer and larger as well as the poorer and smaller choirs, which have more to lose. Each choir secures the collective purpose of its members to collaborate on equal terms in what is necessarily a joint enterprise. The choir only counts as a civic community that is justified in holding its members as obliged to contribute to it in so far as this is the case. Yet, by the same account, their freely made collective decisions can only be justified as worthy of respect and recognition by other choirs in so far as they do not undercut their similarly freely made collective decisions. Moreover, to be non-dominating, ensuring equal respect between choirs requires a settled process parallel to, but not the same as, that within each choir. An obligation thereby rests on each of these interacting choirs to form an association that would allow them to coordinate their activities according to commonly agreed procedures, albeit one that could meet with approval in separate internal democratic processes within each constituent member choir. In this scenario, the members of the constituent choirs join not as individuals but as members of choirs, with each of these choirs possessing different traditions that their members wish to preserve – hence the need for the collective approval of each choir to the shape of the association. In other words, the association of choirs will adopt the normative logic of a two-level game as defended in general terms in Chapter 2 and outlined as a model for democratic decision-making for the EU in Chapter 4.

The formation of such an association need not just be a way of reducing the dominating effects of one choir on another. It could also bring positive advantages stemming from greater collaboration. For example, it might support a shared library of musical scores, enabling them all to perform a wider repertoire of works than might be possible if each choir operated alone. An association might also allow them to cooperate to perform certain large choral works. An association of this kind would extend the civic choral rights and obligations of their members in a variety of ways. The democratic agreements between the original constituent choirs could allow singers to cooperate when necessary on joint larger projects that are mutually agreed and to freely move between these choirs, staying in the Bach choir but singing for extended or shorter periods in the Mozart choir, say, and possibly to switch allegiance permanently to the Mozart choir if they find they prefer it. It might also become necessary to create an administration to run the association's central services, such as the musical score library, and administer its rules, and organise certain association activities, such as the performance of the larger choral works.

In a democratic association, this administration would need to be under the free and equal control of the constituent choirs to ensure it served their needs and did not dominate them either itself, say by raising choir subscriptions simply to increase their salaries, or through favouring some choirs over others. Moreover, it would be strange to suggest that the larger choral works that the association has enabled people to perform were 'better' than the smaller ones each of the choirs standardly performed, or that the repertoire of one choir was superior to that of another. The whole point of the association would be that it allowed diversity to flourish in non self-defeating ways and without requiring excessive standardisation.

An association of this kind operates as an association of choirs, therefore, not of the members of the choirs. Nevertheless, it allows all choir members to gain certain advantages that would be denied them if they were not in an association – notably that of moving and participating in another choir and of performing larger choral works. However, the former possibility would be lost if the choirs all merged. It is precisely through their not merging that the association proves advantageous and non-dominating. As a result, within this association, choir members are primarily members of one of the constituent choirs and have obligations towards sustaining it. That remains true to a degree when they move temporarily to another choir. They may continue to pay their membership fee to their original choir, say, but their commitments to rehearsals are with the choir they have temporarily joined. If they decided to remain permanently in the new choir, then their allegiance would shift. Yet it would be reasonable to allow the receiving choir to limit such transfers to the extent that the very nature of the choir might change if, say, it grew beyond a certain size. In other words, the trans-choir rights of choir members are framed by respect for the rights of the members of each of the constituent choirs and must be compatible with them. After all, in this example, the association exists to uphold the democratic processes of the constituent choirs.

This feature has consequences for voting rights. Some of the constituent choirs might be quite big and have sub choirs. Moving between sub choirs is different to moving from one choir to another choir. That is because the sub choirs are nested within the larger choir in a way the different choirs of the association are not. The sub choir may be funded out of the general subscription to the main choir but also ask members for a small contribution to sub choir events. It may also decide democratically on its own organisation and repertoire, but through consultation with the main choir and according to rules that are decided on by the main choir as a whole, in which all choir members have a say. In other words, authority is delegated down from the main choir to the sub choir and under its control, in the manner outlined in Chapter 2. By contrast, in the association, authority is delegated upwards from the constituent choirs to the association authority and under their joint and equal control and influence in the manner outlined in the final section of Chapter 3. A different arrangement holds to the sub-choir case because the association exists to facilitate the coordination and cooperation of the member choirs in non-dominating ways.

If someone temporarily joins a sub choir of another choir to their own, it would be appropriate to allow them to take part in the sub choir decision-making process along with other members, whose activities they support and make possible, but not in the main choir processes until such time as they decide to move permanently to that choir. For the sub choir's decisions are framed by the rules of the main choir made by long-term members. Moreover, each choir possesses a democratic voice over how the association as a whole operates. It seems suitable that a choir member should exercise influence on this issue in the choir to which they feel principally obligated rather than that to which they have temporarily moved. Nevertheless, as a temporary member of another choir they may have a view on how association rules impact them directly as a trans-choir member. Moreover, regardless of which choir they happen to participate in within the association, they contribute to the collective goods of the association if they pay a choir subscription, a part of which finances association activities. Arguably, if the association also had a choir members' assembly as well as a committee of choir representatives, they should be allowed to vote for that wherever they are located.

The purpose of this simplified picture of an association with parallels to the EU is to draw out how something like Union citizenship can deal with the three issues of the arbitrary exclusion of individuals from a given citizen body, the impact of collective decisions by a group of citizens on non-citizens and the free movement of peoples across borders; while still preserving the integrity of the different citizenship regimes of the member states. By analogy, the prime rights-based obligations of individuals within the EU will be to the system that regulates most of their interactions with others to preserve their rights. At present, and for the foreseeable future, that remains (and, as was argued in Chapter 1, need not cease to remain) their member states. However, through democratic agreements between these member states, their citizens have acquired mutual rights of free movement. As a result, the arbitrariness of exclusion can be partially mitigated by the ability to move from one's polity of birth to another polity within the association to take advantage of the opportunities it provides. Yet, moving per se does not entail automatic inclusion as a citizen of the host state, entitled to all the benefits accorded to its citizens. That would not show equal respect to the civic cultures of all the member states, and would seem arbitrary in its turn. Rather, free movement allows citizens of a member state to enjoy the diffuse benefits provided by the public structures of another member state without discrimination, such as purchasing property, long-term residence without any visa restrictions and, most importantly, equal access to employment. But they must become part of the scheme of social cooperation that funds these public structures to gain an unconditional entitlement to individually targeted benefits within that state, such as health care and social security, and to naturalise as citizens, with a stake in the continuing effectiveness of the state, to obtain the right to a say in how these public structures are shaped and resourced. Likewise, through mutual agreements and the adoption of a common scheme of interstate regulation, member states can seek to prevent the democratic decisions of one state, including their own, undercutting the decisions of another state, while at the same time collaborating in areas where association-level collective goods will be in each of their interests. In both these cases, though, there is no need for the different citizenries of the member states to merge, at least for certain purposes, and become citizens of a supra- (as in federal, super-) or a new form of trans-state Union. Individuals within the association remain citizens of distinct states, yet the associational duties of those states involve showing each other's citizens mutual concern and respect. Borders are open but circumstances of citizenship remain demarcated by different states that support the distinct civic communities among which citizens of these different states can freely move. Indeed, it is the very existence of such a plurality of states between which individuals can freely move that both gives citizens choices and prevents any one of them becoming dominating. Citizens can only vote with their feet if they have somewhere to move to, thereby giving governments an incentive to secure their citizens' rights rather than their state's borders. As Kant noted, the alternatives to such a situation are either the 'souless despotism' of a world state or the 'anarchy' of a world without states (Kant 1796: 113).

A balance is thereby reached between preserving the civic conditions for non-domination provided by the 'circumstances of citizenship and democracy' of the member states, on the one hand, while avoiding them becoming a source of domination in their turn for either their own citizens or, more especially, the citizens of other states, on the other. Therefore, the crucial issue for Union citizenship as international citizenship lies in getting the balance right and providing justifications based on the nature of citizenship itself for where the limits to free movement might lie.

Getting the Balance Right: The Limits to Freedom of Movement

As I noted in the second section of this chapter, citizenship at the national level involves the creation of a condition of civic equality among those subject to a political authority. It involves citizens participating on equal terms in the specification and generation of the collective goods on which their civil and social rights depend in ways that prevent this necessarily collaborative endeavour involving them either dominating each other or being dominated by the political authorities to which they subject themselves. As we saw, such a system generates a degree of reciprocity and solidarity among the members of the political community. Among other things, it underlies support for schemes of social welfare among co-participants in the generation of the collective goods on which citizens' rights depend that is sufficient to ensure a degree of relational equality among citizens such that differences in wealth will not become a source of domination. Not only would the existence of such domination render the political authority illegitimate in the eyes of poorer citizens, but also it fails to recognise that the ability of those with marketable talents to profit from them depends on the existence of the cooperative scheme and the recognition of their rights by all, including those less fortunate than themselves. Given this context, a key concern will be how far the EU as a whole supports or detracts from the capacity of the member states and their citizens to maintain the collective schemes necessary for civic equality. I will consider this issue with regard to the access of EU citizens resident in another member state to welfare rights and to political rights.

Welfare Rights   Most of the worries regarding freedom of movement stem from a concern over the sustainability of domestic welfare systems. The fear is that if similar benefits are offered to those citizens of other member states who exercise the right to free movement as are offered to national citizens, then this might encourage benefit tourism and in various ways undercut national schemes. For example, if a national scheme of rationing access to certain health and educational services to ensure their financial viability is undercut by demands that they be freely open to non-taxpayers, then that might put downward pressure on the provision of these services to nationals as well as non-nationals (Sangiovanni 2013: 233–4). In fact, these concerns were to a large extent anticipated in the TFEU (e.g. Articles 45 and 52) and in Directive 2004/38/EC (e.g. Article 7), which allow certain restrictions to be placed on free movement. However, we saw in the previous section how the various limitations and restrictions on free movement and residence have come under pressure in recent Court decisions, not least with regard to the rights of family members and dependents – including the status of same sex couples, or of the partners and dependents of Union citizens following divorce and separation (e.g. *Iida* 2012, though see *Rahman* 2012). In these cases, the Court has consistently argued against a restrictive reading of the relevant conditions and limitations and linked its decisions to fundamental rights (Nic Shuibhne 2015a). They have encouraged academic commentators to see EU citizenship as not only transforming but also subverting national citizenship, and moving it in a transnational direction by liberating citizens from national restrictions through an appeal to European and ultimately human rights alone (Kochenov 2014).

However, recent cases suggest the Court has at least partly rolled back from these decisions (*Brey* 2013, *Dano* 2014; *Alimanovic* 2015, *Garcia-Nieto* 2016 and *Commission v. UK* 2016). With respect to residence in particular, the Court has appeared to accept that the Directives of the 1990s (90/364, 90/363 and 93/96) should be regarded not as narrow constraints on a fundamental right to free movement, to be applied in a proportionate manner to avoid the extreme case of claimants placing an 'unreasonable' burden on the social assistance system, but more broadly as conditions to be met before a Union citizen can claim equal treatment with a national citizen.

Many legal scholars have regarded this change as turning the reasoning of earlier judgments on their head (Nic Shuibhne 2015b), and even as marking a 'reactionary phase' in the Court's jurisprudence (Spaventa 2017), in which 'the Court has executed a swift dismantling project' of decades of case law establishing the 'fundamental status' of EU citizenship through excessive deference to political pressure (O'Brien 2017: 209). However, the hyperbolic language of *Grzelczyk* (especially paras 3, 44) notwithstanding, the Court has always acknowledged that claims by Union citizens to social assistance in a state other than their own can be limited should residence conditions not be met, and the state has not acted inconsistently or misinformed the claimants about their entitlements; the claim appears meretricious, for example, because it seems motivated purely by benefit tourism rather than genuine need or a temporary period of forced unemployment; or the claim might set a precedent that others would be likely to act on and the state would be unable, or find difficult, to meet.

The issue I want to raise here, however, is not whether the Court's judgments concerning these conditions have been legally well founded or consistent but whether it can be justified to even take such considerations into account. Those who have viewed recent decisions as a retrograde step do so in part because they feel the trajectory of judicial opinion ought to be towards having Union trump national citizenship, with free movement a fundamental right. By contrast, I wish to argue that these factors are relevant and justified if Union citizenship is seen as supplementing rather than supplanting national citizenship. Indeed, developing the argument of the last section, I shall contend that Union citizenship conceived as a right to free movement only makes sense when regarded as a supplementary and complementary rather than as a superior and self-standing status. Within such a conception of Union citizenship, considerations related to the potential impact of free movement on the viability of the civic cultures of host states prove unavoidable.

On the account given here, some restrictions might be justified in principle so long as empirically the worries proved warranted. With respect to workers, given they are participating in the production of the collective goods of the political community, they would seem entitled to equal access to social services even in principle. The exception might be if migrant workers took more from the system than they contributed, lowering benefits for resident citizens, and reduced job opportunities, especially for the low paid and unskilled. In fact, though, far from imposing a fiscal burden on social services, the evidence points to their being net contributors to it (Boeri et al. 2002; Gott and Johnson 2002) – at least at the aggregate level (Martinsen and Werner 2018), although at the disaggregate level the influx of second-country nationals may have diminished the availability of certain scarce resources for particular localities or groups (European Commission 2014). Nor is there any indication of any lowering of either wages or employment opportunities – indeed, some studies suggest the reverse (Hartog and Zorlu 2005). Yet, even if this were the case, so long as the new workers were increasing the fiscal health of the state, then additional resources would exist to offer training and support for those displaced in this way. The appropriate response to this situation, therefore, is something along the lines of Gordon Brown's Migration Impacts Fund of 2009, which was designed to ease the pressure on services and jobs in given localities within the UK.

A somewhat different concern exists with regard to in-work benefits, which were at the heart of the UK's pre-Brexit negotiations. These are designed to help reduce domestic unemployment, are funded by taxpayers, and directly targeted at citizens. If those who move from another state to take up work become immediately eligible for them, then a worry arises that citizens will feel they are subsidising individuals who are not yet part of the domestic social compact. Of course, it may well be that, taken overall, these immigrant workers do enhance domestic labour opportunities and/or increase the tax revenues that fund such schemes. Yet to the extent this scheme is intended as a direct rather than an indirect measure for improving domestic employment opportunities, a case exists for making access to it subject to an additional residence requirement for newly arrived second-country nationals who have not yet shown themselves to have a stake in the future success of the social and economic system of the relevant national political community.

What would be constrained on this account is the sending of posted workers from low cost labour states to higher cost labour states. Posted workers usually reside for a limited period with minimum interaction with the host society, yet their presence does raise the threat of 'social dumping' that can place downward pressure on the degree of social protection and wages in the host state. From this perspective, the above-mentioned judgments in *Laval* (2008), *Viking* (2008) and *Rüffert* (2008) do prove objectionable (see too Sangiovanni 2013: 235 n. 70).

As Juri Viehoff has proposed (Viehoff 2017), one EU level measure that might alleviate these and similar risks stemming from free movement would be an unconditional and universal basic income that he terms a European Social Minimum. This would be funded centrally and be set at a level sufficient to provide a threshold standard of living in poorer if not in richer countries. He observes how this proposal could be justified on what are here called 'thick' cosmopolitan statist grounds precisely as a mechanism that helps reduce domination between states stemming from the arbitrary inclusion and exclusion of individuals in a particular state, while alleviating the potentially dominating impact of free movement on regimes of civic equality within states (Viehoff 2013: 17–20). With regard to diminishing the sources of domination between states, such a mechanism potentially lessens horizontal asymmetries that lead to citizens of poorer countries with less generous welfare systems being disadvantaged. By the same token, it also strengthens non-domination domestically by giving low-waged and less skilled workers enhanced bargaining power. It also alleviates the danger – mainly potential rather than actual, as we saw – of workers from poorer countries temporarily migrating and undercutting local wages. Would an EU-wide scheme enhance potential political domination from the EU at the supranational level? Obviously, on the scheme proposed here, it would require democratic endorsement from each of the member states, who would retain control over its level and operation, merely delegating its organisation upwards. An unconditional, universal and relatively low European basic income also would be minimally disruptive of different national welfare schemes.

Political Rights What about the acquisition of voting rights in another member state? Two concerns seem pertinent: such acquisition must be consistent with:

(1) all those who exercise these rights performing the reciprocal obligations needed to sustain the public policies on which the continued enjoyment of these rights equally by all citizens within the member state depend, and

(2) the mutual recognition of the citizenship regimes of all member states and their consequent equal representation within the EU's political system.

On these criteria, Union citizenship seems legitimate in granting rights to vote in local and EP elections anywhere within the EU based on residence alone but not to national elections. If a Union citizen moves to another state long enough to register as a resident, they will be participating in the local community and be impacted by its decisions sufficiently to meet the first criterion. Of course, they may not intend to stay long-term, but that will be the same for many national citizens. However, local communities are nested within a national political framework of those who do have an equal stake in the long-term interests of the political community. Regardless of where they reside in the EU, Union citizens have an equal interest in influencing how the EU operates. Moreover, granting second-country nationals a vote in EP elections arguably reinforces the second criterion, since they perhaps have a greater interest in the ability to choose between diverse citizenship regimes than those who stay put. It cannot be assumed that they would favour a merging of national citizenships. Either way, the significant if small minority who exercise transnational citizenship – a group larger than the populations of several of the member states – deserve a voice in EU decision-making. However, national citizenship ought to be reserved to those committed long term to the national community – who are willing to become stakeholders. If they intend to return to their member of state of origin, then they ought not – as is the case in many jurisdictions – to be denied the right to vote in that state's national elections. Over time, though, citizens who have moved ought to be allowed to shift their civic obligations entirely to the chosen member state by becoming citizens of it – as they are currently entitled to do – indeed, arguably they have a duty to do so if their rights become increasingly dependent on that member state (de Schutter and Ypi 2015, although Bauböck 2018: 153–4 questions this last step). Yet, even if they retain dual citizenship, being able to vote in national elections of two states becomes problematic in the EU context since it gives them a double vote with regard to EU decision-making. Indeed, the rationale for retaining a vote in their state of origin becomes lessened within the EU given that the power of all states to dominate citizens living in other member states has been constrained.

Third-Country Nationals and Human Rights

I have said almost nothing so far regarding third-country nationals – that is, about citizens from outside the EU. Those who regard Union citizenship as an extension of human rights norms more generally find few justifiable grounds for distinguishing between second-country nationals, who have Union citizenship and can move from one member state to another within the EU, and those third-country nationals who lack this status despite being long-term residents in the EU (Benhabib 2002: 455, 458–61). By contrast, the model advocated here does allow for such a distinction because what legitimises Union citizenship and the status it provides to second-country nationals derives from the terms and conditions of this status being under the equal control and influence of the representatives of the member states of the association. To that extent, those outside the association are appropriately treated differently. Nevertheless, third-country nationals do rightly benefit in some ways from the existence of such an association, while most democratic states have committed themselves to international conventions supporting the basic human rights of refugees, thereby acknowledging certain duties to third-country nationals outside the association.

When third-country nationals enter a member state belonging to such an association, they gain certain of the benefits stemming from its membership. For example, within the EU they can benefit from the absence of border checks resulting from a member state being part of the twenty-six states currently forming the Schengen Area. The Schengen countries have shared standards for crossing the external borders of the Area, with harmonised entry and short-stay visa conditions so that nationals of any country can cross the internal borders of Schengen countries free from passport or other controls. Of course, these arrangements may make it harder to get access to the association in the first place. It can also make it easier in some respects for third-country nationals to be removed, given the Schengen states also have enhanced police and judicial collaboration for the identification and extradition of criminals. However, third-country nationals do gain some additional rights from the association, not least as beneficiaries under Article 3 of Directive 2004/38, which gives derivative rights in the host member state to family members and dependents of Union citizens irrespective of their nationality.

For example, in its decisions in *Chen* (2004) and, more emphatically, in *Zambrano* (2011), the Court of Justice argued that the third-country-national parents of a dependent minor who was a EU citizen could not be denied a right of residence or a work permit in a member state, as that would damage the rights of a Union citizen who might be obliged to leave the territory of the EU to follow his or her parents (*Zambrano* 2011: paras 43–44). Third-country-national partners and dependents of Union citizens have likewise benefitted from having a legal union in one member state recognised in another when they move with their partner, including when their partner returns to his or her own member state which may have stricter immigration and family reunion laws than the member state in which he or she had married or been living and working previously (e.g. *Singh* 1992: paras 19–20). Along with second-country nationals, family members also gain from enhanced protection in the case of death, divorce or departure of the Union citizen from the host state, retaining their right of residence by virtue of Articles 12 and 13 of the Directive.

These strengthened rights ought not to be seen as reflecting human rights *per se*. As with other Union citizenship rights, these rights are extrapolated from free movement rather than human rights – they do not reflect a human right to family life as found in Article 8 ECHR, for example (A. G. Mengozzi in *Reyes* 2014: para 32). Moreover, the definition of family member in Article 2 (2) of the Directive is fairly narrowly drawn to include only partners and direct descendants under 21. It also leaves the definition of 'partnership' to be legislated nationally, so that same-sex relationships in particular gain different degrees of recognition in different member states – an issue that disadvantages second country as well as third country nationals, given not all member states recognise same-sex marriage or even same-sex registered partnerships. In addition, many states also have different immigration regimes. As a result, inequalities of treatment of third country nationals can be found across the Union – as indeed is also the case in related areas with Union citizens more generally.

Such inequalities have been rightly condemned as infringements of the EU's more general commitment to the prohibition of discrimination on grounds of sexual orientation (as in Article 21 (1) of the Charter). Yet, pressure exists for states not to dominate either their own citizens or those of other states from the interaction that results from membership of an association of states. From the republican perspective adopted here, it proves more legitimate to engage states in a dialogue between governments and their peoples over issues of equal treatment within and across their borders than to impose a particular judicial decision of what equal concern and respect entails. Given the circumstances of justice lie within those of political legitimacy, as we saw in Chapter 2, the top-down judicial approach risks appearing or being illegitimate, and so dominating in its turn those to whom it is applied if they have been denied equal influence and control over its determination and implementation. I shall return to this point in the next chapter.

That said, the current migration crisis in Europe might be taken as an instance of the need to adopt a more rights-based judicial approach, given the dominating effects of the political reluctance of some countries to an on-going humanitarian tragedy. Statelessness is perhaps the paradigmatic case of contemporary domination, as the stateless individual has neither the rights protections nor the basic socio-economic conditions required to pursue a plan of life (Nicolaïdis and Viehoff 2017). Yet, the migration crisis has not only led to a hardening of the EU's external borders but also of its internal borders, given that once migrants enter a member state they can move about the Schengen area.

Three points are relevant here (the discussion that follows is indebted to Miller 2016: Postscript). First, as we saw in Chapter 2, a commitment to address issues of justice politically rather than coercively implies the avoidance of domination. As such, that gives all democratic states that recognise such a commitment a reason to support citizenship as the 'right to have rights' of all individuals. On this reasoning, at least one rationale for such states to join associations such as the EU or the Council of Europe stems from precisely this commitment to upholding the 'circumstances of citizenship' for all. Consequently, a duty – similar to the one incurred in the example, given above, of the beach stroller who finds him or herself helping in the rescue of a fishing vessel – exists on all states and their citizens to support those effectively denied citizenship by virtue of their state of origin being oppressive, unsafe due to invasion or civil war, or failing in some way for which those fleeing cannot be held responsible, such as a natural disaster.

Second, quite what form such an obligation should take can prove hard to specify. A standard distinction would be between refugees who count as what Alexander Betts terms 'survival migrants', who are 'outside their country of origin because of an existential threat for which they have no access to a domestic remedy or resolution' (Betts 2013: 23), on the one hand, and 'economic migrants' seeking improved opportunities, on the other (for this distinction, see Miller 2016: 77). Though this distinction is disputed, many people would agree that the duty of 'hospitality' that Benhabib (2002: 442) takes from Kant, and that was adverted to above, does operate in the former case if not necessarily in the latter, as she appeared to suggest. As a result, it might seem the EU has a moral obligation to accommodate as best it can the very large number of migrants fleeing North Africa and the Middle East – or at least those whose very survival seems at risk from staying where they are. However, deciding who precisely fits this category poses a difficult task, especially at a time when the numbers are truly overwhelming, even if the extreme risks taken to leave on invariably unseaworthy craft attest to a high degree of desperation on the part of all the prospective immigrants.

At the same time, an equal obligation also exists to ensure that the citizenship regimes of the host states are not themselves undermined and those of the states of origin made hard to re-establish. I suggested above that the former concern proves far less of a constraint for wealthy countries with declining birth rates, as is the case across Western Europe, than has been often suggested, though in the short term the sheer numbers of those seeking admission have created problems. The latter concern has perhaps received less attention. Yet, providing positive incentives for would-be survival migrants to stay or return, not only by providing safer and more hospitable camps as near as possible to the state of origin but also training and employment that could be transferred back to their home state once conditions improve (see Miller 2016: 170–1 for proposals along this line), could – if practicable – address both the humanitarian disaster of migrant deaths at sea and the prospect of permanently failing states. On the republican account, EU member states clearly have a duty to properly fund such schemes in order to promote the access of all individuals to citizenship of their own state as a context for non-domination within and between states.

Third, and relatedly, an association such as the EU also exists to ensure fair burden sharing in meeting these obligations. The EU's current migration policy, the 'Dublin Regulation', maintains that the first member state in which an asylum seeker enters has legal responsibility for him or her. This rule places a heavy burden on countries on the EU's southern border – especially Italy, Greece and Hungary. As relatively small countries, they can be hardly expected to police their borders unaided or absorb almost two million migrants. The Commission has attempted a top-down solution to the internal challenge via quotas, while offering financial aid to those countries bearing the brunt of the external challenge, including the possibility of relocating some of their refugees elsewhere in Europe. The problem is that these arrangements have proven too little to alleviate the burdens of the states on the EU's external border while quotas only work to the extent that free movement is constrained. Arguably, as a rough measure, states should be willing to take a similar proportion of refuges relative to the size of their populations and GDP. If so, it could be that matters would regulate themselves without quotas given that most migrants will naturally gravitate to the northern countries where employment opportunities are greatest. Therefore, the problem comes from those countries, notably the UK, that have refused to undertake their fair share by either measure and closed their borders. In so doing, they are dominating not only the migrants but also their partners within the association, particularly Italy and Greece – the main receiving states.

Conclusion

This chapter has defended the existing character of Union citizenship as supplementing rather than either subsuming or supplanting member state citizenship, let alone subverting the very notion of territorially based citizenship altogether. It supplements it by removing the potential domination that might arise from systems of national citizenship through either the exclusion of non-citizens from the borders of a given state or the impact of the democratic decisions of one state's citizens on another state's citizens. On the one hand, it allows free movement among member states on the basis of non-discrimination; on the other hand, it imposes justified conditions on access to benefits and national voting rights, while allowing local and EU rights and facilitating naturalisation for those wishing to remain in the host state. As such, it serves the purposes of a republican association of sovereign states. By contrast, the supra- and post-national accounts of citizenship would entail dominating existing political communities, while the transnational account relies upon national citizenship for its coherence yet opens up possibilities for its undermining and exploitation.

In line with a cosmopolitan statism, this approach aims to ensure states treat the citizens of other states with equal concern and respect, while preserving their capacity to protect the rights of their citizens in diverse ways. For this diversity is itself a source of non-domination. Within a republican association of states, the existence of different states not only allows them to check and balance each other, encouraging both non-domination within each state as well as between them, but also provides a variety of experiments in living to their citizens. However, the integration process has often been seen as necessarily involving the overcoming of such diversity through the creation of a uniform regulatory framework. The Court in particular has been seen as the prime agent of such an approach, not least in seeing the EU legal order as distinct from and having primacy over those of the member states, and applying with direct effect to the inhabitants of all the member states. As we saw in certain citizenship judgments, the Court can be regarded as undercutting republican intergovernmental decision-making with supra-national decisions that aim at subordinating the diversity of different national citizenships to a common European citizenship of a supra-, post- or trans-national character. The next chapter challenges the view that such an approach is morally and practically warranted. It argues that there are strong democratic and pragmatic grounds for allowing differentiated integration among the states of a republican association, and suggests how EU law and the role of the Court might be reconceived accordingly.

Differentiated Integration and the *Demoi*cratic
Constitution of the EU

Introduction

The normative goal of an EU conceived as an association of sovereign democratic states is to ensure fair terms of cooperation between them. As has been noted in earlier chapters, such fair terms entail treating their different and often divergent economic, social and political systems with equal concern and respect, not least by avoiding any state or group of states dominating another state or group of states. However, these differences and divergences can be considerable. States vary greatly in their geography and population, possess different kinds and degrees of natural and social capital, with some much wealthier than others, and have made diverse policy choices about the character of their social and economic arrangements (Hall and Soskice 2001). Likewise, although being a democracy forms a precondition for a state to join such an association, the legal and political systems of democratic states can differ in certain key respects: from their electoral systems and the distribution and division of legislative, executive and judicial powers, to the competences allocated between central, regional and local government, the terms and forms of constitutional arrangements (Finer 1995), and – most important of all – their languages and modes of public discourse (Kymlicka 2001). These and various other dissimilarities and disparities in both the socio-economic and legal and political systems of democratic states reflect their individual responses to numerous contingent human and natural events and circumstances that have resulted in distinctive, and occasionally contrary, historical traditions and paths of development (Greenfield 1992; Brubaker 1996). A core challenge confronting any international association of states, therefore, is how to encompass such demographic, socio-economic, legal, political and cultural heterogeneity. For example, treating all states equally may involve treating their citizens unequally if some states are either more populous or have a greater stake in a given collective decision than other states. There are also the problems of consistent or discreet and isolated minorities familiar from domestic political systems. Addressing such issues poses a number of dilemmas that are explored in this chapter.

Chapter 3 suggested an important criterion in this regard. Namely, that such an association should be voluntary. As we saw, the importance of this criterion follows from the association's democratic legitimacy requiring the consent of all its members, such consent being obtained through its abiding by the normative logic of a two-level game. This provision allows for opt-outs or special arrangements for those who have less of a stake in a given collective policy, or who fear discrimination or domination as a minority with regard to certain of their core values or interests. Yet, the prospect of some members of an association not collaborating across all policies, or opting out of common standards in those areas where they do collaborate, might be thought to allow for free riding and backsliding from important obligations, including those cosmopolitan duties that most people would acknowledge as morally obligatory, such as tackling global warming or providing aid to what Rawls referred to as 'burdened' societies. The possibility of withdrawal may also incline states to structure their interactions according to what Chapter 4 described as an ontology of singularity, characterised by self-interested bargaining, and result in those collective agreements that are reached requiring consensus. As we saw in Chapter 4, such circumstances can increase the transaction costs in adopting any common policy, with those that are adopted proving insufficient or suboptimal. For example, settlements may be more likely to reflect the lowest common denominator.

The EU offers a good laboratory for exploring these issues, given that what is called 'differentiated integration' (DI) has become an increasingly prevalent feature of its organisation. DI allows member states to integrate at different speeds, to collaborate more intensively with some states than with others, and to opt out of certain policies or apply them in different ways. As a result, European integration is more complex than many people seem to appreciate, being multi-speed, multi-tiered and multi-menu. However, DI has been viewed with suspicion and regarded as problematic from a legal and practical point of view, especially on the part of those who see the developing EU legal and political system as part of an emerging cosmopolitan constitutional and democratic order.

The task for this chapter, therefore, is to investigate whether valid reasons can be given for DI that avoid the pitfalls of allowing free riding or backsliding, while being consistent with the rule of law and effective and equitable decision-making. As I observed in the Introduction and at greater length in Chapter 1, many commentators believe that globalisation poses moral and functional challenges to states that can only be met through ever greater political and social, as well as economic, integration than the EU has hitherto achieved, and that require the creation of common legal and political institutions at the EU level possessing authority over a range of shared economic and social policies. However, as I noted in Chapters 3 and 4, and will detail further below, political and cultural heterogeneity, on the one side, and socioeconomic heterogeneity, on the other, detract from the legitimacy and efficacy of such a democratic and constitutional reordering of the EU. Instead, to meet the two challenges fairly and efficiently requires a much more flexible and demoicratic association of sovereign states, which allows for a considerable degree of DI. After all, the existence of political, cultural and socio-economic heterogeneity within most of the member states has led to various degrees of devolution of sovereign powers to different regions, often creating asymmetries in the structure of the state's polity in the process; and mechanisms to achieve near-consensus decision-making to protect minority rights at the central level, that have added complexity to the organisation of its regime; with both allowing for considerable differentiation in core areas of public policy. Given there is even greater variation within the EU than in any member state, it would be strange if it failed to adopt similar devices. Yet, that very diversity has increasingly made even necessary attempts at unity ever more controversial and hard to achieve.

The argument progresses in two main steps. The first step defends the demoicratic legitimacy of DI at the 'polity' level – namely, how far member states need to integrate and collaborate and adopt shared standards and norms in order to achieve certain collective goals. I start by offering a descriptive typology of the various kinds of DI within the EU, distinguishing 'instrumental', 'constitutional' and 'legislative' DI. The first consists of various kinds of opt-outs or exclusions from participating in policies designed to produce collective goods at the EU level, be these non-excludable 'public' goods, or excludable 'club' goods. The second involves an opt-out from a given policy or measure because it conflicts with a domestic constitutional norm or cultural practice. The third arises when all states participate in a common measure but there are derogations from, or variations within, shared standards for 'instrumental' or 'constitutional' reasons. As we shall see, the first type of DI can be related to socio-economic and the second type to politico-legal and cultural forms of heterogeneity, with the third type responding to lesser forms of both. I conclude this step by showing how the three types of DI can be demoicratically justified in so far as they correspond respectively to modifications required if collective decision-making is to accord with the three democratic values of fairness, impartiality and equity. Step two then turns to the consequences of DI at the 'regime' level, and the processes of collective decision-making. I look at the potential difficulties

DI poses for equitable and effective collective decision-making within the EU, and the ways it is challenged by what has been called the constitutionalisation of EU law by the ECJ (Grimm 2016: chs 13 and 14), on the one side, and demands for a shift towards majority decision-making, on the other (Scharpf 2015, 2017). These moves have been defended as necessary to address the aforementioned moral and functional challenges of an interdependent world, yet run counter to the arguments put forward in step one. While they have some purchase, I argue that both can be resolved within a demoicratic political constitution of the EU that permits flexible agreements allowing different groups of states to integrate to a greater or lesser extent while still addressing the moral and functional objectives required for the sustainability of the EU as a whole. I conclude by turning to the Euro crisis. I argue it offers a case study of the problems associated with ignoring heterogeneity and the resulting need for both DI and demoicratic decision-making. Contrary to those suggesting that the crisis can only be resolved by moving to political and fiscal union, I suggest such moves would compound the crisis and suggest a demoicratic alternative.

Differentiated Integration and Heterogeneity

DI involves EU member states having different rights and obligations in regard to specific EU programmes or rules, as some member states agree to cooperate on a specific policy or conform to a given standard, whilst others either opt out or adopt different standards. This section starts by offering a typology of the various forms DI can take, each of which can be found in the EU, and then relates their occurrence to the two dominant forms of heterogeneity noted above.

Conceptual research about DI began in the mid-1990s (Stubb 1996), leading to no less than thirty models of DI. Since then, a variety of conceptualisations have been proposed, most of which can be grouped in one of three categories – time, space and policy. Conceptualisations focused on time are commonly linked to the idea of a 'multi-speed Europe', whereby some member states advance with integration and others are expected to follow later. Space-related differentiation is often associated with a 'variable geometry', whereby different geographic tiers have different levels of integration. Finally, policy-related differentiation is allied to a 'Europe à la carte', where member states pick the policies they wish to join. The three forms of DI can be combined and all can be time limited or permanent, and can operate either inside or outside the treaties.

Among both academics and politicians, the 'multi-speed' concept has generally been regarded as the most acceptable and a 'Europe à la carte' the least. The dominant view has held that DI is at best of pragmatic and temporary value, and at worst a hindrance to the just and successful functioning of the EU. On the plus side, many acknowledge that DI addresses a classic collective-action problem. A policy that is advantageous to most or all concerned can get blocked or rendered suboptimal, say by the adoption of lowest common denominator policies (Tsoukalis 2016: 199), by those who disagree with, feel disadvantaged by, or have less of an interest in it. By letting states integrate to different degrees and at different speeds, DI allows potential veto players to opt out rather than blocking further integration by others. Likewise, the divergent views of member states on the general purpose and ultimate goal of the EU, and growing questioning of the trend towards a political union, make it more difficult to achieve a consensus on the course EU integration should take. Here too DI helps. By permitting certain members to adopt different policies to others, member states can leave their fundamental disagreements about the *finalité* of European integration unresolved (Dehousse 2003). Therefore, a multi-speed approach combined with some variable geometry allows member states to choose policies more aligned to their needs and preferences, and potentially makes decision-making more efficient and effective. As such, it provides 'one of the main sources of pragmatic compromise in EU politics' (Lord 2015: 784).

Notwithstanding these advantages, though, most scholars and policy makers have emphasised DI's drawbacks. On the negative side, they caution that opt-outs undermine the legal unity and authority of the EU (de Burca and Scott 2000; Curtin 1993), as well as the uniform composition of EU institutions. They fear it will create a differentiated citizenship that threatens the liberal model of universalist citizenship characteristic of modern constitutionalism. They also worry it erodes solidarity between member states and constitutes a challenge to any prospect of developing the EU into a political community based on shared rights and obligations of membership. They charge DI with weakening mutual trust between states, especially when accompanied by a narrative of insiders and outsiders, as is partly the case with the Eurozone members (Adler-Nissen 2016). Moreover, they are concerned DI strengthens the power of strongly pro-integration member states by improving their bargaining position, since negotiating beyond the limits of a specific policy area is more difficult for states that only participate in some of the relevant areas. As a result, those who opt out of certain policies lose influence in the EU, thereby creating different classes of citizens (Jensen and Slapin 2012).

These reservations led earlier scholarship to assume that DI would erode over time (Kölliker 2001), with member states converging on the same policies at different speeds (Stubb 1996), rather than dividing permanently into 'ins' and 'outs'. However, the ensuing integration process has disproved this expectation. Instead, DI has steadily increased as European integration has extended into 'core state powers' (Genschel and Jachtenfuchs 2016) of increasing political salience due to their impact on national economic, financial and welfare policies. Consequently, domestic electorates have become more aware and often more critical of the integration process than before. This growing critical awareness on the part of voters correlates with the increased use of DI (Thym 2016), though various forms of DI have always existed (Schimmelfennig 2014). Post Maastricht, DI has substantially increased. Indeed, the Conclusions of the European Council of 26/ 27 June 2014 noted that 'the concept of ever closer union allows for different paths of integration for different countries', while the leaders of the founding member states responded to the British vote to leave by announcing an initiative aimed at more 'flexible' integration, recognising that the 'one-size-fits-all model simply cannot work' (Tsoukalis 2016: 199). DI even forms one of five scenarios for the future of Europe outlined by the Commission (2017).

Both the positive, yet purely pragmatic, view of DI, and the more negative view, privilege the supposed functional and moral necessity of producing collective goods and adopting common norms over the empirical constraints and normative value of the existing heterogeneity among member states. Consequently, they underestimate the extent to which this heterogeneity impacts both the economic space for integration and the political willingness of the peoples of these states to integrate further. Yet, if heterogeneity is seen as part of the ineliminable diversity and pluralism of any Union as large as the EU, then DI becomes functionally inescapable and normatively imperative. Rather than seeing DI as a failure to integrate in a uniform way or as confining certain member states to a 'second-class' status within the EU, I shall argue DI offers a tool which allows for the demoicratic accommodation of heterogeneity and thereby the stabilisation of European integration, particularly in times of a severe nationalist and/or populist backlash against it. The rest of this section relates DI descriptively with various forms of heterogeneity, while the next section will do so normatively.

As I noted above, heterogeneity comes in two main versions, each of which can be related to two main forms of DI. The first version consists of economic and social heterogeneity. This version means that not all the member states may have the same stake in given collective goods – be these goods public goods, such as clean air, that are non-excludable; or club goods, such as a custom union, that are excludable. In both cases, costs may be distributed asymmetrically and not all those involved may value the benefits to an equal degree. Without compulsion, there can also be incentives for free riding. The deciding factor is the ratio between the advantages of reducing production costs by sharing them among as many members as possible, and the loss of benefits as the gap between average collective preferences and individual preferences widens (see Kölliker 2001). Therefore, the more heterogeneous the group of participating states becomes, the greater the likelihood that either the EU will refrain from producing a given collective good, leaving it to member states, or that some members states will decide to set up a 'club' that excludes others – thereby leading to DI.

Schimmelfennig and Winzen partly captured the resulting form of DI with the term 'instrumental differentiation', which 'is motivated by efficiency and distributional concerns' (Schimmelfennig and Winzen 2014: 355). Like other scholars, they contend it is by definition transitional. It occurs either when existing member states temporarily *exclude* new member states from certain policy areas because they 'fear economic and financial losses as a result of market integration with the new member states, the redistribution of EU funds or weak implementation capacity' (ibid.: 361); or when new member states seek to be *exempted* temporarily from integration and be granted more time to adapt to EU rules and market pressures. In such constellations, temporary differentiation aids at least one side of the equation and ideally both, thereby overcoming deadlock in accession negotiations. However, their analysis fails to address the increased *structural* economic and social heterogeneity, which implies less space for uniform integration overall and might lead to some more durable forms of DI than the transitional ones linked to enlargement rounds. Nevertheless, I will use their term of *instrumental* differentiation to typify forms of DI that stem from considerations of fairness and efficiency among socially and economically heterogeneous states.

The second version of heterogeneity relates to the differing politico-legal and cultural values of different member states. It has given rise to what Schimmelfennig and Winzen (2014) term *constitutional* differentiation. This version of heterogeneity comes in two types. The first type concerns policies involving cultural differences, often rooted in religious traditions, such as those related to marriage and divorce, abortion, the use of stem cell research or euthanasia. In such areas, some governments may be reluctant to integrate a policy or seek to opt out if it is integrated, so as to respect the predominant cultural values of their demoi. Traditional integration theories do not sufficiently take into account the continuing importance of these identity-related forces. Legal scholars, by contrast, have noted how EU law has faced demands for a degree of differentiation since the 1970s so as to accommodate cultural diversity, leading to new concepts of differentiated citizenship (de Witte 1991).

The second type of value heterogeneity involves issues of sovereignty and diverging views about how much political integration is desirable. In the context of the Euro and migration crises, it has become clear that member states differ as to how much integration they wish to achieve, and of which kind. The alarming electoral successes of right-extreme parties, which typically defend anti-EU positions, indicate how, for some citizens, the boundaries of European integration have been pushed too far. As a result, governments of largely Eurosceptic countries, who are either ideologically opposed to further integration themselves or fear domestic opposition to it, are either unwilling or incapable of negotiating a compromise at the EU level and instead seek a potentially permanent opt-out from further integration. Heterogeneity of this kind proves particularly salient when core state competences are transferred to the EU in the context of treaty revisions, and is usually associated with a discourse of 'sovereignty' (Winzen 2016).

Finally, both socio-economic and value heterogeneity may lead not to opt-outs from a collective policy or a given measure, but rather to what can be called *legislative* differentiation, whereby different regulations or standards apply to different states participating in a given common policy area. Currently, almost 40 per cent of EU legislation is differentiated in this way. Although many Court of Justice decisions acknowledge, often tacitly rather than explicitly, that different regulations may apply in different jurisdictions, a tension exists between the trend in EU law to regard non-discrimination as requiring uniform standards that apply in the same way everywhere, and growing claims to special rights which argue that non-discrimination within an economically and culturally heterogeneous legal sphere requires differentiated law (de Witte 2005).

Three Demoicratic Justifications for Differentiated Integration: Proportionality, Partiality and Difference

The accounts of DI discussed above are essentially descriptive and analytical categories. This section develops a democratic rationale for DI that can legitimise some, if not all, forms of instrumental, constitutional and legislative DI. Drawing on the account of democratic decision-making offered in earlier chapters, democracy can be defended as offering members of a political community a legitimate mechanism for making necessary collective decisions about which they may disagree by giving them an equal say (the fairness argument), on the basis of a common process and criteria (the impartiality argument), to produce decisions likely to treat those involved with equal concern and respect (the equity argument)

(Christiano 2008). However, as has been noted, all three arguments assume a degree of homogeneity among the decision-makers.

Chapter 3 indicated two types of relations as providing the preconditions for a group of individuals to form a *demos*, among whom a democratic process based on majority rule and common constitutional arrangements will be legitimate. These preconditions consisted of shared and roughly equal interests in the totality of collective decisions they proposed to take together, on the one hand, and a conception of themselves as forming a public, on the other hand. The two types of heterogeneity outlined above as prevailing between the member states unsettle respectively these two preconditions. The social and economic heterogeneity of the member states makes it likely they will have divergent interests in the various schemes for collaboration on offer. Certain schemes may impose greater costs on some or yield them fewer benefits than others. It may also be harder for all states to relate to each other as equals within particular arrangements – they may often have unequal stakes, which may hinder fair cooperation in an entirely common scheme. Meanwhile, their legal-political and cultural heterogeneity can give rise to them employing different public reasons and constitutional norms to evaluate these schemes. Even if the member states agree at the most abstract level on a number of very general norms, they may reasonably disagree as to their ranking and application to specific cases.

As is the case within a number of the member states, both forms of heterogeneity can justify differentiation with regard to the polity dimensions of a political community with knock-on effects for the organisation of its regime. The first form of heterogeneity impacts the fairness of democratic decisions that fail to accommodate differences of stake in the collective decision, while the second form of heterogeneity can affect the impartiality of decisions that fail to accommodate incommensurable and conflicting evaluative perspectives. Meanwhile, both these forms of heterogeneity can undermine the equity of common rules that do not accommodate relevant differences among those to whom they apply. The rest of this section explores three classic political aphorisms guiding the fairness, impartiality and equity arguments for democracy respectively, noting how heterogeneity raises a problem for each that can justify differentiation as to which collective decisions may be taken, among whom and in what form. As the next section will show, these arguments offer a demoicratic rationale for instrumental, constitutional and legislative DI respectively.

The first aphorism decrees that 'what touches all should be decided by all'. This aphorism appeals to the fairness argument but assumes a roughly equal stake in the relevant collective decision (Christiano 2008). On this view, if each individual is the best guardian of his or her interests, and the interests of every individual in the polity are equally at stake in the decision, then, in fairness, all these individuals are entitled to play an equal part in making the decision to ensure their interests are equally taken into account. Therefore, a democratic system based on one person, one vote assumes that all involved have a roughly equal stake in the overall package of decisions, if not in each and every one. If that was not the case and a significant group had less of a stake in the generality of collective decisions than most others, an equal vote might lead to the underfunding of public services or the rejection of public regulations on which many people's well-being depends. Consequently, a democratic case exists for either so shaping the demos that all those involved do have a roughly equal stake or in giving individuals a vote proportional to their stake, and thereby treating them fairly and with equal respect, if not literally equally in the sense of exactly the same (Brighouse and Fleurbaey 2010). I shall call this the 'proportionality problem'.

Demos-shaping to create an equal stake among citizens is fairly common within most democracies. For example, most states devolve certain public services to local communities for reasons of fairness as well as efficiency. States are generally heterogeneous: urban areas differ from rural areas, some regions have an aging population and others a higher proportion of children and young people, and so on. The central state may have certain regulations that can be generally regarded as in the equal interest of all, but there will be a reasonable case for a domestic form of differentiated integration in other respects. Demographic and socio-economic differences can make the spending priorities of one region legitimately different to another, at least on those matters that impact mainly local residents. A democratic system that allowed, say, urban areas to determine all the policies of rural areas (or *vice versa*) could be regarded as failing to take account of the unequal stakes citizens had in the relevant collective decisions, so that a disproportionate stake was given to some citizens.

A different but related issue concerns the way those with less of a stake in making a collective decision may be able to exploit those for whom the benefits of a collective decision or the costs of not making it are much greater. As Thomas Christiano has noted (Christiano 2015: 997), fairness in individual transactions turns on there being a rough equality in what he calls the *ex ante* stakes the parties have in a given system of transactions as a way of furthering their legitimate interests. Here the problematic issue, well known in labour relations, consists of rendering power in bargaining proportionate to stakes (Christiano 2015: 998). Although a given worker may have more at stake in a possible labour contract than their potential employer, he or she may have fewer resources, time and information to devote to securing a good deal. In these circumstances, the making of labour contracts may be formally free, but the background conditions in which they are made are unfair. Within most democratic states, public systems of justice and welfare have developed that to some degree serve to compensate for inequalities in information and other resources by providing legal regulations and certain social protections, such as a minimum wage and a system of social benefits, designed to work against fraud and force in private transactions. However, this public framework has been able to develop through individuals being roughly equal as citizens even if they are unequal as market actors. Even so, a system of public protection has only evolved and been sustained to the extent workers and the underprivileged have been able to organise themselves through unions and parties able to promote their interests, and because legal and democratic channels exist through which they can influence the political agenda (Hirschl and Rosevear 2011). As critics of the so-called overloading of the state complained in the 1970s and 80s (Brittan 1975), to some degree these social achievements arose from inequalities in the apportionment of bargaining power deriving from neo-corporatist political structures that recognised the greater stake of labour organisations in promoting certain public services and structures that advanced and supported social equality. As Christiano observes (Christiano 2015: 999–1006), such considerations prove even more significant in international negotiations, where inequalities between states are not counterbalanced by a democratically constructed public safety net, and the opportunities for exploitation prove greater. Hence, there is a more urgent need to design institutional mechanisms for international negotiations that compensate for differences of wealth and economic power (Christiano 2015: 1006–10).

The second aphorism enters here. It holds that 'for justice to be done, it must be seen to be done'. This aphorism underlies the impartiality argument and the need for democracy to be not only fair but also publically and demonstrably so. As I have noted in earlier chapters, one reason for insisting all have a fair say in collective decision-making rather than trusting in a benevolent dictator arises from people's inevitable partiality to their own point of view. Such partiality results from the unavoidable limitations in our reasoning about others, particularly in large societies where the details of most people's lives are a mystery to us (Christiano 2008: chs 3 and 6). Even the most conscientious, well intentioned and best informed of us cannot avoid drawing on our own experiences and reasoning in the light of values and facts that resonate with us but may not do so with others. A democratic system of one person, one vote offers a formally impartial system that endeavours to integrate our multifarious points of view and so promote policies that reflect our various concerns and circumstances. Nevertheless, to do so, the process must incorporate incentives for us – or, more realistically, the decision-makers we elect – to go beyond a partial perspective and 'hear the other side' in ways that move policy-making towards an impartial consideration of what is in the public interest rather than simply responding to the private interests of various particular groups.

To achieve this result, the process must involve a more substantive notion of impartiality, whereby policy-makers address the commonly avowable interests of citizens by appealing to reasons that are widely shared as suitable criteria for collective decision-making and justifying decisions in terms of their contribution to the common good (Miller 2009; Christiano 2010). As was argued in Chapters 3 and 4, to achieve this result citizens must share a sense of what count as public reasons, and the ability to reason in public – notions typically associated with the presence of a shared public sphere, involving a common language and media. Democratic systems that lack these public qualities are likely to allow politicians to play different groups off against each other. It also gives rise to the danger of consistent minorities, in which particular groups with distinctive cultural or other priorities are persistently excluded from collective decisions. These issues create what I shall call the 'partiality problem'.

Again, many member states contain cultural and national minorities and adopt various types of differentiation when making and applying collective policies to address this problem. These mechanisms standardly take the form of differentiated group rights. Following Will Kymlicka, one can divide these rights into self-government rights, special representation rights, and poly-ethnic rights (Kymlicka 1995). All involve asymmetrical arrangements between regions or groups of citizens. These types of differentiation address the partiality problem by seeking to incorporate heterogeneous groups of citizens in a unified public decision-making process. Self-government rights involve the devolution of particular competences to certain territorially concentrated cultural or other minorities, as in Scotland or Catalonia; or the ability for such groups to control certain services, such as publically funded faith schools that are run by particular religious groups. Special representation rights involve giving such groups a guaranteed level of representation to ensure their voice gets heard. Finally, poly-ethnic rights involve special dispensations from certain general laws for particular groups, such as allowing the slaughter of animals in ways that are otherwise prohibited to accommodate the dietary code of certain religious groups.

The third aphorism enters here. Related to the equity argument, it dictates that democracy involves the 'rule of law, not persons'. On this view, democracy ideally removes the possibility for arbitrary rule by preventing any person or group of persons from ruling in a wilful and capricious way, without consulting the interests of those subject to their rule (Pettit 2012). Instead, they must rule by a duly constituted democratic process. Suitably adjusted to take into account the proportionality and partiality problems, such a democratic process creates incentives to govern as equitably as possible by placing governments under the equal influence and control of the governed, and removable and replaceable by them, making all citizens rulers and ruled in turn.

An appealingly simple account of how laws can meet the equity requirement of the rule of law is that one should have 'one law for all' (Burke 1794). As Edmund Burke famously deployed the phrase in the impeachment trial of former Governor-General of India Warren Hastings, it suggests all should be equal before the laws and subject to the same standards and punishments no matter how well esteemed, connected, rich or powerful they may be. Yet, despite its undoubted force in this sort of context, this simple account turns out to be simplistic (Bellamy 2007: 63–6; Waldron 1990: 40–1). Most people accept that exceptions can exist – for example, that ambulances may exceed speed limits when rushing a sick person to hospital, even if we expect them to exercise due care and attention when doing so. Likewise, it seems reasonable to look at the heterogeneity of different types of provider of a given service when setting and applying regulatory standards. So certain health and safety rules may differ with regard to small and large firms. Similarly, there can be rules designed to benefit specific groups of people, albeit in the interests of equity, such as regulations aimed at facilitating access to buildings for the disabled. As a result, a more accurate principle of equity in the case of laws would be the Aristotelian maxim that 'one treats like cases alike, and unalike cases differently' (Aristotle 1996: III.9.1280 a8–15, III. 12. 1282b18–23: at pp. 74–5, 78–80). Yet, a difficulty arises in deciding when a difference is relevant or not with regard to the policy at hand. Let's call this the 'difference problem'. A well-designed democratic system responds to this problem by allowing different groups within society to 'hear the other side' and share the costs and benefits of differential treatment reciprocally (Bellamy 2007: 80–83). However, this process will only operate in a fair and impartial manner that respects difference to the extent the proportionality and partiality problems are taken into account.

Democratic decision-making about common policies can only be fair, impartial and equitable to the extent it takes into account the proportionality, partiality and difference problems, therefore, all of which can arise within heterogeneous states. Such heterogeneity creates different demoi, making it necessary to conceive how these different groups can 'govern together but not as one' (Nicolaïdis 2013). Applying the argument of this section to the EU, the next section shall maintain that the proportionality problem can justify some member states opting out or being excluded, temporarily or permanently, from participation in certain club goods. It proves less justified for public goods, where they cannot either avoid adding to or be excluded from the negative or positive externalities these goods produce. Fair-play arguments of political obligation suggest that in such cases all should contribute (Rawls 1964). Nevertheless, unless such goods are morally obligatory, in that they relate to upholding basic rights, it would be illegitimate to force people into accepting benefits they do not value (Nozick 1974: 90–95). At some point, all the member states would need to be involved in deciding whether and how far such goods should be provided. The partiality problem enters here, since this allows for those who conceive of themselves as a distinct public, with divergent public norms, to make their own decisions as to which collective goods they should support or how they should be provided in circumstances where they feel their distinct but reasonable views will not get an impartial hearing. Finally, the difference problem suggests that when groups with different interests and values belong to a club, then collective rules need to accommodate these differences to some degree. Figure 6.1 summarises the argument so far, indicating how the three arguments will be related respectively to instrumental, constitutional and legislative differentiation in the next section.

Democratic value	Fairness	Impartiality	Equity
Social/cultural preconditions	Equal stake	Shared values	Co-incidence of equal with uniform treatment
Type of heterogeneity	Different socio-economic stakes in a given collective good	Cultural differences; lack of identification as a public or absence of shared public reasons	Moderate relevant differences of either stakes or diversity
Form of DI	Instrumental	Constitutional	Legislative

Figure 6.1: Democratic Values, Type of Heterogeneity and Form of Differentiated Integration

Three Types of Differentiated Integration: Instrumental, Constitutional and Legislative

As the EU slogan 'unity in diversity' indicates, the EU recognises the proportionality, partiality and difference problems to some degree, not least in the demoicratic character of many of its governance structures (Cheneval and Schimmelfennig 2013), as we have already seen in Chapter 4 and will discuss further in the next section. So far as the treaty-making and accession processes are concerned, the EU remains a union of member states and their peoples rather than straightforwardly of European citizens. This feature has allowed the proportionality, partiality and difference problems to be partly accommodated through temporary opt-outs, exclusions and differentiated legislation. The emphasis on subsidiarity and the use of national parliaments to police it also reflects an awareness of these problems (Kröger and Bellamy 2016). Issues better regulated at the European than at lower levels are likely to be those where member states possess an equal stake and a shared perspective. Where they have different stakes, subsidiarity operates in a similar manner to the devolution of many services to local government even within unitary states. Where cultural differences exist, subsidiarity operates similarly to granting self-government rights to different linguistic and other cultural communities within multinational and multicultural federal systems, which can extend to different legal, health and education systems and include extensive tax-raising powers. As in many domestic systems, countries have also requested Treaty opt-outs that lead to an asymmetric retention of power by certain member states in matters that most countries agree can be EU competences. Thus, Denmark and the UK have four Treaty opt-outs each, Ireland two and Poland one. Meanwhile, much EU legislation is increasingly differentiated so as to apply differently in different member states. Below, I explore the case for such derogations and exclusions on grounds of fairness, impartiality and equity in the context of a heterogeneous EU.

With regarded to fairness, I noted above how economic and social heterogeneity can be problematic in the case of collective goods. Even when all countries have an equal stake in a common measure, they may not have equal incentives to resource it. However, differences in population size, varieties of capitalism, economic specialisation and wealth may lead to different stakes, giving rise to the proportionality problem. Giandomenico Majone has observed how the logic of collective action often militates against the optimal provision of a collective good, particularly among a large and heterogeneous group (Majone 2016). If all members benefit from a collective good because it is a public good or membership of the club producing it is automatic, they will have an incentive to free ride on the efforts of others and to contribute less than their fair share to its provision. In a small group, wealthier participants may be willing to cover more than their fair share, accepting that they gain more from the good and would suffer a greater loss from its not being supplied than in paying disproportionally to provide it. Selective incentives can also be offered to encourage compliance. For instance, the Common Agricultural Policy originated as part of a grand bargain between France and Germany to gain French support for further European integration in other areas. As the club gets bigger, such trade-offs get harder to arrange, especially if the balance between wealthier and poorer countries tips decisively towards the latter, as has happened post Eastern enlargement whereby Denmark has a nominal GDP/capita that is around seven times that of Bulgaria (European Commission 2018). The poorer and/or smaller states will tend to exploit the wealthier and/ or larger states. Clubs with a larger membership that possess such asymmetries are also more likely to include members for whom the costs outweigh the benefits associated with the good. There are also likely to be disagreements as to which collective goods should be provided in the first place, increasing the transaction costs of obtaining consensual agreement among all concerned – a point I address in the next section.

In these circumstances, it becomes rational to employ instrumental forms of DI that reduce the club involved in producing a given collective good to a smaller group than the whole so as to overcome the proportionality problem. Two mechanisms have been employed to achieve this result. One approach, suggested as early as 1975 in the 'Leo Tindemans Report', involves allowing a small 'pioneer' group to forge ahead with cooperation in a given policy (Piris 2012: 67). However, since Amsterdam, the Treaties have authorised both 'in-built' cooperation for certain members in policy areas specifically mentioned in the Treaties, such as the Schengen and Euro areas, and allowed certain members to employ EU institutions for 'enhanced cooperation' on a case-by-case basis should at least nine member states wish to do so (Piris 2012: 70–5). A corollary of such measures has been to exclude those states that fail to reach a given threshold sufficient to make them fair participants in a particular club good, although hitherto such exclusions have been seen as temporary. The most significant example of this approach is participation in the Euro, which depends on the fulfilment of certain preconditions, although arguably these criteria have proved neither stringent enough nor been applied with appropriate rigour.

The formation of exclusive clubs such as these might be thought to go against a modern democratic principle in which all have an equal vote regardless of their wealth. However, apportioning stakes relative to wealth makes more sense if we see certain collective decisions as more like a joint investment decision, where power and benefits tend to be apportioned according to the amount invested (Christiano 2015: 1006–7). However, there are areas where this parallel does not hold. Take the exclusion of Bulgaria, Romania and Croatia from the Schengen Area. This might also be justified on the grounds that they had a disproportionate interest in free movement in order to access better jobs in other member states. However, an injustice might be thought to be committed where the stake an excluded and poorer country has in a collective arrangement is greater than those of the richer states that are included. For example, in the case of free movement, the potential costs to existing member states of an influx of cheap labour was arguably less than the benefit to the new member states when such temporary arrangements were introduced, so that the latter were unfairly treated in having their interests weighed equally with those of the former.

This latter sort of example illustrates a paradox noted by Christiano (2015: 1008–10), and remarked on in the last section, whereby those who have more of a stake in international trade decisions are often the smaller and poorer states, yet they invariably have less rather than more bargaining power in a voluntary scheme than richer countries with less of a stake. That disparity in bargaining power can be to some degree alleviated by multilateral treaty making and the sort of consociational governance mechanisms that typify the EU (Costa and Magnette 2003; Papadopoulos and Magnette 2010). These arrangements allow coalitions to develop among the smaller and poorer states and facilitate their pooling informational resources. Most importantly, their possession of a veto can allow them to force concessions and compromises. For example, the Wallonia regional parliament was able to hold up the Canada-EU Trade Agreement (CETA) in order to put in place measures aimed at protecting the various democratically determined public services and regulations of the various states and regions of the EU from being undermined on the grounds they formed barriers to free trade.

A second approach to the proportionality problem involves taking subsidiarity seriously and accepting that different functional tasks may be assigned to a wide variety of different levels involving different groups of states and even of regions not only for reasons of efficiency but also to reflect the degree of interest each of the participants has in it. Such a solution would extend the EU's variable geometry, yet no more than is common within many unitary federations that allow the asymmetrical devolution of various competences to different regions. Again, a Treaty basis already exists for such flexibility (Piris 2012: 75–7). Protocol 25 on the exercise of shared competences makes explicit that even in areas where the EU has adopted legislation, member states can legislate nationally and conclude agreements with other states in those areas not specifically governed by the relevant EU act. Indeed, since the 1980s, the Commission has limited many measures to 'minimum' or 'partial' harmonisation. Article 100A(4) of the Single European Act even introduced the possibility of a partial opt-out from a given harmonisation if 'a member state deems it necessary to apply national provisions on grounds of major needs referred to in Article 36'.

Public goods raise a potential problem for DI through being non-excludable. Consequently, they generate positive externalities from which non-club members still benefit or negative externalities that disadvantage them further. However, EU policies with this property are exceptions not the norm. Not even all environmental policies tackle EU-wide public goods or bads. Negative or positive externalities cannot provide a justification for a common policy on beach cleanliness, for example. Here, the advantages or disadvantages accrue largely to local residents and so can be differentiated.

Likewise, since Maastricht, the Treaties have recognised the possibility of constitutional differentiation to address the partiality problem. For example, Article 3 TEU asserts the Union 'shall respect its rich cultural and linguistic diversity', Article 67 (1) TFEU that it will 'respect ... the different legal systems and traditions of the member states' and Article 4 (2) TEU that it 'respect the equality of Member States before the Treaties as well as their national identities, inherent in their fundamental structures, political and constitutional, inclusive of regional and local self-government'. More specifically, Articles 83 (3) and 151 TFEU assert that relevant Union measures must respect national practices in the operation of the criminal justice system and social policy. These and similar articles reflect tensions from the 1970s onwards between national constitutional courts and certain rulings of the Court of Justice regarding areas where the former held domestic constitutional norms legitimated restrictions on the free movement of goods, services, capital and labour that the latter sought to uphold. This conflict was at the heart of a whole series of key cases where the Court of Justice was criticised for extending the range of its jurisdiction and interpreting rights in a largely market manner that showed scant respect for national constitutional values: notably, *Cinéthèque, Groener, Bond, ERT* and *Grogen* (de Witte 1991, Coppel and O'Neill 1992). Such issues have played an important role in a number of key opt-outs, such as the Danish Protocol allowing a permanent derogation prohibiting the purchase of second homes by non-Danes and regarding its non-participation in the European Policy on Defence and Security, or the Irish Protocol on Article 40.3.3 concerning the prohibition of abortion. Denmark and the United Kingdom also have opt-outs from certain central EU policies relating to the free movement of persons and the Euro, on the grounds that these are core sovereign competences. Calls for such opt-outs have spread to other countries in the wake of the pressure to share the burden of refugees in response to the migrant crisis and to introduce constitutional measures regarding public spending following the Euro crisis.

The rationale behind the insistence on constitutional differentiation lies in the fact that the different demoi of the member states have already developed their own constitutional and juridical orders that reflect the distinctive and diverse public cultures of their citizens. As a result, impartiality in the application of constitutional norms may not be possible at the EU level. Even if all the member states endorse broadly the same set of rights and democratic principles, they may have legitimately different views about their scope and relative weighting with regard to both each other and other important values and interests that reflect valid cultural differences. The right to freedom of expression is accepted by all member states, for example, but in certain countries it is interpreted as warranting the special protection of linguistic minorities or a national language on the grounds that a people's culture provides the necessary context within which they express themselves as possessors of a specific identity. As I have remarked in earlier chapters, such reasoning led the German Federal Court to affirm in its 2009 Lisbon Judgment that European unification should 'not be achieved in such a way that not sufficient space is left to the member states for the political formation of economic, cultural and social living conditions'.

Nevertheless, basic rights, if not EU law, can limit how much constitutional differentiation is justifiable. The Polish stance on homosexuality, for example, is problematic in itself, not just because it can restrict mobility and non-discrimination in the EU. Likewise, the degree to which Hungary and Poland are currently adhering to the principles of democracy and the rule of law outlined in Article 2 TEU (and 6), and hence should have certain rights of membership of the EU curtailed as allowed under Article 7, has become increasingly debateable for a number of commentators (Kelemen 2017).

Of course, constitutional opt-outs are the exception rather than the rule. However, we noted how 40 per cent of EU legislation involves derogations and differences among member states in applying a given measure. During the 1960s and 70s, European institutions took the view expressed in the landmark *Costa* judgment that the 'executive force of Community law cannot vary from one state to another ... without jeopardizing the attainment of the objectives of the treaty'.

However, as the membership has grown and become more varied, so the formulation of specific EU secondary law has allowed for flexibility that acknowledges the need on grounds of equity to recognise relevant differences. This need involves both economic and social differences involving the proportionality problem and constitutional differences involving the partiality problem. For example, with regard to the proportionality problem, although the UK Transport Minister, Chris Grayling, declared that as a result of Brexit the UK would now be able to set the height of its own railway platforms, the relevant EU regulation, (EU) No 1299/2014, allows considerable diversity to accommodate the extraordinary variety of gauges and heights currently present across Europe. The interoperability of trains across Europe is an important collective good but not at a cost that would undermine the likely benefits – especially when it can be achieved in cheaper ways, such as adding steps to carriages. Similarly, with regard to the partiality problem, the, Commission has proposed amending Regulation (EC) No 1829/2003 to give member states decisional power regarding the use on their territory of genetically modified food or feed that has been authorized at the EU level.

The heterogeneity of member states makes DI normatively and morally necessary, therefore. Even in the case of cooperation for morally obligatory goals, the interests of different states in the various ways these obligations might be met are likely to differ, while there can be reasonable disagreement as to the best ways to address them. States can sensibly diverge as to which measures they view as most equitable, effective, or efficient, and about the most appropriate way to balance these desiderata. As a result, with regard to even morally obligatory global goods, such as the alleviation of climate change or global poverty, it may be normatively legitimate and also more effective for states to opt out of certain collective arrangements so long as they continue to address the issues in alternative ways that can claim to have a similar chance of success or that place a more justifiable burden upon them. For example, in Chapter 5, I noted legitimate differences in the welfare arrangements of different states that modified their obligations towards second- and third- country nationals. Such considerations have even more weight in the case of collective goods that go beyond what might be commonly regarded as the morally obligatory. In these cases, the probability of divergent interests and the scope for reasonable disagreement is likely to be greater. Given that the vast majority of what the EU does is of this character, it is unsurprising that member states have regularly sought to opt out of common programmes or to modify their involvement and commitments to them in various ways.

Towards the Demoicratic Constitution of the EU: Overcoming Constitutional Supremacy and the Allure of Majority Rule

The argument so far has focused mostly on the impact of DI on the structure of the EU's polity and the legitimacy of the challenge DI poses to the view that all member states should integrate at the same pace, within the same areas and adopt the same policies. However, DI in these areas also motivates and gives rise to a more differentiated regime. Political systems that compensate for the proportionality, partiality and difference problems necessarily depart from a strict equality of voting weights and a system of majority rule, and involve differentiation in both the mechanisms for making collective decisions, and the distribution of political authority between territorial and functional units. For example, states with national and cultural minorities, or even a plurality of ideological positions, standardly adopt forms of consociational governance (Lijphart 1977). This political arrangement involves representing the various groups separately in collective decision-making in ways that give them a proportionate say or protect them from partial views – usually via mechanisms such as a Grand Coalition at the executive level, mutual veto of policies by the various groups, and a highly proportional system of electoral representation, with considerable devolution of decisions to the relevant regions or groups, often to different degrees and in different policy areas.

Given that economic, cultural and political heterogeneity within the EU is 'extreme' compared to most consociational democracies (Lijphart 1999: 42–7; Scharpf 2015: 395), it is unsurprising that the EU has adopted a range of similar super-majoritarian and consensus requirements for Treaty making and legislation (Costa and Magnette 2003), that taken together characterize what is called the 'Community Method' (Scharpf 2017: 326). However, two related problems arise from this system. First, as I noted in Chapter 4, the difficulty with such arrangements lies in their allowing multiple veto points that encourage the self-interested bargaining and gridlock typical of what I called the 'ontology of singularity'. While the blocking measures allowed by such a system can be used in the legitimate ways detailed in the last two sections, they can also be used illegitimately as a way of extracting additional resources by less involved states who can up the price of their vote, thereby increasing the transaction costs of collective action. As a result, EU legislation can be a cumbersome and time-consuming process, and less than fit for purpose. Second, as a result of these inconveniences, the temptation has been to bypass the political process by integrating through law and, when judicial intervention fails, by shifting to bilateral negotiations outside the treaties, as has been the case during the Euro crisis in order to rescue the Monetary Union. This section starts by criticising these latter developments. It then turns to how they might be rolled back, while at the same time addressing some of the above mentioned problems with the consensus mechanisms of the Community Method that partly led to them in the first place. As we shall see, DI facilitates both moves.

Integration by Law and the Challenge to Democracy

Law constrains both DI and the related demoicratic political process in two main ways. First, these cooperative and multilateral political mechanisms only operate once states have joined the EU. Accession negotiations are bilateral, even in the case of the major Enlargement post-1989 to Central and Eastern European states. As a result, these latter states were largely obliged to adopt a more or less full and, post the Single European Act, much expanded, legal *acquis communautaire* of prevailing uniform rules. These had been designed for the rich and more competitive Western states and most parties appreciated at the time that they might prove unfeasible for the new members, at least in part (Scharpf 2003: 94–5). As we saw, some requirements were postponed, most particularly adoption of the Euro and entry into Schengen. However, as I remarked above, the general expectation was that these were temporary, transitional, measures, and that in time these states would catch up.

The experience of German unification suggests such beliefs are misplaced. Despite massive financial transfers – far beyond anything the EU can achieve for its poorer members – the application of West German regulations and currency to the East resulted in the collapse of Eastern industries and continuing comparative disadvantages, unemployment and growing political alienation, none of which are likely to disappear soon (Carlin 1998). Meanwhile, the historical process of Italian unification and the continuing North-South divide in Italy arguably offers an even more apposite, and rather more discouraging, analogy to the challenges currently confronting the enlarged EU (Carlin 2015). The initial response to this dilemma post-Enlargement was lax implementation that involved subterfuge and hypocrisy by all concerned (Héritier 1999). Yet this tactic has invested the Commission and Court of Justice with a degree of arbitrary discretionary power of a dominating and haphazard kind (Scharpf 2003: 90), while – as we saw – also being suboptimal for the collective production of common goods.

Second, and relatedly, moving beyond this situation confronts the constraints of EU law and a given ideological approach to it and the

Court of Justice (on ideological discourse and the Court of Justice, see Weiler 1999: 86–99). The term ideological is used advisedly and is not intended to be derogatory. Rather, it serves to indicate that views on the role of courts and the character of law are political in the broad sense of having implications for the kind of policies that can be pursued and the way the political system operates that can often be reasonably contested rather than being 'neutral' or purely 'functional' requirements of a liberal democratic regime, and so 'above' politics (Bellamy 2007; Isiksel 2016). Moreover, the Court of Justice, like other Courts, has political agency and its behaviour cannot be attributed simply to a correct (or incorrect) application of legal rules and norms alone. The Court's adoption of particular strategies also reflects the available political opportunity structure and context, and involves and responds to mobilisation by various legal actors of a political character (Alter 2001, 2009). For example, the longer time horizon of the Court gives it a strategic advantage over governments subject to the shorter time scale of the electoral cycle, allowing for incremental changes, each of which is of low political salience relative to their cumulative effect (Weiler 1999: 50–1; Conant 2002; Scharpf 2009: 191). Meanwhile, it has tended to be most activist when not only was there a relatively solid legal basis for doing so, but also there was a political vacuum (Weiler 1999: 63), and/or its action had broad support among member states (Maduro, 1998), and/or could draw on a doctrinal basis that had been widely disseminated by a transnational network of Euro-Law associations (Alter 2009: ch. 4). When these features have been absent or less favourable than had been assumed, the Court has regularly stepped back (Alter 2009: ch. 3, Weiler 1999: 99–101).

From this political perspective, complaints about the lack of a full and uniform 'acquis', to be applied equally across all the member states (Curtin 1993), reflect a disputable and arguably misplaced belief that such an approach provides a basis for European solidarity, collective identity and common citizenship, while being inherent to the rule of law. As we saw in earlier sections, cultural and other differences can often be best accommodated through forms of 'differentiated citizenship' (Young 1989). Likewise, equal treatment needs to be distinguished from treating everyone the same. Relevant differences often require differential treatment to be equitable. By contrast, the insistence on common rules has often served simply to support an economic commitment to free trade and the removal of barriers to provide a level playing field. As I remarked with regard to the Court's jurisprudence concerning Union citizenship in Chapter 5, and will detail further below, the conjunction of judicial and economic reasoning has had the effect of constitutionalising the rules of the single market and treating the four market freedoms as the logical and morally necessary extensions of the exercise of basic rights.

The Court affected this shift from the mid-1960s onwards as a result of two revolutionary judgments that provided the legal basis for its subsequent constitutionalisation of the Treaties (Weiler 1999: ch. 2, especially 10–63). In *Van Gend and Loos vs Netherlands* in 1963, the Court declared EU law to have direct effect with regard to the member states, allowing individuals to derive rights from it they could claim through national courts. A year later, in *Costa v. ENEL*, the Court declared the Treaties and European law in general had primacy over national law, including national constitutions (Grimm 2016: 300–1). The implications of these judgments have not gone uncontested. As I noted above, the willingness of national political and legal actors to accept Court of Justice rulings that progressively integrated the economies of the member states within the single market has depended on a set of factors that have varied in their force. However, my aim here is not so much to trace or explain this development, as to note its accumulative effect in depoliticising core aspects of EU decision-making.

Four aspects of this development are relevant to the current argument (Grimm 2016: 302–8; Scharpf 2017: 316–20). First, this move involved regarding EU law as a distinct and autonomous legal system rather than as international law, possessing an objective purpose of its own, that could be detached from the will of the contracting state parties and the constraints of national legal orders, and which the Court came to conceive itself as obliged to realise to the utmost extent. Moreover, this approach gradually extended beyond the Treaty provisions to encompass European directives that were likewise treated as binding on the member states. Second, the main focus of integration through law became the construction of the single market. Some scholars have traced this commitment to the influence of a particular 'ordoliberal' vision of the economy (Scharpf 2010). Certainly, the Court is limited by its competences and those of the EU to the promotion of what Scharpf has termed 'negative' integration – the market making dismantling of regulatory barriers to interstate trade (Scharpf 1999: 43). However, 'positive' integration, in the sense of an EU-level market constraining social and welfare policy, is not only largely absent at the EU level but also has come under increasing pressure from the Court at the national level. Its teleological reasoning has led anti-protectionist provisions to be interpreted to encompass any regulation deemed to constrain the four freedoms, so that almost any law could be treated as an impediment to free trade regardless of its purpose (Offe 2003; Joerges 2010; Streek 2014). Third, these moves have been further supported by the incorporation of the

Charter of Fundamental Rights into the Lisbon Treaty. Although technically only applicable to member states when implementing Union law (Art. 51 of the Charter), the intertwined character of national and EU law means that can easily cover whatever the Court considers appropriate. Notwithstanding the safeguards offered to national levels of rights protection by the Charter (Art. 51 and 52), given the Court had already raised the four freedoms to the level of fundamental rights and claims the competence to adjudicate on the balance between them and national levels of rights protection, this measure has largely served to further buttress its tendency to challenge rights-based checks to integration by national courts, such as the *Solange* judgments of the German Federal Constitutional Court, that had hitherto formed a key source of resistance by member state constitutional courts to its ascendency (Grimm 2016: 305, 282–9; 2017: 172–3). Finally, the result of the Court of Justice's jurisprudential entrepreneurship has been to allow integration to be achieved not only though the Treaty-making process but also through the judicial interpretation of existing provisions and directives. This channel has empowered the Commission as well as the Court, while allowing the collusive delegation of powers by the executives of the member states desirous of discouraging or disabling domestic democratic scrutiny of contentious, market enhancing policies (Curtin 2014).

All four aspects, but especially this last, undercut to varying degrees the demoicratic character of EU decision-making and challenge the possibility for the form of normative legitimacy defended here. True, the member states remain the Masters of the Treaties so far as Treaty making is concerned, with these Treaties having to conform to the normative logic of 'republican intergovernmentalism'. In other words, governments can only agree to Treaty changes that prove consistent with their respective domestic constitutional arrangements and can obtain the requisite democratic consent of their respective demoi. Yet, we have seen how that constraint gets weakened so far as the accession of new members is concerned. The governments of these states are pressurised into adopting the entirety of an *acquis communitaire* they played no part in negotiating. The advantages of joining may outweigh the disadvantages of not joining at all, but for poorer states the result may be a Faustian bargain that keeps them at a permanent disadvantage. Once members, they have the possibility of clawing back some ground through multilateral bargaining that allows them to find common cause and pool resources with similarly situated states. Moreover, the consensual decision-making of the EU and its multiple checks and balances serve to ensure at the very least that subsequent decisions remain Pareto optimal for all concerned, including through allowing DI. However, as I detailed above, the Treaties place certain obligations directly on states that confer rights on individuals and firms. Infringements of these conditions can be pursued by the Commission and through the Court of Justice. Moreover, the Court has the capacity to offer binding and enforceable interpretations of these obligations (Scharpf 2009: 190–8).

By and large, this mechanism operates in areas related to economic integration and market liberalisation. The rationale has been that this arrangement avoids a potential Prisoner's Dilemma in those cases where a mutually beneficial collective agreement might be undermined by potential free riding by states selectively adopting protectionist measures (Scharpf 2003: 82–3). So conceived, it becomes in the enlightened self-interest of the states to bind themselves to a degree of supranational centralised decision-making, with enforcement by an impartial and independent judiciary (Moravcsik 1998). Yet, this arrangement risks becoming dysfunctional to the extent such legal self-binding removes flexibility to revise these obligations as circumstances change and gets extended into areas where no win-win solutions exist through the creative and evolving interpretation of legal agreements by the Court, admittedly often due to an inability or unwillingness of state governments to take decisions in contentious areas. The crux, therefore, is whether the demoicratisation of the EU – its reconnection to its constituent peoples – remains achievable and, if so, can be sustainable.

The Demoicratic Constitution of the EU and Majority Rule

As I have remarked in earlier chapters, especially Chapter 4, there have been two important steps towards reasserting the demoicratic constitution of the EU following the Lisbon Treaty. First, Article 4 (2) TEU commits the EU to showing equal respect to the national constitutional identities of the member states, albeit – as I noted above – subject to upholding the democratic values outlined in Articles 2 and 6, with the possibility of suspending certain rights of membership under Article 7 of those states that fail to do so. Second, Articles 10 and 12 TEU gave a role to national parliaments as part of the EU decision-making process.

As we saw, the German Federal Constitutional Court's Lisbon and OMT judgments testify to a continued willingness by national constitutional courts to push back against incursions by EU law on national understandings of constitutional essentials. So have similar references by the Spanish and Italian courts in *Melloni* and *Taricco* concerning, respectively, the European Arrest Warrant and the right to a fair trial under the Spanish Constitution, and EU VAT law and the nature of legality in Italian constitutional law. Such moves suggest that the picture of a steady erosion of national constitutional provisions can be exaggerated. As other commentators have noted, the EU's legal structures as often as not exemplify a remarkable degree of constitutional pluralism (MacCormick 1993; 1995; Jaklic 2014). Indeed, some claim 'constitutional toleration' – whereby the European legal order involves member states and the EU mutually recognising and accommodating their legal systems in a non-hierarchal manner to each other – to offer the distinctive EU model (Weiler 2003: 20–1). That claim may be under increasing strain (Weiler 2012; Kelemen 2016, although see Walker 2016), as its chief advocate acknowledged from the start (Weiler 1999: 90–101), but it suggests the possibility of a demoicratic constitutional alternative (Weiler 1999: 346–7).

The German Court's OMT ruling had turned on its interpretation of Article 38(1) of the German Basic Law as requiring that state authority could not be transferred to the extent to which it makes democratic control nugatory, and that Germany's obligations under outright monetary transactions could not be such as to undermine the Bundestag's budgetary oversight (Bellamy and Weale 2015: 264–5; Grimm 2017: 170–1). That judgment has served to reinforce the role of national parliaments in other member states. Although the preparedness and capacity of national parliaments to take on their new functions varies between member states, Chapter 4 suggested that the possibility for them being the agents of a demoicratic reconnection to EU policy-making existed. In particular, when allied to a suggested Parliamentary Legislative Initiative, or Green Card, allowing qualified minorities among national parliaments to initiate legislative proposals, with enhanced oversight of the Executive also legitimating qualified minorities in the European Council doing likewise, they provide potential mechanisms for politicising EU policy making in constructive ways typical of a 'civicity'. Part of the problem of demoicractic disconnection has been that it has handed the political initiative on EU matters to populist, Eurosceptic parties. This proposal seeks to allow pro-EU parties back in the game of normal politics, by enabling different policies to be advocated and debated.

However, these steps of themselves are insufficient. On the one side, they may not suffice to challenge the incremental constitutionalisation of the Treaties by the Court of Justice and the resulting process of ever more negative integration through law. On the other side, there remains the problem of the cumbersome and often dysfunctional character of the Community Method as a mode of EU policy making. Fritz Scharpf has offered two related sets of suggestions that might address each of these issues to some degree.

The first set of suggestion explores the possibility of a political override of Court of Justice decisions by the European Council (Scharpf 2009: 199–200). Although constitutional pluralists regard the validity of EU law as ultimately resting on domestic sources of law as interpreted by national constitutional courts, that raises the worry of a potential clash between national courts and the Court of Justice should the former consider the latter to have overreached its competence – a challenge the Court of Justice has viewed as *per se* illegitimate given its own claim to Kompetenz-Kompetenz. In fact, both sides have carefully steered clear of such a clash, fearing it represents a nuclear option (Weiler 1999: 320–1). Yet, in the long term, such avoidance strategies ultimately play into the hands of the Court of Justice as it increases the sway of European law by a kind of ratchet effect.

Scharpf (2009: 199–200) suggests that a supermajority decision in the Council offers an appropriate mechanism for addressing such situations – and indeed, it would make them possible by offering a demoicratically legitimate mechanism for resolving them. In essence, this mechanism would reduce the role of the Court of Justice to that of 'weak-form review', in which judicial decisions are open to legislative challenge and amendment (Tushnet 2006: 3–11). It would remove judicial supremacy by making clear that elected governments are the Masters of the Treaties. In line with the norms of 'republican intergovernmentalism', a democratic government disputing a Court of Justice ruling would be submitting to the judgement of its peers among other member states and asking to be treated with equal concern and respect. On the one hand, other democratic governments can be expected to be appreciative of the need to attune decisions to different domestic contexts and in particular the two forms of heterogeneity that motivate DI. They will also understand the adverse reaction a Court of Justice decision perceived as insensitive to such considerations and in error might arouse. On the other hand, that need not mean they would tolerate almost any objection to a ruling that proved inconvenient for the government concerned – quite the contrary. For they would also be fully alive to the dangers of allowing states to renege on their solidaristic obligations and of undermining the Court's authority through frivolous or self-serving challenges. A parallel move for undoing the constitutionalisation of the Treaties by the Court would involve (a) only permitting litigation and infringement proceedings based on regulations and directives adopted under Articles 289–291 TFEU (Scharpf 2017: 322), and (b) allowing the proposed legislative proposals from national parliaments and the Council to involve partial or total abandonment of parts of the *acquis* for some or all states, subject to the approval of a qualified majority in the Council and a majority in the European Parliament (Scharpf 2009: 403). This measure would enable the removal of aspects of the *acquis* that no longer command political support, not least because they have outlived their usefulness.

This last proposal links up with the second set of suggestions (Scharpf 2009: 400–4; 2017: 330–2). If instrumental, constitutional and legislative DI become normalised, not least by allowing challenges to the Court of Justice and opt-outs from the *acquis*, then majority rule also becomes more legitimate. Indeed, there is a certain symmetry between the two. In areas where majority or qualified majority rule prevails, there should be the possibility for member states to opt out of ordinary legislation. To guard against that occurring in areas where either free riding or negative externalities might arise, it should be possible to block such requests by qualified majority in the Council and an absolute majority in the EP. Meanwhile, the Community Method and consensus would prevail with regard to Treaty making.

These suggestions aim to facilitate effective and equitable decision-making that remains consistent with the norms and practices of democratic legitimacy. Given the heterogeneity of the EU, that cannot be achieved by simply scaling up democracy to the EU level. However, it can be achieved if the EU adopts a demoicratic constitution that allows for mutually agreed variable geometry among its constituent members. Moreover, it would be wrong to regard such a Union as a pragmatic ragbag, consisting of 'ins' and 'outs'. Rather, it reflects a principled conception of an international community of democratic states based on equal concern and respect. In particular, it allows a shift from free trade to fair trade, not least in distinguishing anti-protectionism at the borders from de-regulation within borders. The first has been broadly beneficial in improving efficiency by allowing countries to play to their comparative advantage. However, the second has led to disembedding markets from the social and political structures that have been democratically negotiated at the state level to maintain production and labour standards and offer social support and training to the potential losers of freer trade (Ruggie 1982: 382–3, 393–8; Gilpin 1987: 355). It has been pushed for, and exploited by, those multinational corporate interests able to benefit from such changes, but has served to enhance the gap between the winners and losers by eroding social protection in the name of market liberalisation (Scharpf 2010: 223; Isiksel 2016: 173–9). Allowing DI restores a degree of national regulatory autonomy that provide incentives for the EU itself to adopt countervailing measures, such as protection of labour standards and the coordination of corporate tax levels, that can increase domestic political buy-in to a scheme of free trade by allowing its benefits to be balanced against its inegalitarian redistributive costs by upholding the capacity of states to mitigate these last.

Differentiated Integration and the Euro Crisis

Even many commentators who might otherwise support the arguments made so far for DI might object that, for good or ill, the adoption of the Euro and the current fiscal crisis has rendered them unworkable. In Claus Offe's telling metaphor, the EU has become 'entrapped' by the fact that, while adopting the Euro was a mistake, its abandonment would be an even greater mistake (Offe 2015: 55). It is worth noting that the original mistake instructively reinforces the argument of this chapter and the book more generally. As a number of economists had warned (Bordo and Jonung 2003: 43–4), the EU has proven insufficiently socially and economically homogenous to form an optimal currency area. At the same time, monetary union was promoted well in advance of any serious attempt to integrate the highly diverse social policies and labour-market institutions of the member states, let alone to take steps towards fiscal and political integration. As ever, the hope of the European politicians and policy-makers promoting this measure was that the requisite increase in social and political integration would almost automatically follow on from enhanced economic integration, with market pressures pushing the social and political as well as the economic systems of the member states to converge. The introduction of the Euro did indeed produce a convergence of borrowing costs. Yet this development had the effect of enabling borrowers to steadily accumulate problematic amounts of external debt through inadequate regulation of the banks by either national governments or the EU. Rather than fostering cross-border trade, favourable access to foreign credit fuelled a domestic boom, most notably in the construction sector, that has given way to sustained slumps in the midst of an inevitable depression and credit crunch. Meanwhile, the only mechanisms readily available to the EU to handle the resulting crisis remain those of negative integration, resulting in the adoption of austerity measures aimed at reducing the swollen public debt – even though, by and large, this burgeoning indebtedness had resulted from bailing out the banks rather than excessive public spending.

These measures have given rise to the most egregious example of the constitutionalisation, and consequent attempted depoliticisation, of economic policy (Bellamy and Weale 2015). As a result of the Fiscal Compact contained in the Treaty on Stability, Coordination and Governance in the Economic and Monetary Union (TSCG), member states must undertake to ensure that national budgets are in balance or in surplus 'through provisions of binding force and permanent character, preferably constitutional, or otherwise guaranteed to be fully respected and adhered to throughout the national budgetary processes' (TSCG, Article 3.2). These policies attempt to codify general, and contentious, economic norms that constrain state intervention even further. As such, they deliberately override all three forms of DI, ignoring not only the social and economic but also the cultural and constitutional heterogeneity that motivates them. Unsurprisingly, they have prompted a democratic backlash in the form of populist and often Eurosceptical parties of the left and, especially, the nationalist right, as well as challenges from member state Constitutional courts – most notably in Germany (*Lisbon Judgment* 2 BvE 2/08) and Portugal (Acordão 187/2013). As I noted above, the German Court has insisted that the right to democracy guaranteed by the German Basic Law requires that the national parliament exercise budgetary oversight (*European Stability Mechanism*, 2 BvR 1390/12), an insistence that has encouraged parliaments in other member states, such as Spain, France and Italy, to develop their budgetary powers (Bellamy and Weale 2015: 270–1).

Wolfgang Streeck (2014: 97–103) and Philippe Van Parijis (2016) have argued that the EU's entrapment by its pursuit of an ambitious single market and currency agenda had been foreseen and advocated by the economic liberal philosopher Friedrick Hayek in his 1939 essay on 'The Economic Conditions of Interstate Federalism'. Hayek's argument was twofold. On the one hand, he believed the free movement of labour, capital, goods and services would drastically constrain the capacity of national governments to intervene in the economy, curtailing their use of indirect or direct taxation to regulate prices, labour or investment. For similar reasons, the bargaining power of trade unions, professional associations and businesses would likewise be weakened. Hayek gleefully remarked that even 'the restriction of child labour or of working hours' would become problematic if labour, capital and production could move elsewhere. On the other hand, he predicted that cultural heterogeneity would mean political integration would be unable to compensate for this loss of state capacity at the national level by replacing it at the supranational level. Such a multi-state federation would lack an overarching national identity that might foster solidarity of the kind that allowed redistribution from one economic sector to another within states. He doubted the 'French peasant will be willing to pay more for his fertiliser to help the British chemical industry' (Hayek 1948: 262). As a result, the central government of a federation of multiple demoi would need to avoid taking action that might provoke resistance from one or more of its constituent peoples, and, hence, be restricted in scope.

Like many other commentators, Van Parijs and Offe contend that the EU is currently impaled on the first horn of Hayek's dilemma, with an ordo-liberal spin on Hayekian reasoning explicitly informing the construction of monetary union (Issing 2008; James 2012: 6–7; Bellamy and Weale 2015: 259, 263). However, they believe the only escape from Hayek's trap is to risk being caught on the second horn by hastening political and fiscal integration, and shifting more sovereign authority to the EU level by the traditional means of increasing the powers of the EP, directly electing the Commission and weakening the role of state governments in the European Council. In sum, they advocate a shift from republican intergovernmentalism and demoicracy to a EU level democracy. They consider the depth of the crisis opens up an opportunity for political leaders to hazard a passionate appeal beyond national divisions to an ideal of pan-European solidarity grounded in a fair division of the costs and benefits of maintaining an integrated economy. Yet such a strategy seems more likely to compound the original error and complete the Hayekian entrapment. The 'constraining dissensus' towards further integration has grown across Europe (Hobolt and Tilley 2016), with right-wing Eurosceptical populist nationalist parties now commanding large minorities, and in some cases majorities, in many of the main creditor member states, including the two countries that have traditionally formed the vanguard of European unification, France and Germany. As the vote for Brexit indicated, even purely prudential appeals to economic self-interest only carry so much weight and may even be dismissed. True, certain left wing movements, such as Podemos and Syriza, have developed in the debtor states that envisage a more solidaristic and socially just EU. However, as the experience of the Syriza administration in Greece has graphically demonstrated, the electoral pressures in the creditor states operate precisely as Hayek anticipated, rendering the price of financial support the imposition of yet tighter fiscal controls on public spending and taxation.

This objection might be regarded as contingent and prudential rather than suggesting an inherent and principled weakness in the unionist argument. To suggest that a given strategy may be difficult to realise does not suggest it cannot or should not be realised. However, this type of argumentation confuses the various ideal views of the EU different people might hold with a legitimate view of the EU that people might be willing to agree on despite their disagreements. The broadly acceptable, and hence legitimate, view provides the context within which we might try and convince our fellow citizens to adopt our preferred ideal view. It is the legitimate view that leads individuals to regard themselves as citizens of the EU in the first place, and see it as deserving their support (Sangiovanni, forthcoming). A legitimate conception of the EU and the kind of policies it might pursue needs to be capable of securing widespread endorsement and to involve policies that could be plausibly implemented in current circumstances and that most people have good reason to support in the here and now. It cannot be partisan or utopian in the manner advocated by Van Parijis (2016) and rest on highly disputable assertions that no reasonable alternative exists or similarly debateable claims about the benefits to be gained in some imagined future. Such arguments may reflect a given ideal but they cannot provide a content-independent view of the nature and purpose of the EU that citizens might agree on despite their disagreements. As with the introduction of the Euro, a policy may be advanced by formally legitimate means and be achievable, yet still be a mistake. The mistake is ontological and not just instrumental, because, by overreaching the politically acceptable and undermining reasonable expectations, it has put into question the legitimacy of the EU itself. Ignoring the current demoicratic and heterogeneous character of the EU in favour of a putatively superior unified and homogenous future EU risks being similarly mistaken in just this sense. As such, it can only prove self-defeating, producing ineffective and inefficient polices that arouse increasingly vocal popular opposition that will threaten the legitimacy of not only of the EU's proposed new regime but also of its claims as a polity.

Fortunately, an alternative exists that requires neither fiscal nor political union and adopts instead the demoicratic logic of differentiated integration advocated here. The key problem of the Euro crisis was the linking of private to public finance so that states had to bail out the banks (Sandbu 2015). An endemic weakness of financial globalisation lies in inadequate regulation – precisely the sort of market failing that the EU should tackle. A banking union, combined with strict rules limiting concentrated holdings of capital bonds to prevent banks holding too much government debt, would effectively share risks between creditors and borrowers regardless of where they are geographically located (Eichengreen 2018).

At the same time, completing the banking union would allow fiscal policy to be returned to national governments by reducing the danger that fiscal mismanagement in one country could spread to others and potentially upset the banking system. If governments make bad decisions and overspend, they would need to restructure their debts rather than receiving a bailout from other states. A genuine European Monetary Fund would replace the ECB and European Commission as lender of last resort, able to ensure liquidity, providing for a European debt-restructuring programme. The fund could be overseen by the Interparliamentary Conference on Economic and Financial Governance of the European Union that was set up under Article 13 of the TSCG, giving the process of granting an emergency loan a demoicratic legitimacy it currently lacks (for a parallel scheme, see Hennette et al. 2017). The crucial element is that fiscal policy would not be quasi-constitutionalised through attempting to enforce discipline through a binding set of common spending rules. Even if further political integration allowed genuine budgetary powers to be given to the EP, such a policy would create a demoicratic deficit in not recognising the socio-economic, let alone the constitutional, heterogeneity of the EU. Returning such capacity to states would help them escape the first prong of the Hayekian trap by embedding market liberalism without the risk of becoming impaled on the second prong.

Pace Hayek, neither free trade nor openness to foreign direct investment need result in a lowering of state expenditure or intervention or a weakening of labour regulation (Hay 2007: 143–50). That only happens if the rules that shape these process are designed to produce these results, as has occurred through the market reinforcing negative integration imposed by the EU legal order (Rodrick 2011, ch. 3). Absent such conditions, a strong correlation actually operates in the opposite direction, with a robust positive association existing between economic openness to both trade and finance and state expenditure as a proportion of GDP (Rodrik 1996; Cooke and Noble 1998; Mosely 2003). In part, that results from democratic pressures towards compensating welfare measures that provide collective social insurance against the risks of depending on export markets. In part, it reflects the competitive economic advantages of having a highly skilled work force and a quality public infrastructure. However, for the EU to foster such possibilities requires the demoicratic reconnection and the resulting differentiated integration advocated in this book. Only then will global markets be effectively and equitably regulated in demoicratically legitimate, and as a result, mutually beneficial, ways (Rodrick 2011: 249–50, ch. 12).

Conclusion

This chapter has argued that social and economic heterogeneity, on the one side, and political and cultural heterogeneity, on the other, can render different categories of DI democratically legitimate. Democracy provides a fair and impartial process for the legitimate making of equitable collective decisions. However, the suitability of such a process assumes that all citizens have an equal stake in the collective decision and conceive themselves as a public capable of arguing from a shared set of public reasons. I have argued that, to the degree groups of citizens are heterogeneous and have unequal stakes in a collective decision, then one can expect instrumental differentiation, which reflects the proportionate degree of interest given groups may have in any policy. Likewise, to the extent groups have heterogeneous public cultures and feel they belong to distinct demoi, collective decision-making risks being partial. Such circumstances justify an asymmetric distribution of self-government between different member states and a number of exemptions typical of constitutional differentiation. Both types of heterogeneity will also produce legislative differentiation even when all adopt common policies but need to tailor them to reflect local conditions and partialities. All three forms of DI enable the moderation of the market liberalisation promoted by the EU through the rigorous pursuit of the four freedoms. At the member-state level, they allow for domestic regulation that takes into account the relevant social and economic differences and divergent preferences of national demoi. At the EU level, they allow departures from consensual decision-making and the use of majoritarian voting that facilitates the politicisation of EU policy making not just negatively, by Eurosceptic parties antagonistic to the very idea of the EU, but also positively, by pro-EU parties that see it as a means for supporting proactive domestic policies aimed at moderating globalisation to ensure its costs do not outstrip its benefits. It opens the way for a demoicratic constitution of the EU in which the peoples of Europe can reach fair terms of cooperation that derive mutual advantages from the equal recognition of their diversity and differences.

Conclusion: The Global Trilemma, the Future of the EU and Brexit

This book has argued that in a globalising world democratic states have compelling functional and moral reasons to cooperate and to create supranational organisations that resemble the EU in key respects. However, I have also contended that need not involve a transfer of democratic authority and sovereignty upwards to the supranational level. The normative and empirical requirements of an interdependent global order can be satisfied most appropriately and effectively through a form of what I have called cosmopolitan statism: that is, an association of states that govern the interactions between their respective *peoples* according to cosmopolitan norms, rather than considering all *individuals* across the globe – or even across Europe – as forming a single people. Within such an arrangement, democratic legitimacy needs to be provided in the form of a two-level game I have termed 'republican intergovernmentalism'. According to this approach, the decisions of governments and other political representatives and agencies at the supranational level must operate under the equal influence and control of their respective peoples at the domestic level, whilst recognising the obligation of all other associated states to operate similarly. The aim of such a decision-making structure is to avoid domination of either one state by another or by the supranational structures they create to regulate their mutual interrelations.

The *demoi*cratic logic of this two-level game entails that such an association needs to show equal concern and respect for the capacity for collective self-rule of its constituent peoples, supporting and sustaining and where necessary supplementing that capacity rather than substituting for it. Such an arrangement ensures that supranational institutions remain democratically connected to the peoples who have conferred competences on them. It works against a supranational democratic deficit by avoiding the creation of a domestic democratic deficit through treating such associations as mechanisms for retaining and enhancing, rather than losing, control at the national level.

If Part 1 outlined the general argument summarised above, Part 2 applied that argument in detail to the EU. Here I suggested that the EU possesses many features of such a cosmopolitan statist association of sovereign states, while many of its decision-making processes could be characterised as conforming to 'republican intergovernmentalism', or at least are capable of being plausibly developed in that direction. I contended against neo-functionalists that the social and cultural preconditions were lacking for a well performing democracy at the EU level while conceding that the current form of liberal intergovernmental bargaining was likewise suboptimal. I proposed changes, especially in the role played by national parliaments in EU decision-making, which could move intergovernmentalism in a more republican direction that might foster a demoicratic reconnection of EU institutions with the various peoples of Europe. I also argued that considerations of fairness, impartiality and equity justify the EU being characterised by a high degree of variable geometry, whereby the member states need not be uniformly integrated into all EU policy areas or adopt the same regulations.

The overarching aim of this account of the EU is to provide a structure that can realise 'unity with diversity', to cite an oft-quoted formula coined by the architects of the EU's ill-fated Constitutional Treaty, which dismally failed to achieve either. Bringing the argument for differentiated integration together with the previous argument for republican intergovernmental decision-making, I proposed that we should conceive EU law not as a legal constitution but as a political constitution, ultimately under the equal and several control of the member states. As such, the tendency of the Court of Justice to turn the rules of the single market into a uniformly binding economic constitution would be considerably constrained, as in practice it often has been. This proposal would also have important implications for the governance of the Euro zone, which has often been regarded – mistakenly in my view – as requiring yet more political and fiscal integration of a supranational kind to operate effectively. I also drew out the implications of this account for how we should understand the rights and duties of Union citizenship. Again, this has been misguidedly interpreted as destined to supplant national citizenship with a supra- and post-national form of citizenship. Instead, I argue that it provides a mechanism for the mutual recognition of different member state citizenship regimes, to which it is intimately connected. It embodies the ethos of cosmopolitan statism and reflects a political system of republican intergovernmentalism.

The overall argument can be seen as a response to Dani Rodrik's global trilemma (Rodrik 2011: xix, 200–5), which I outlined in the Introduction.

As I reported there, this trilemma consists of the difficulty of preserving national self-determination, democracy and globalisation – Rodrik suggests one of the three has to give way. That has led many to assume that democracy can only be combined with globalisation by shifting democratic authority above the nation state. However, the EU experience indicates such a shift is easier said than done, suggesting undermining national self-determination may leave us simply with globalisation. Yet, few would regard an unconstrained and unregulated globalisation as desirable. The alternative, advocated by Rodrik himself, addresses the trilemma through moderating globalisation in ways that retain scope for the national self-determination of different varieties of capitalism. That suggests the trilemma as stated is under described. Rather, the challenge for those wishing to retain political diversity and embed economic liberalism within social welfare systems, and thereby maintain the equal value of basic liberties for the citizens of all states, must be to combine all three so that each moderates the other. That is precisely the goal of the form of international governance advocated in this book.

As I noted in the Preface, this argument was not conceived as a response to Brexit. However, it does offer a political response to the claim of Leavers that by exiting the EU the UK could 'take back control'. As Sir Ivan Rogers remarked on resigning as the UK's representative to the EU (reported in Rogers 2018), free trade only happens through legal agreements, be they global, regional, bilateral or internal to a bloc. An association such as the EU provides the most developed structure that currently exists for ensuring such legal agreements and the regulations that result from them are negotiated and overseen in ways that treat all states equitably and respect their domestic democratic systems of authorisation and accountability. As I have suggested, this structure can undoubtedly be improved from a demoicratic perspective. However, the potential exists for such improvements. But outside such a structure, a single country carries significantly less clout and inevitably loses control, becoming a rule taker rather than a rule maker. The EU already allowed significant variable geometry for the UK to be a semi-detached member of the EU. Yet, as Ivan Rogers's notes, the UK's new status as a semi-attached non-member will greatly reduce its bargaining power and influence. Assertions of unilateral sovereignty cut both ways, and the EU has considerably more negotiating power than the UK and an understandable desire to maintain the integrity and legitimacy of the regulatory framework agreed by its members. Given the UK cannot avoid having a series of legal agreements with the EU governing much of what was covered by its earlier membership, it can be anticipated that any post-Brexit arrangements will favour the political and economic interests of the larger partner and involve losing much of the control the UK previously possessed as a member of the EU (Bellamy 2018).

None of the above denies that the EU requires reform to meet the requirements of republican intergovernmentalism and ensure the decision-making process, as well as the resulting agreements and their implementation, all avoid domination and show equal concern and respect and mutual recognition to the different peoples of the member states. As I acknowledged at the end of the last chapter, the greatest challenge in this regard remains the governance of the Euro. But it is not an insurmountable challenge, and an opportunity exists even here for strengthening rather than weakening inter-parliamentary influence and control of the ECB and banking regulations more generally, including the terms of any bail outs, while allowing a high degree of fiscal autonomy to the member states. In sum, like most pro-Europeans, I am sceptical of the legitimacy and efficacy of many features of the EU as currently organised while believing that inter-state cooperation of a kind made possible by an organisation such as the EU offers the only credible path for ensuring the interactions between states and their citizens operate in fair and non-dominating ways. This book constitutes a modest effort towards achieving that goal.

Bibliography

Cases Cited

European Court Cases

Case 120/78 (Cassis de Dijon) *Rewe-Zentral AG v Bundesmonopolverwaltung für Branntwein* [1979] ECR 649.

Case C-263/86, *Belgian State v René Humbel and Marie Thérèse Edel* [1988] ECR 5365.

Case C-370/90, *The Queen v Immigration Appeal Tribunal and Surinder Singh* [1992] ECR I-04265.

Case C-64/96 and C-65/96, *Land Nordrhein-Westfalen v Kari Uecker and Vera Jacquet v Land Nordrhein-Westfalen* [1997] ECR I-03171.

Case C-158/96, *Raymond Kohll v Union des caisses de maladie* [1998] ECR I-01831.

Case C-85/96, *María Martínez Sala v Freistaat Bayern* [1998] ECR I-02691.

Case C-157/99, *B.S.M Geraets-Smits v Stichting Ziekenfonds VGZ and H.T.M. Peerbooms v Stichting CZ Groep Zorgverzekeringen* [2001] ECR I-05473.

Case C-184/99, *Grzelczyk v Centre Public d'Aide Sociale d'Ottignies-Louvain-la-Neuve* [2001] ECR I-6193.

Case C-413/99, *Baumbast and R v Secretary of State for the Home Department* [2002] ECR I-07091.

Case C-148/02, *Carlos Garcia Avello v Belgian State* [2003] ECR I-11613.

Case C-405/01, *Marina Mercante Española v Administración del Estado* [2003] ECR I-10391.

Case C-385/99, *V.G. Müller-Fauré v Onderlinge Waarborgmaatschappij* [2003] ECRI-04509.

Case C-200/02, *Kunquian Catherine Zhu and Man Lavette Chen v Secretary of State for the Home Department* [2004] ECR I-09925.

Case C-138/02, *Brian Francis Collins v Secretary of State for Work and Pensions* [2004] ECR I-02703.

Case C-456/02, *Michel Trojani v Centre public d'aide sociale de Bruxelles* (CPAS) [2004] ECR I-07573.

Case C-147/03, *Commission of the European Communities v Republic of Austria* [2005] ECR I-05969.

Case C-372/04, *Yvonne Watts v Bedford Primary Care Trust and Secretary of State for Health* [2005] ECR I-04325.

Case C-76/05, *Herbert Schwarz and Marga Gootjes-Schwarz v Finanzamt Bergisch Gladbach* [2007] ECR I-06849.

Case C-319/06, *Commission v Luxembourg* [2008] ECR I-4323.

Case C-346/06, *Dirk Rüffert v Land Niedersachsen* [2008] ECR I-01989.

Case C-135/08, *Janko Rottman v Freistaat Bayern* [2010] ECR I-01449.

Case C-434/09, *Shirley McCarthy v Secretary of State for the Home Department* [2011] ECR I-03375.

Case C-34/09, *Gerardo Ruiz Zambrano v Office national de l'emploi (ONEm)* [2011] ECR I-01177.

Case C-83/11, *Secretary of State for the Home Department v Muhammad Sazzadur Rahman and Others* [2012] ECLI:EU: C:2012: 174.

Case C-40/11, *Yoshikazu Iida v Stadt Ulm* [2012] ECLI:EU: C:2012:691.

Case C–399/11 *Stefano Melloni v Ministerio Fiscal* EU:C:2013:107.

Case C-423/12, *Flora May Reyes v Migrationsverket* [2014].

Case C-140/12, *Pensionsversicherungsanstalt v Peter Brey* [2013].

Case C-333/13 Dano v Jobcenter Leipzig [2014].

Case C-67/14 *Alimanovic* [2015].

Case C-299/14 *García-Nieto and others* [2016].

Case C-308/14 *Commission v UK* [2016].

Case C-105/14, *Taricco* EU:C:2015:555.

Industrial Relations Law Reports

Case C-438/05, *International Transport Workers' Federation, Finnish Seamen's Union v Viking Line ABP* [2008] IRLR 143.

Case C-341/05, *Laval un Partneri Ltd v Svenska Byggnadsarbetareförbundet* [2008] IRLR 160.

National Constitutional Courts

Germany

German Federal Constitutional Court (BVerfG) Case No 2 BvL 52/71 *Internationale_ Handelsgesellschaft_mbH_v_ _Einfuhr-und _Vorratsstelle für_Getreide und Futtermittel_37 BVerfGE 271* (Solange I) [1974] 2 CMLR 540.

German Federal Constitutional Court (BVerfG) Case No 2 BvE 2/08, 30 June 2009. (Lisbon Judgment).

German Federal Constitutional Court (BVerfG) Case 2 BvR 1390/12, 12 September 2012. (European Stability Mechanism Treaty, Temporary Injunctions).

Portugal
Portuguese Constitutional Tribunal Acordão 187/2013.

References

Abizadeh, A. (2008). Democratic Theory and Border Coercion: No Right to Unilaterally Control Your Own Borders, *Political Theory*, 36(1): 37–65.

Adler-Nissen, R. (2016). The Vocal Euro-outsider: The UK in a Two-speed Europe, *Political Quarterly*, 87(2): 238–46.

Adonnino, P. et al. (1985). First report of the Adonnino Committee, Bull. EC Supp. 7/85.

(1988). Second report *A People's Europe*, Bull. EC Supp. 2/88.

Alter, K. (2001). *Establishing the Supremacy of European Law*, Oxford: Oxford University Press.

(2009). *The European Court's Political Power*, Oxford: Oxford University Press.

Archibugi, D. (1998). Principi di democrazia cosmopolita in D. Archibugi and D. Beetham (eds.), *Diritti umani e democrazia cosmopolita*, Milan: Feltrinelli, pp. 66–121.

(2008). *The Global Commonwealth of Citizens: Toward Cosmopolitan Democracy*, Princeton, NJ: Princeton University Press.

Arendt, H. (1958). *The Origins of Totalitarianism*, new edn., Orlando, FL: Harcourt Brace.

Aristotle. (1996). *The Politics and the Constitution of Athens*, ed. S. Everson, Cambridge: Cambridge University Press.

Balibar, E. (2004). *We the Peoples of Europe: Reflections on Transnational Europe*, Princeton, NJ: Princeton University Press.

Barbalet, J. (1988). *Citizenship: Rights, Struggle and Class Inequality*, London: Open University Press.

Barker, A. (2017). Brexit: EU and UK Battle Over 'An Accession in Reverse', *Financial Times*, 3 December. www.ft.com/content/e4824a0a-d373-11e7-8c9a-d9c0a5c8d5c9.

Barroso, J. (2012). European Commission Press Release, 1 September, http://e uropa.eu/rapid/press-release_IP-12-930_en.htmp.

Barry, B. (1999). Statism and Nationalism: A Cosmopolitan Critique in I. Shapiro and L. Brilmayer (eds.), *Nomos: Global Justice*, New York: New York University Press., pp. 12–66.

Bartolini, S. (2005). *Restructuring Europe: Centre Formation, System Building and Political Restructuring between the Nation State and the European Union*, Oxford: Oxford University Press.

(2006). Should the Union Be 'Politicised'? Prospects and Risks. *Politics: The Right or the Wrong Sort of Medicine for the EU?* Notre Europe, Policy Paper No. 19.

Bauböck, R. (2007). Stakeholder Citizenship and Transnational Political Participation: A Normative Evaluation of External Voting, *Fordham Law Review*, 75(5): 2393–448.

(2015). Morphing the Demos into the Right Shape. Normative Principles for Enfranchising Resident Aliens and Expatriate Citizens, *Democratization*, 22 (5): 820–39.

(2018). *Democratic Inclusion*, Manchester: Manchester University Press.

Beaud, O. (1995). La Fédération entre l'état et l'empire in B. Théret (ed.), *L'État, la finance et le sociale*, Paris: La Decouverte, pp. 282–304.

Beitz, C. (1983). Cosmopolitan Ideals and National Sentiment, *Journal of Philosophy*, 80(10): 591–600.

(1990). *Political Equality: An Essay in Democratic Theory*, Princeton, NJ: Princeton University Press.

(1994). Cosmopolitan Liberalism and the State System in C. Brown (ed.), *Political Structuring in Europe*, London: Routledge, pp. 119–32.

(1998). International Relations, Philosophy of in E. Craig (ed.), *The Routledge Encyclopaedia of Philosophy*, 10 vols, London: Routledge, p. 831.

Bellamy, R. (1999). *Liberalism and Pluralism: Towards a Politics of Compromise*, London: Routledge.

(2001). The 'Right to have Rights': Citizenship Practice and the Political Constitution of the EU in R. Bellamy and A. Warleigh (eds.), *Citizenship and Governance in the European Union*, London: Continuum, pp. 41–70.

(2003). Sovereignty, Post-Sovereignty and Pre-Sovereignty: Reconceptualising the State, Rights and Democracy in the EU in N. Walker (ed.), *Sovereignty in Transition*, Oxford: Hart, pp. 167–90.

(2004). Introduction: The Making of Modern Citizenship, in R. Bellamy, D. Castiglione, and E. Santoro (eds.), *Lineages of European Citizenship*, Basingstoke: Palgrave, pp. 1–21.

(2006). Still in Deficit: Rights, Regulation and Democracy in the EU, *European Law Journal*, 12(6): 725–42.

(2007). *Political Constitutionalism: A Republican Defence of the Constitutionality of Democracy*, Cambridge: Cambridge University Press.

(2008a). The Democratic Constitution: Why Europeans Should Avoid American Style Judicial Review, *European Political Science*, 7(1): 9–20.

(2008b). Evaluating Union Citizenship: Belonging, Rights and Participation within the EU, *Citizenship Studies*, 12(6): 597–611.

(2008c). *Citizenship: A Very Short Introduction*, Oxford: Oxford University Press.

(2010). Democracy without Democracy?: Can the EU's Democratic 'Outputs' Be Separated from the Democratic 'Inputs' Provided by Competitive Parties and Majority Rule?, *Journal of European Public Policy*, 17(1): 2–19.

(2012a). Rights as Democracy, *Critical Review of International Social and Political Philosophy*, 15(4): 449–71.

(2012b). The Liberty of the Moderns: Civic and Market Freedom in the EU, *Global Constitutionalism: Human Rights, Democracy, Rule of Law*, 1 (1): 41–72.

(2013). An Ever Closer Union of Peoples: Republican Intergovernmentalism, Demoi-cracy and Representation in the EU, *Journal of European Integration*, 35(5): 499–516.

(2014). The Democratic Legitimacy of International Human Rights Conventions: Political Constitutionalism and the European Convention on Human Rights, *European Journal of International Law*, 25(4): 1019–42.

(2015). A Duty-Free Europe? What's Wrong with Kochenov's Account of EU Citizenship Rights, *European Law Journal*, 21(4): 558–65.

(2016). Which Republicanism, Whose Freedom?, Review Essay on P. Pettit, *The People's Terms, Political Theory*, 44 (5): 669–78.

(2018). Losing Control: Brexit and the Demoi-cratic Disconnect in U. Staiger and B. Martill (eds.), *Brexit and Beyond: Rethinking the Futures of Europe*, London: UCL Press, pp. 222–7.

Bellamy, R. and Castiglione, D. (2003). Legitimising the Euro-polity and Its Regime: The Normative Turn in EU Studies, *European Journal of Political Theory*, 2(1): 7–34.

(2004). Debate: Lacroix's European Constitutional Patriotism: A Response, *Political Studies*, 52(1): 187–93.

(2013). Three Models of Democracy, Political Community and Representation in the EU, *Journal of European Public Policy*, 20(2): 206–23.

(2019). *From Maastricht to Brexit: Citizenship, Constitutionalism and Democracy in Europe's Mixed Polity*, London: Rowman and Littlefield/ ECPR Press.

Bellamy, R. and Lacey, J. (2018). Balancing the Rights and Duties of Union and National Citizenship: A Demoicratic Approach, *Journal of European Public Policy*, 25(10): 1403–1421.

Bellamy, R. and Kröger, S. (2014). Domesticating the Democratic Deficit? The Role of National Parliaments in the EU's System of Governance, *Parliamentary Affairs*, 67(2): 437–57.

Bellamy, R. and Weale, A. (2015). Political Legitimacy and European Monetary Union: Contracts, Constitutionalism and the Normative Logic of Two-Level Games, *Journal of European Public Policy*, 22(2): 257–74.

Beitz, C. (1979). *Political Theory and International Relations*, Princeton, NJ: Princeton University Press.

Benhabib, S. (2002). Transformations of Citizenship: The Case of Contemporary Europe, *Government and Opposition*, 37(4): 439–65.

(2004). *The Rights of Others: Aliens, Residents and Citizens*, Cambridge: Cambridge University Press.

(2007). Twilight of Sovereignty or the Emergence of Cosmopolitan Norms? Rethinking Citizenship in Volatile Times, *Citizenship Studies*, 11(1): 19–36.

(2008). *Another Cosmopolitanism*, Oxford: Oxford University Press.

Besson, S. (2006). Deliberative Demoi-cracy in the European Union. Towards the Deterritorialization of Democracy, in S. Besson and J.L. Martí (eds.), *Deliberative Democracy and Its Discontents*, Aldershot: Ashgate, pp. 181–214.

Betts, A. (2013). *Survival Migration: Failed Governance and the Crisis of Development*, Ithaca, NY: Cornell University Press.

Beyers, J. and Kerremans B. (2007). Critical resource dependencies and the Europeanization of domestic interest groups, *Journal of European Public Policy*, 14(3): 460–48.

Blake, M. (2013). We Are All Cosmopolitans Now in G. Brock (ed.), *Cosmopolitanism versus Non-Cosmpolitanism*, Oxford: Oxford University Press, pp. 35–54.

Boeri, T., McCormick, B., and Hanson, G.H. (2002). *Immigration Policy and the Welfare System: A Report for the Fondazione Rodolfo Debendetti*, Oxford: Oxford University Press.

Bohman, J. (1996). *Public Deliberation*, Cambridge, MA: MIT Press.

(2004a). Republican Cosmopolitanism, *Journal of Political Philosophy*, 12(3): 336–32.

(2004b). Constitution Making and Institutional Innovation: The European Union and Transnational Governance, *European Journal of Political Theory*, 3(3): 315–37.

(2005). From *Demos* to *Demoi*: Democracy Across Borders, *Ratio Juris*, 18(3): 293–314.

(2007). *Democracy across Borders: From Demos to Demoi*, Cambridge, MA: MIT Press.

Bolleyer, N. and Reh, C. (2012). EU legitimacy revisited: the normative foundations of a multilevel polity, *Journal of European Public Policy*, 19(4): 472–90.

Bordo, M.D. and Jonung, L. (2003). The Future of EMU: What Does the History of Monetary Unions Tell Us? in F.H. Capie and G.E. Wood (eds.), *Monetary Unions: Theory, History, Public Choice*, London and New York: Routledge, pp. 42–69.

Börzel, T.A. (2016). From EU Governance of Crisis to Crisis of EU Governance: Regulatory Failure, Redistributive Conflict and Eurosceptic Publics, *Journal of Common Market Studies*, 54(1): 8–31.

Boxill, B. (1987). Global Equality of Opportunity and National Integrity, *Social Philosophy and Policy*, 5(1): 143–68.

Brighouse, H. and Fleurbaey, M. (2010). Democracy and Proportionality, *Journal of Political Philosophy* 18.2: 137–55.

Brittan, S. (1975). The Economic Contradictions of Democracy. *British Journal of Political Science*, 5(2), 129–59.

Bromley, S., Hirst, P., and Thompson, G. (2009). *Globalisation in Question*, 3rd edn., Cambridge: Polity Press.

Brubaker, R. (1996). *Nationalism Reframed: Nationhood and the National Question in the New Europe*, Cambridge: Cambridge University Press.

Brunkhorst, H. (2002). *Solidarität -Von der Bürgerfreundschaft zur globalen Rechtsgenossenschaft*, Frankfurt: Suhrkamp Verlag.

Bruter, M. (2005). Developments in the 'Old' Member States, *Journal of Common Market Studies*, 43(1): 147–62.

Buchanan, A. (2000). Rawls's Law of Peoples: Rules for a Vanished Westphalian World, *Ethics*, 110(4): 697–721.

Buchanan, A. (2002). `Political legitimacy and democracy, *Ethics*, 112(4): 689–719.

(2004). *Justice, Legitimacy and Self-Determination*, New York: Oxford University Press.

Burgess, M. (2000). *Federalism and the EU*, London: Routledge.

Burke, E. (1774). Speech to the Electors of Bristol in I. Hampshire-Monk (ed.), *The Political Philosophy of Edmund Burke*, Harlow: Longman (1987), pp. 108–10.

(1794). Speech on the Impeachment of Warren Hastings in I. Kramnick (ed), *The Portable Edmund Burke*, Harmondsworth: Penguin Books (1999), pp. 388–408.

Burns, T, Jaeger, C., Liberatore, A., Meny, Y., and Nanz, P. (2000). *The Future of Parliamentary Democracy: Transition and Challenge in European Governance* (Green Paper prepared for the Conference of the European Union), AS/D.

Cabrera, L. (2004). *Political Theory of Global Justice: A Cosmopolitan Case for the World State*, London: Routledge.

Caney, S. (2001). Cosmopolitan Justice and Equalizing Opportunities, *Metaphilosophy*, 32(1&2): 113–34.

(2005). *Justice beyond Borders: A Global Political Theory*, Oxford: Oxford University Press.

Canovan, M. (1998). *Nationhood and Political Theory*, Cheltenham: Edward Elgar.

Caporoso, J.A. and Tarrow, S. (2008). Polanyi in Brussels: European Institutions and the Embedding of Markets in Society. Paper presented at APSA 2008 annual meeting, Boston, MA.

Carens, J. (1987). Aliens and Citizens: The Case for Open Borders, *Review of Politics*, 49(2): 251–73.

Carens, J. (2000). *Culture, Citizenship and Community*, Oxford: Oxford University Press.

Carlin, W. (1998). The New East German Economy: Problems of Transition, Unification and Institutional Mis-match, *German Politics* 7(3): 14–32.

(2015). Institutions, Integration and Divergence: Lessons from Europe. Max Weber Lecture 17 June 2015, www.youtube.com/watch?v=DYbUQdE-ETY.

Carter, I. (2008). How Are Power and Unfreedom Related? in C. Laborde and J. Maynor (eds.), *Republicanism and Political Theory*, Oxford: Blackwell, pp. 58–82.

Chalmers, D; Jachtenfuchs, M., and Joerges, C. (eds.). (2016). *The End of the Eurocrat's Dream*, Cambridge: Cambridge University Press.

Cheneval, F. (2008). Multilateral Democracy: The Original Position, *Journal of Social Philosophy*, 39(1): 42–61.

(2011). *The Government of the Peoples: On the Idea and Principles of Multilateral Democracy*, New York: Palgrave Macmillan.

Cheneval, F. and Nicolaïdis, K. (2016). The Social Construction of Demoicracy in the European Union. *European Journal of Political Theory*, OnlineFirst. DOI: 10.1177/1474885116654696.

Cheneval, F. and Schimmelfennig, F. (2013). The Case for Demoicracy in the European Union, *Journal of Common Market Studies*, 51(2): 334–50.

Christiano, T. (2006). A Democratic Theory of Territory and Some Puzzles about Global Democracy, *Journal of Social Philosophy* 37(1): 81–107.

(2008). *The Constitution of Equality*, Oxford: Oxford University Press.

(2010). Democratic Legitimacy and International Institutions in S. Besson and J. Tasioulis (eds.), *The Philosophy of International Law*, Oxford: Oxford University Press, pp. 119–37.

(2011a). An Instrumental Argument for a Human Right to Democracy, *Philosophy & Public Affairs*, 39(2): 142–76.

(2011b). Is Democratic Legitimacy Possible for International Institutions? in D. Archibugi, M. Koenig-Archibugi, and R. Marchetti (eds.), *Global Democracy: Normative and Empirical Perspectives*, Cambridge: Cambridge University Press, pp. 69–95.

(2012). The Legitimacy of International Institutions in A. Marmor (ed.), *The Routledge Companion to Philosophy of Law*, New York: Routledge, pp. 380–93.

(2015). Legitimacy and the International Trade Regime, *San Diego Law Review*, 52: 981–1012.

(2016). Replies to David Álvarez, David Lefkowitz, and Michael Blake, *Law, Ethics and Politics*, 4: 221–36.

Christiansen, T. (2016). After the Spitzenkandidaten: Fundamental Change in the EU's political system?, *West European Politics*, 39:5, 992–1010.

Cohen, G.A. (2003). Facts and Principles, *Philosophy & Public Affairs* 31(3): 211–45.

Cohen, J. (2012). *Globalization and Sovereignty*, Cambridge: Cambridge University Press.

Cohen, J. and Sabel, C. (2005). Global Democracy, *International Law and Politics*, 37: 763–97.

Conant, L. (2002). *Justice Contained: Law and Politics in the European Union*, Cornell: Cornell University Press.

Constant, B. (1813). *De l'esprit de conquete et de l'usurpation*, Paris: Normant et Nicolle.

Cooke, W.N. and Noble, D.S. (1998). Industrial Relations Systems and US Foreign Direct investment Abroad, *British Journal of Industrial Relations*, 36(4): 581–609.

Cooper, I. (2013). Bicameral or Tricameral? National Parliaments and Representative Democracy in the European Union. *Journal of European Integration* 35(5): 531–46.

(2016). The Politicization of Interparliamentary Relations in the EU: Constructing and Contesting the 'Article 13 Conference' on Economic Governance, *Comparative European Politics*, 14(2): 196–214.

Coppel, J. and O'Neill, A. (1992). The European Court of Justice: Taking Rights Seriously?, *Common Market Law Review*, 29: 669–92.

Council Directive 2004/38/EC 29 April 2004 on the right of citizens of the Union and their family members to move and reside freely within the territory of the Member States. Available at http://eur-lex.europa.eu/LexUriServ/LexUriSe rv.do?uri=OJ:L:2004:158:0077:0123:en:PDF.

Costa, M. V. (2016). Republican Liberty and Border Controls, *Critical Review of International Social and Political Philosophy*, 19(4): 400–15.

Costa, O. and Magnette, P. (2003). The EU as a Consociation: A Methodologial Assessment, *West European Politics*, 26(3): 1–18.

Cram, L. (2009). Introduction: Banal Europeanism: European Union Identity and National Identities in Synergy, *Nations and Nationalism*, 15(1): 101–8.

Curtin, D. (1993). The Constitutional Structure of the Union: A Europe of Bits and Pieces, *Common Market Law Review*, 30:17–69.

(2014). Challenging Executive Dominance in European Democracy, *Modern Law Review*, 77(1): 1–32.

Dahl, R.A. (1989). *Democracy and Its Critics*, New Haven and London: Yale University Press.

(1998). *On Democracy*, New Haven and London: Yale University Press.

(1999), Can International Organisations Be Democratic? A Skeptic's View in I. Shapiro and C. Hacker-Cordón (eds.), *Democracy's Edges*, Cambridge: Cambridge University Press, pp. 19–36.

(2001). *How Democratic Is the American Constitution?* New Haven, CT: Yale University Press.

Dehousse, R. (2003). La méthode communautaire a-t-elle encore un avenir?, *Mélanges en hommage à Jean-Victor Louis*, 1(5): 95–107, Bruxelles: Presses de l'ULB.

de Burca, G. and Scott, J. (eds.). (2000). *Constitutional Change in the EU: From Uniformity to Flexibility*, Oxford: Hart Publishing.

de Schutter, H. and Ypi, L. (2015). Mandatory Citizenship for Immigrants, *British Journal of Political Science*, 45(2): 235–51.

De Vries, C. (2018). *Euroscepticism and the Future of European Integration*. Oxford: Oxford University Press.

de Witte, B. (1991). Community Law and National Constitutional Values, *Legal Issues of European Integration*, 2: 1–22.

(2005). Regional Autonomy, Cultural Diversity and European Integration: The Experience of Spain and Belgium in S. Ortino, M. Zagar and V. Mastny (eds.), *The Changing face of federalism. Institutional Reconfiguration in Europe from East to West*. Manchester: Manchester University Press, pp. 202–25.

de Witte, F. (2016). Freedom of Movement Under Attack: Is It Worth Defending as the Core of EU Citizenship. EUDO Blog, Available at: http://eudo-citizenship.eu/commentaries/citizenship-forum/1586-freedom-of-movement-under-attack-is-it-worth-defending-as-the-core-of-eu-citizenship.

Duff, A. (2011). *Federal Union Now*, London: The Federal Trust.

Eichengreen, B. (2018). *The Populist Temptation Economic Grievance and Political Reaction in the Modern Era*, Oxford: Oxford University Press.

Eleftheriadis, P. (2007). The Idea of a European Constitution, *Oxford Journal of Legal Studies*, 27(1): 1–21.

Eriksen, E.O. (2009). *The Unfinished Democratization of Europe*, Oxford: Oxford University Press.

Eriksen, E.O. and Fossum, J.E. (2004). Europe in Search of Legitimacy: Strategies of Legitimation Assessed, *International Political Science Review*, 25(4): 435–59.

Estlund, D. (2014). Utopophobia, *Philosophy & Public Affairs*, 42(2): 113–34.

European Commission. (2001). *European Governance. A White Paper*, Brussels: Commission of the European Commission (2001).

(2007). Open Method of Coordination. *Europa Glossary*, http:// 18uropa.eu/s cadplus/glossary/open_method_coordination_en.htm.

(2014). Evaluation of the Impact of the Free Movement of EU Citizens at Local Level. Final Report. January 2014, Brussels.

(2014). Press Release. European Commission Upholds Free Movement of People. http://europa.eu/rapid/press-release_MEMO-14-9_en.htm.

(2015). *Standard Eurobarometer 83*, Spring, http://ec.europa.eu/public_opi nion/index_en.htm.

(2017). White Paper on the Future of Europe. COM(2017) 2025 of 1 March 2017.

(2018). Eurostat GDP/capita 2017. https://ec.europa.eu/eurostat/statistics-explained/index.php/GDP_per_capita,_consumption_per_capita_and_pric e_level_indices#Relative_volumes_of_GDP_per_capita.

Everson, M. (1995). The Legacy of the Market Citizen in G. More and J. Shaw (eds.), *New Legal Dynamics of European Union*, Oxford: Clarendon Press, pp. 73–89.

Fabbrini, S. (2010). *Compound Democracies: Why the United States and Europe Are Becoming Similar*, Oxford: Oxford University Press.

Favell, A. (2008). *Eurostars and Eurocities*, Oxford: Blackwell.

Ferry, J. H. (1992). Une 'philosophie' de la communaute in J.H. Ferry and P. Thibaud (eds.), *Discussion sur l'Europe*, Paris: Calmann-Levy, pp. 127–212.

Ferrera, M. (2014). Social Solidarity after the Crisis, *Constellations*, 21(2): 222–38.

Finer, S. (ed.). (1995). *Comparing Constitutions*, Oxford: Clarendon Press.

Fligstein, N. (2008). *Euroclash: The EU, European Identity and the Future of Europe*, Oxford: Oxford University Press.

Flikschuh, K. (2010). Kant's Sovereignty Dilemma: A Contemporary Analysis, *Journal of Political Philosophy*, 18(4): 469–93.

Follesdal, A. and Hix, S. (2006). Why There Is a Democratic Deficit: A Reply to Majone and Moravcsik, *Journal of Common Market Studies*, 44(3): 533–62.

Forsyth, M. (1981). *Unions of States*, Leicester: Leicester University Press.

Friedrich, D. and Kröger, S. (2013). Democratic Representation in the EU: Two Kinds of Subjectivity, *Journal of European Public Policy*, 20(2): 171–89.

Friedman, D. (2014). *The Machinery of Freedom*, 3rd edn., New York: Chu Hartley.

Ganghof, S. and Genschel, P. (2008). Taxation and Democracy in the EU, *Journal of European Public Policy*, 15(1): 58–77.

Gellner, E. (1983). *Nations and Nationalism*, Ithaca: Cornell University Press.

Genschel, P. and Jachtenfuchs, M. (2016). More Integration, Less Federation: The European Integration of Core State Powers, *Journal of European Public Policy*, 23(1): 42–59.

George, S. (1991). *Policy and Politics in the European Community*, Oxford: Oxford University Press.

Giddens, A. (2014). *A Turbulent and Mighty Continent: What Future for Europe?*, Cambridge: Polity Press.

Gilpin, R. (1987). *The Political Economy of International Relations*, Princeton, NJ: Princeton University Press.

Goodin, R.E. (1988). What Is So Special about Our Fellow Countrymen?, *Ethics*, 98(4): 663–86.

Gott, C. and Johnston, K. (2002). *Migrant Population in the UK: Fiscal Effects*, London: Great Britain Home Office.

Greenfield, L. (1992). *Nationalism: Five Roads to Modernity*, Cambridge, MA: Harvard University Press.

Grimm, D. (1995). Does Europe Need a Constitution?, *European Law Journal*, 1 (3): 282–302.

(2016). *Constitutionalism: Past, Present, Future*, Oxford: Oxford University Press.

(2017). *The Constitution of European Democracy*, Oxford: Oxford University Press.

Haas, E. (1958). *The Uniting of Europe: Political, Social and Economic Forces 1950–1957*, Stanford: Stanford University Press.

Habermas, J. (1984, 1987). *Theory of Communicative Action*, 2 vols, Cambridge, MA: MIT Press.

(1992). Citizenship and National Identity: Some Reflections on the Future of Europe, *Praxis International*, 12(1): 1–19.

(1996). *Between Facts and Norms*, Cambridge: Polity Press.

(1999). *The Inclusion of the Other*, Cambridge: Polity Press.

(2000). *The Postnational Constellation*, Cambridge: Polity Press.

(2001). Why Europe Needs a Constitution, *New Left Review*, 11(September-October): 4–26.

(2012). *The Crisis of the European Union: A Response*, Cambridge: Polity Press.

(2015). Democracy in Europe: Why the Development of the EU into a Transnational Democracy Is Necessary and How It Is Possible, *European Law Journal*, 21(4): 546–57.

Hale, T. and Koenig-Archibugi, M. (2016). Are Europeans Ready for a More Democratic European Union? New Evidence on Preference Heterogeneity, Polarisation and Crosscuttingness, *European Journal of Political Research*, 55 (2): 225–45.

Hall, P.A. and Soskice, D.W. (2001). (eds.), *Varieties of Capitalism: The Institutional Foundations of Capitalism*, Oxford: Oxford University Press.

Haltern, U.R., Mayer F.C., and Weiler, J.H.H. (1995). European Democracy and Its Critique in J. Haywood (ed.), *The Crisis of Representation in Europe*, New York: Frank Cass, pp. 4–39.

Hamilton, A., Madison, J., and Jay, J. ('Publius') (2003 [1778]). *The Federalist*, ed. T. Ball, Cambridge: Cambridge University Press.

Hartog, J. and Zorlu, A. (2005). The Effect of Immigration on Wages in Three European Countries, *Journal of Population Economics*, 18(1): 113–51.

Hay, C. (2007). *Why We Hate Politics*, Cambridge: Polity Press.

Hayek F.A. (1948 [1939]). The Economic Conditions of Interstate Federalism in F.A. Hayek (ed.), *Individualism and Economic Order*, Chicago, IL: University of Chicago Press, pp. 255–72.

(1960). *The Constitution of Liberty*, Chicago, IL: University of Chicago Press.

Held, D. (1995). *Democracy and the Global Order: From the Modern State to Cosmopolitan Governance*, Cambridge: Polity Press.

Hennette, S., Piketty, T., Sacriste, G., and Vauchez, A. (2017). *Pour un Traité de Democratisation de l'europe*, Paris: Seuil.

Héritier, A. (1999). *Policy-Making and Diversity in Europe: Escape from Deadlock*, Cambridge: Cambridge University Press.

Hinsley, F.H. (1986). *Sovereignty*, 2nd edn., Cambridge: Cambridge University Press.

Hirschl, R. and Rosevear, E. (2011). Constitutional Law Meets Comparative Politics: Socio-economic Rights and Political Realities in T. Campbell, K.D. Ewing and A. Tomkins (eds.), *The Legal Protection of Rights: Sceptical Essays*, Oxford: Oxford University Press, pp. 207–28.

Hix, S. (2008). *What's Wrong with the European Union and How to Fix It*, Cambridge: Polity Press.

Hix, S. and Marsh, M. (2011). Second-Order Effects Plus Pan-European Political Swings: An Analysis of European Parliament Elections Across Time, *Electoral Studies* 30(1): 4–15.

Hobolt, S.B. and Tilley, J. (2016). Fleeing the Centre: The Rise of Challenger Parties in the Aftermath of the Euro Crisis, *West European Politics*, 39(5): 971–91.

Hobbes, T. (1651). *The Leviathan*, ed. R. Tuck, Cambridge: Cambridge University Press, 1996.

Hooghe, L. and Marks, G. (2009). A Postfunctionalist Theory of European Integration: From Permissive Consensus to Constraining Dissensus, *British Journal of Political Science*, 39(1): 1–23.

Hoffman, S. and Keohane, O. (1991). Institutional Change in Europe in the 1980s in Hoffman and Keohane (eds.), *The New European Community: Decision Making and Institutional Change*, Boulder, CO: Westview Press, pp. 1–39.

Holmes, S. (1993). *The Anatomy of Antiliberalism*, Cambridge, MA: Harvard University Press.

Honoré, T. (1993). The Dependence of Morality on Law, *Oxford Journal of Legal Studies*, 13(1): 1–17.

Ingram, A. (1996). Constitutional Patriotism, *Philosophy and Social Criticism*, 22 (6): 1–18.

Irti, N. (2005). *Nichilismo giuridico*, Rome: Laterza.

Isiksel, T. (2016). *Europe's Functional Constitution: A Theory of Constitutionalism beyond the State*, Oxford: Oxford University Press.

Issing, O. (2008). *The Birth of the Euro*, Cambridge: Cambridge University Press.

Jaklic, J. (2014). *Constitutional Pluralism in the EU*, Oxford: Oxford University Press.

James, H. (2012). *Making the European Monetary Union: The Role of the Committee of Central Bank Governors and the Origins of the European Central Bank.* Cambridge, MA: The Belknap Press.

Jančić, D. (2012). The Barroso Initiative: Window Dressing or Democracy Boost?, *Utrecht Law Review*, 8(1): 78–91.

Jensen, C.B. and Slapin, J.B. (2012). Institutional Hokey-Pokey: The Politics of Multispeed Integration in the European Union, *Journal of European Public Policy*, 19(6): 779–95.

Joerges, C. (2010). *Rechtsstaat* and Social Europe: How a Classical Tension Resurfaces in the European Integration Process, *Comparative Sociology*, 9: 65–85.

Jones, C. (1999). *Global Justice*, Oxford: Oxford University Press.

Jones, R.J.B. (1993). The Economic Agenda in G. Wyn Rees (ed.), *International Politics in Europe: The New Agenda*, London and New York: Routledge, pp. 87–110.

(1995a). The United Nations and the International Political System in D. Bourantonis and J. Weiner (eds.), *The United Nations in the New World Order: The World Organization at Fifty*, Basingstoke: Macmillan, pp. 19–40.

(1995b). *Globalisation and Interdependence in the International Political Economy: Rhetoric and Reality*, London and New York: Pinter.

Kant, I. (1781, 1787). *Critique of Pure Reason*, ed. P. Guyer and A.W. Wood, Cambridge: Cambridge University Press (1999).

(1796). *Perpetual Peace: A Philosophical Sketch* in *Political Writings*, ed. H. Reiss, Cambridge: Cambridge University Press (1991), pp. 93–130.

(1797). *The Metaphysics of Morals* in *Political Writings*, ed. H. Reiss, Cambridge: Cambridge University Press (1991), pp. 131–75.

Karlas, J. (2012). National Parliamentary Control of EU Affairs: Institutional Design after Enlargement, *West European Politics*, 35(5): 1095–113.

Kelemen R.D. (2016). On the Unsustainability of Constitutional Pluralism. European Supremacy and the Survival of the Eurozone, *Maastricht Journal of European and Comparative Law*, XXIII(1): 136–50.

(2017). Europe's Other Democratic Deficit, *Government and Opposition*, 52(2): 211–38.

Keohane, R., Macedo, S., and Moravcsik, A. (2009). Democracy-Enhancing Multilateralism, *International Organization*, 63(1): 1–31.

King, D.S. (1987). *The New Right: Politics, Markets and Citizenship*, Basingstoke: Macmillan.

Kleingeld, P. (2004). Approaching *Perpetual Peace*: Kant's Defense of a League of States and His Ideal of a World Federation, *Journal of European Philosophy*, 12: 304–25.

Kochenov, D. (2009). *Ius Tractum* of Many Faces: European Citizenship and the Difficult Relationship between Status and Rights, *Columbia Journal of European Law*, 15(2): 169–234.

(2011). A Real European Citizenship: A New Jurisdiction Test: A Novel Chapter in the Development of the Union in Europe, *Columbia Journal of European Law*, 18(1): 55–109.

2013). The Essence of EU Citizenship Emerging from the Last Ten Years of Academic Debate: Beyond the Cherry Blossoms and the Moon?, *International and Comparative Law Quarterly*, 62(1): 97–136.

(2014). EU Citizenship without Duties, *European Law Journal*, 20(4): 482–98.

Koenig-Archibugi, M. (2011). Is Global Democracy Possible?, *European Journal of International Relations*, 17(3): 519–42.

Kohler-Koch, B. (2011). Civil Society and EU Democracy: 'Astroturf' Representation?, *Journal of European Public Policy*, 17(1): 100–16.

Kölliker, A. (2001). Bringing Together or Driving Apart the Union? Towards a Theory of Differentiated Integration, *West European Politics*, 24(4): 125–51.

Koopmans, R. (2007). Who Inhabits the European Public Sphere? Winners and Losers, Supporters and Opponents in Europeanised Political Debates, *European Journal of Political Research* 46: 183–210.

Kostakopoulou, D. (2007). European Union Citizenship: Writing the Future, *European Law Journal*, 13(5): 623–46.

(2008). *The Future Governance of Citizenship*, Cambridge: Cambridge University Press.

Kramer, M. (2008). Liberty and Domination in C. Laborde and J. Maynor (eds.), *Republicanism and Political Theory*, Oxford: Blackwell, pp. 34–57.

Kriesi, H. (2016). The Politicization of European Integration, *Journal of Common Market Studies*, 54(S1): 32–47.

Kröger, S. (2007). The End of Democracy as We Know It? The Legitimacy Deficits of Bureaucratic Social Policy Governance, *Journal of European Integration*, 29(5): 565–82.

(2016). *Europeanised or European?: Representation by Civil Society Organisations in EU Policy Making*, Colchester: ECPR Press.

Kröger S. and Bellamy, R. (2016). Beyond a Constraining Dissensus: The Role of National Parliaments in Domesticating and Normalising the Politicization of European Integration, *Comparative European Politics*, 14(2), pp. 131–53.

Kröger S. and Friedrich, D. (2013). Democratic Representation in the EU: Two Kinds of Subjectivity, *Journal of European Public Policy*, 20(2): 171–89.

Kukathas, C. (2003). Immigration in H. LaFollette (ed.), *The Oxford Handbook of Practical Ethics*, Oxford: Oxford University Press, pp. 567–90.

Kumm, M. (2009). The Cosmopolitan Turn in Constitutionalism: On the Relationship between Constitutionalism in and beyond the State in J.L. Dunoff and J.P. Tractman (eds.), *Ruling the World? Constitutionalism, International Law, and Global Governance*, Cambridge: Cambridge university Press, pp. 258–324.

Kymlicka, W. (1989). *Liberalism, Community and Culture*, Oxford: Oxford University Press.

(1995). *Multicultural Citizenship: A Liberal Theory of Minority Rights*, Oxford: Oxford University Press.

(1999). Citizenship in an Era of Globalization: A Commentary on Held in C. Hacker-Cordón and I. Shapiro (eds.), *Democracy's Edges*. Cambridge: Cambridge University Press, pp. 112–26.

(2001). *Politics in the Vernacular: Nationalism, Multiculturalism and Citizenship*, Oxford: Oxford University Press.

Laborde, C. (2002). From Constitutional to Civic Patriotism, *British Journal of Political Science*, 32(4): 591–612.

Laborde, C. and Ronzoni, M. (2015). What Is a Free State? Republican Internationalism and Globalisation, *Political Studies*, 64(2): 279–96.

Lacey, J. (2014). Must Europe Be Swiss? On the Idea of a Voting Space and the Possibility of a Multilingual Demos, *British Journal of Political Science*, 44(1): 61–82.

(2016). Conceptually Mapping the European Union: A Demoi-cratic Analysis, *Journal of European Integration*, 38(1): 61–77.

(2017). *Centripetal Democracy: Democratic Legitimacy and Political Identity in Belgium, Switzerland and the European Union*, Oxford: Oxford University Press.

Lavdas, K. and Chryssochoou, D. (2011). *A Republic of Europeans: Civic Potential in a Liberal Milieu*, Cheltenham: Edward Elgar.

Lenaerts, K. and Gerard, D. (2004). The Structure of the Union According to the Constitution for Europe: The Emperor Is Getting Dressed, *European Law Review*, 29(3): 289–322.

Lijphart, A. (1977). *Democracy in Plural Societies: A Comparative Exploration*, New Haven, CT: Yale University Press.

Lijphart, A. (1999). *Patterns of Democracy*, New Haven, CT: Yale University Press.

Lindseth, P. (2010). *Power and Legitimacy: Reconciling Europe and the Nation State*, Oxford: Oxford University Press.

Lodge, J. (1994). The European Parliament and the Authority–Democracy Crisis, *Annals of the American Academy of Political and Social Sciences*, 531 (1): 69–83.

Lord, C. (2015). Utopia or Dystopia? Towards a Normative Analysis of Differentiated Integration, *Journal of European Public Policy*, 22(6): 783–98.

Lovett, F. (2001). Domination: A Preliminary Analysis, *The Monist*, 84(1): 98–112.

(2010). *A General Theory of Domination and Justice*, Oxford: Oxford University Press.

Luban, D. (1985). Just War and Human Rights in C. Beitz et al. (eds.), *International Ethics*, Princeton, NJ: Princeton University Press, pp. 195–216.

MacCormick, N. (1993). Beyond the Sovereign State, *The Modern Law Review*, LVI(1): 1–18.

(1995). The Maastricht-Urteil: Sovereignty Now, *European Law Journal*, 1(3): 259–66.

(1999). *Questioning Sovereignty*, Oxford: Oxford University Press.

Macdonald, T. and Ronzoni, M. (2012). Introduction: The Idea of Global Political Justice, *Critical Review of Social and Political Philosophy*, 15(5): 521–33.

Macedo, S. (2004). What Self-Governing Peoples Owe to One Another: Universalism, Diversity and The Law of Peoples, *Fordham Law Review*, 72 (5): 101–17.

Macpherson, C.B. (1977). *The Life and Times of Liberal Democracy*, Oxford: Oxford University Press.

Maduro, MP (1998). *We the Court: The European Court of Justice and the European Economic Constitution*, Oxford: Hart.

Mair, P. (2011). Smaghi vs. the Parties: Representative Government and Institutional Constraints. Paper prepared for the Conference on Democracy in Straightjackets: Politics in an Age of Permanent Austerity, Ringberg Castle, Munich, 23–26 March.

Majone, G. (1996). Regulatory Legitimacy in G. Majone (ed.), *Regulating Europe*, London: Routledge, pp. 284–301.

    (1998). Europe's Democratic Deficit: The Question of Standards, *European Law Journal*, 4(1): 5–28.

    (2001). Nonmajoritarian Institutions and the Limits of Democratic Governance: A Political Transaction Cost Approach, *Journal of Institutional and Theoretical Economics*, 157(1): 57–78.

    (2012). Rethinking the European Integration after the Debt Crisis. European Institute UCL Working Paper No. 3/2012.

    (2016). The Limits of Collective Action and Collective Leadership in D. Chalmers, M. Jachtenfuchs and C. Joerges (eds.), *The End of the Eurocrat's Dream*, Cambridge: Cambridge University Press, pp. 218–40.

Malcolm, N. (1991). *Sense on Sovereignty*, London: Centre for Policy Studies.

Mancini, G.F. (1989). The Making of a Constitution for Europe, *Common Market Law Review*, 26(4): 595–614.

    (1998). Europe: The Case for Statehood, *European Law Journal*, 4(1): 29–42.

Manin, B. (1997). *The Principles of Representative Government*, Cambridge: Cambridge University Press.

Marti, J. (2010). A Global Republic to Prevent Global Domination, *Diacritica*, 24 (2): 31–72.

Marshall, T.H. (1950). *Citizenship and Social Class*, Cambridge: Cambridge University Press.

Martinsen, D.S. and Werner, B. (2018). No Welfare Magnets – Free Movement and Cross-Border Welfare in Germany and Denmark Compared, *Journal of European Public Policy*, forthcoming.

Mason, A. (2012). *Living Together as Equals: The Demands of Citizenship*, Oxford: Oxford University Press.

May, K. (1952). A Set of Independent, Necessary and Sufficient Conditions for Simple Majority Decision, *Econometrica*, 20(4): 680–84.

Maurer, A. and Wessels, W. (eds.). (2001). *National Parliaments on Their Ways to Europe: Losers or Latecomers?* Baden-Baden, Nomos.

McNamara, K.R. (2015). *The Politics of Everyday Europe: Constructing Authority in the European Union*, Oxford: Oxford University Press.

Meinhof, U.H. (2004). Europe Viewed from Below: Agents, Victims and the Threat of the Other in R. Hermann et al. (eds.), *Transnational Identities:*

Becoming European in the EU, Oxford: Rowman and Littlefield, pp. 214–46.

Mill, J.S. (1972 [1861]). Considerations on Representative Government, in H.B. Acton (ed.), *Utilitarianism, On Liberty and Considerations on Representative Government*, London: Dent, pp. 171–393.

Miller, D. (1995). *On Nationality*, Oxford: Clarendon Press.

(2005). Against Global Egalitarianism, *The Journal of Ethics*, 9(1&2): 55–79.

(2007). *National Responsibility and Global Justice*, Oxford: Oxford University Press.

(2008). Republicanism, National Identity and Europe in C. Laborde and J. Maynor (eds.), *Republicanism and Political Theory*, Oxford: Blackwell, pp. 133–58.

(2009). Democracy's Domain, *Philosophy & Public Affairs*, 37(3): 201–28.

(2010). Against Global Democracy in K. Breen and S. O'Neill (eds.), *After the Nation: Critical Reflections on Post-Nationalism*, Basingstoke: Palgrave MacMillan, pp. 141–60.

(2013). Lea Ypi on Global Justice and Avant-Garde Political Agency: Some Reflections, *Ethics & Global Politics*, 6(2): 93–97.

(2016). *Strangers in Our Midst: The Political Philosophy of Immigration*, Cambridge, MA: Harvard University Press.

Miller, R.W. (1998). Cosmopolitan Respect and Patriotic Concern, *Philosophy & Public Affairs*, 27(3): 202–24.

Milward, A. (1992). *The European Rescue of the Nation State*, London: Routledge.

Moellendorf, D. (2002). *Cosmopolitan Justice*, Boulder, CO: Westview Press.

Moore, M. (2001). *The Ethics of Nationalism*, Oxford: Oxford University Press.

Moravcsik, A. (1993). Preferences and Power in the European Community: A Liberal Intergovernmental Approach, *Journal of Common Market Studies*, 31(4): 473–524.

(1998). *The Choice for Europe: Social Purpose and State Power from Messina to Maastricht*, London: UCL Press.

(2002). In Defence of the Democratic Deficit: Reassessing Legitimacy in the EU, *Journal of Common Market Studies*, 40(4): 603–24.

(2004). Is There a Democratic Deficit in World Politics? A Framework for Analysis, *Government and Opposition*, 39(2): 336–63.

(2008). The Myth of Europe's 'Democratic Deficit', *Intereconomics*, November/December: 331–40.

(2012). Europe after the Crisis: How to Sustain a Common Currency, *Foreign Affairs*, 91(3): 54–68.

Morgan, G. (2005). *The Idea of a European Superstate*, Princeton, NJ: Princeton University Press.

Mosely, L. (2003). *Global Capital and National Governments*, Cambridge: Cambridge University Press.

Müller, F. (2003). *Demokratie zwischen Staatsrecht und Weltrecht*, Berlin: Duncker & Humblot.

Müller, J.W. (2011). *Contesting Democracy: Political Ideas in Twentieth Century Europe*, New Haven, CT: Yale University Press.

Müller, J.W. (2016). *What Is Populism?*, Philadelphia, PA: Pennsylvania University Press.

Nagel, T. (2005). The Problem of Global Justice, *Philosophy & Public Affairs*, 33 (2): 113–47.

Newdick, C. (2006). Citizenship, Free Movement and Healthcare: Cementing Individual Rights by Corroding Social Solidarity, *Common Market Law Review*, 43(6): 1645–68.

Nic Shuibhne, N. (2010). The Resilience of EU Market Citizenship, *Common Market Law Review*, 47(6): 1597–628.

(2015a). The Developing Legal Dimensions of Union Citizenship in A. Arnull and D. Chalmers (eds.), *The Oxford Handbook of European Union Law*, Oxford: Oxford University Press, pp. 477–507.

(2015b). Limits Rising, Duties Ascending: The Changing Legal Shape of Union Citizenship, *Common Market Law Review*, 52(4): 889–938.

Nicolaïdis, K. (2004). The New Constitution as European 'Demoi-cracy'?, *Critical Review of International Social and Political Philosophy* 7(1): 76–93.

(2013). European Demoicracy and Its Crisis, *Journal of Common Market Studies*, 51(2): 351–69.

Nicolaïdis, K. and Viehoff, J. (2017). Just Boundaries for Demoicrats, *Journal of European Integration*, 39(5): 591–607.

Nili, S. (2013). Who's Afraid of a World State? A Global Sovereign and the Statist-Cosmopolitan Debate, *Critical Review of International Social and Political Philosophy*, 18(3): 241–63.

Nozick, R. (1974). *Anarchy, State, and Utopia*, New York: Basic Books.

Nussbaum, M. (1996). Patriotism and Cosmopolitanism in J. Cohen (ed.), *For Love of Country: Debating the Limits of Patriotism*, Boston, MA: Beacon Press, pp. 3–17.

O'Brien, C.R. (2017). The ECJ Sacrifices EU Citizenship in Vain: Commission v. United Kingdom, *Common Market Law Review*. 54(1): 209–43.

Offe, C. (2000). The Democratic Welfare State in an Integrating Europe in M. Greven and L. Pauly (eds.), *Democracy beyond the State? The European Dilemma and the Emerging Global Order*, Lanham, MD: Rowman and Littlefield, pp. 63–90.

(2003). The European Model of Social Capitalism: Can It Survive Integration?, *Journal of Political Philosophy*, 11(4): 437–69.

(2015). *Europe Entrapped*, Cambridge: Polity Press.

O'Leary, S. (1996). *The Evolving Concept of Community Citizenship: From the Free Movement of Persons to Community Citizenship*, The Hague: Lewer.

O'Neill, O. (2000). *Bounds of Justice*, Cambridge: Cambridge University Press.

Papadopoulos, Y. and Magnette, P. (2010). On the Politicisation of the EU: Lessons from Consociational National Polities, *West European Politics*, 33(4): 711–29.

Patberg, M. (ed.). (2017). Symposium 2017: The EU's *Pouvoir Constituant Mixte*, *Journal of Common Market Studies*, 55(2): 163–222.

Pettit, P. (1997). *Republicanism: A Theory of Freedom and Government*. Oxford: Oxford University Press.

(2005). Rawls's Political Ontology, *Politics, Philosophy and Economics*, 4(2): 157–174.

(2006). Rawls's Peoples in R. Martin and D. Reidy (eds.), *Rawls's Laws of Peoples: A Realistic Utopia?*, Oxford: Blackwell, pp. 38–56.

(2008). Republican Freedom: Three Axioms, Four Theorems in C. Laborde and J. Maynor (eds.), *Republicanism and Political Theory*, Oxford: Blackwell, pp. 102–31.

(2010a). A Republican Law of Peoples, *European Journal of Political Theory*, 9 (1): 70–94.

(2010b). Legitimate International Institutions: A Neo-Republican Perspective in S. Besson and J. Tasioulis (eds.), *The Philosophy of International Law*, Oxford: Oxford University Press, pp. 139–60.

(2012). *On the People's Terms*, Cambridge: Cambridge University Press.

(2014). *Just Freedom: A Moral Compass for a Complex World*, New York: W.W. Norton.

(2015). On the People's Terms: A Reply to Five Critiques, *Critical Review of International Social and Political Philosophy*, 18(6): 687–96.

Piris, J.-C. (2012). *The Future of Europe: Towards a Two-speed EU?*, Cambridge: Cambridge University Press.

Pitkin, H. (1967). *The Concept of Representation*, Berkeley, Los Angeles, London: University of California Press.

Pocock, J.G.A. (1995). The Ideal of Citizenship Since Classical Times in R. Beiner (ed.), *Theorizing Citizenship*, New York: SUNY Press, pp. 29–52.

Pogge, T. (1992). Cosmopolitanism and Sovereignty, *Ethics*, 103(1): 48–75.

(1994). An Egalitarian Law of Peoples, *Philosophy & Public Affairs*, 23(3): 195–224.

(1997). Creating Supra-National Institutions Democratically: Reflections on the European Union's Democratic Deficit, *Journal of Political Philosophy*, 5 (2): 163–82.

(2008). *World Poverty and Human Rights*, 2nd edn., Cambridge: Polity Press.

Przeworski, A. (2010). *Democracy and the Limits of Self-Government*, Cambridge: Cambridge University Press.

Puntscher Riekmann, S. and Wydra, D. (2013). Representation in the European state of emergency: Parliaments against governments?, *Journal of European Integration*, 35(5): 565–82.

Putnam, R.D. (1988). Diplomacy and Domestic Politics: The Logic of Two-Level Games, *International Organization*, 42(3): 427–60.

Rabkin, J. (1998). *Why Sovereignty Matters*, Washington, DC: AEI Press.

Rawls, J. (1964). Legal Obligation and the Duty of Fair Play in S. Hook (ed.), *Law and Philosophy*, New York: New York University Press, pp. 3–18.

(1971). *A Theory of Justice*, Oxford: Oxford University Press.

(1993). *Political Liberalism*, New York: Columbia University Press.

(1997). The Idea of Public Reason Revisited, *The University of Chicago Law Review*, 64(3): 765–807.

(1999). *The Law of Peoples*, Cambridge, MA: Harvard University Press.

Rawls, J. and Van Parijs, P. (2003). Three Letters on *The Law of Peoples* and the European Union, *Revue de philosophie economique* 7: 7–20.

Ripstein, A. (2009). *Force and Freedom: Kant's Legal and Political Philosophy*, Cambridge, MA: Harvard University Press.

Risse, T. (2005). Neofunctionalism, European Identity and the Puzzles of European Integration, *Journal of European Public Policy*, 12(2): 291–309.

(2010). *A Community of Europeans? Transnational Identities and Public Spheres*, Ithaca, NY: Cornell University Press.

Rittberger, B. (2005). *Building Europe's Parliament: Democratic Representation beyond the Nation State*, Oxford: Oxford University Press.

(2014). Integration without Representation? The European Parliament and the Reform of Economic Governance in the EU, *Journal of Common Market Studies*, 52(6): 1174–83.

Rodrik, D. (1996). Why Do More Open Economies Have Bigger Governments? NBER Working Paper no 5537, Cambridge, MA, National Bureau of Economic Research.

(2011). *The Globalization Paradox*, Oxford: Oxford University Press.

Rogers, I. (2018). Lecture on 'The real post-Brexit options' at the University of Glasgow on 23 May 2018. https://policyscotland.gla.ac.uk/blog-sir-ivan-rogers-speech-text-in-full/.

Rokkan, S. (1974). Dimensions of State Formation and Nation-Building in C. Tilly (ed.), *The Formation of National States in Western Europe*, Princeton, NJ: Princeton University Press, pp. 562–600.

Ronzoni, M. (2017). The European Union as Demoi-cracy: Really a Third Way?, *European Journal of Political Theory*, 16(2): 210–34.

Rousseau, J.J. (1762). *The Social Contract*, ed. V. Gourevitch, Cambridge: Cambridge University Press (1997).

Ruggie, J.G. (1982). International Regimes, Transactions and Change: Embedded Liberalism in the Postwar Economic Order, *International Organisation*, 36(2): 379–415.

Sandel, M. (1987). The Political Theory of the Procedural Republic in G. Bryner and N. Reynolds (eds.), *Constitutionalism and Rights*, Provo, UT: Brigham Young University Press, pp. 141–55.

Sandbu, M. (2015). *Europe's Orphan: The Future of the Euro and the Politics of Debt*, Princeton, NJ: Princeton University Press.

Sangiovanni, A. (2007). Global Justice, Reciprocity, and the State, *Philosophy & Public Affairs*, 35(1): 3–39.

(2008). Justice and the Priority of Politics to Morality, *Journal of Political Philosophy*, 16(2): 137–64.

(2013). Solidarity in the European Union, *Oxford Journal of Legal Studies*, 33 (2): 213–41.

(Forthcoming). On the Relation between Legitimacy and Justice: A Framework for the EU, *JCMS: Journal of Common Market Studies*.

Sassen, S. (1996). *Losing Control?*, New York: Columbia University Press.

Saward, M. (2010). *The Representative Claim*, Oxford: Oxford University Press.

Savage, D. and Weale, A. (2009). Political Representation and the Normative Logic of Two-Level Games, *European Political Science Review*, 1(1): 63–81.

Scharpf, F.W. (1988). The Joint-Decision Trap: Lessons from German Federalism and European Integration, *Public Administration*, 66(3): 239–78.

(1999). *Governing in Europe: Effective and Democratic*, New York: Oxford University Press.

(2003). Legitimate Diversity: The New Challenge of European Integration in T.A. Börzel and R. Cichowski (eds.), *The State of the European Union, 6: Law, Politics and Society*, Oxford: Oxford University Press, pp. 79–104.

(2009). Legitimacy in the Multilevel European Polity, *European Political Science Review*, 1(2): 173–204.

(2010). The Assymetry of European Integration or Why the EU Cannot Be a Social Market Economy, *Socio-Economic Review*, 8: 211–50.

(2015). After the Crash: A Perspective on Multilevel European Democracy, *European Law Journal*, 21(3): 384–405.

(2017). De-Constitutionalisation and Majority Rule: A Democratic Vision for Europe, *European Law Journal*, 23(3): 315–34.

Schimmelfennig, F. (2014). EU Enlargement and Differentiated Integration: Discrimination or Equal Treatment?, *Journal of European Public Policy*, 21 (5): 681–698.

Schimmelfennig, F. and Winzen, T. (2014). Instrumental and Constitutional Differentiation in the European Union, *Journal of Common Market Studies*, 52(2): 354–70.

Schmidt, V.A. (2006). *Democracy in Europe: The EU and National Polities*, Oxford: Oxford University Press.

Schön, W. (2015). Neutrality and Territoriality – Competing or Converging Concepts in European Tax Law?, *Bulletin for International Taxation* (April/May): 271–93.

Schumpeter, J. (1947). *Capitalism, Socialism, and Democracy*, New York: Allen and Unwin.

Scruton, R. (2016). Le Brexit est un choix éminemment culturel, *Figaro*, 28 June, www.lefigaro.fr/vox/monde/2016/06/28/31002-20160628ARTFIG00064-roger-scruton-le-brexit-est-un-choix-eminemment-culturel.php.

Sheehan, J.J. (2006). The Problem of Sovereignty in European History, *American Historical Review*, 111(1): 1–15.

Shore, C. (2000). *Building Europe: The Cultural Politics of European Integration*, New York and London: Routledge.

(2004). Whither European Citizenship?: Eros and Civilization, *European Journal of Social Theory*, 7(1): 27–44.

(2011). 'European Governance' or Governmentality? The European Commission and the Future of Democratic Government, *European Law Journal*, 17(3): 287–303.

Shue, H. (1996). *Basic Rights: Subsistence, Affluence, and U.S. Foreign Policy*, 2nd edn., Princeton, NJ: Princeton University Press.

Simmons, A.J. (1979). *Moral Principles and Political Obligation*, Princeton, NJ: Princeton University Press.

(2001). *Justification and Legitimacy*, Cambridge: Cambridge University Press.

Skinner, Q. (1998). *Liberty before Liberalism*, Cambridge: Cambridge University Press.

(2008). Freedom as the Absence of Arbitrary Power in C. Laborde and J. Maynor (eds.), *Republicanism and Political Theory*, Oxford: Blackwell, pp. 83–101.

(2010). The Sovereign State: A Genealogy in H. Kalmo and Q. Skinner (eds.), *Sovereignty in Fragments: The Past, Present and Future of a Contested Concept*, Cambridge: Cambridge University Press, pp. 26–46.

Slaughter, A.M. (2004). Disaggregated Sovereignty: Toward the Public Accountability of Global Governance Networks, *Government and Opposition*, 39(2): 159–90.

(2005). *A New World Order*, Princeton, NJ: Princeton University Press.

Soysal, Y.N. (1994). *Limits of Citizenship: Migrants and Postnational Membership in Europe*, Chicago, IL: University of Chicago Press.

Spaventa, E. (2017). Earned Citizenship – Understanding Union Citizenship through Its Scope in D. Kochenov (ed.), *EU Citizenship and Federalism: the Role of Rights*, Cambridge: Cambridge University Press, pp. 204–25.

Sprungk, C. (2013). A New Type of Representative Democracy? Reconsidering the role of national parliaments in the European Union, *Journal of European Integration*, 35(3): 547–63.

Steinberg, J. (2015). *Why Switzerland?*, 3rd edn., Cambridge: Cambridge University Press.

Steiner, H. (1994). *An Essay on Rights*, Cambridge, MA: Blackwell Publishers.

Stilz, A. (2009). *Liberal Loyalty: Freedom, Obligation and the State*, Princeton, NJ: Princeton University Press.

Streeck, W. (2014). *Buying Time: The Delayed Crisis of Democratic Capitalism*, London: Verso.

Stubb, A. (1996). A Categorization of Differentiated Integration, *Journal of Common Market Studies*, 34(2): 283–95.

Sunstein, C. R. (1991). Preferences and Politics, *Philosophy & Public Affairs* 20 (1): 3–34.

Tamir, Y. (1993). *Liberal Nationalism*, Princeton, NJ: Princeton University Press.

Taylor, C. (1989). Cross-Purposes: The Liberal-Communitarian Debate in N. Rosenblum (ed.), *Liberalism and the Moral Life*, Cambridge, MA: Harvard University Press, pp. 159–82.

Thibaud, P. (1992). L'Europe par les nations (et réciproquement) in J.H. Ferry and P. Thibaud (eds.), *Discussion sur l'Europe*, Paris: Calmann-Levy, pp. 19–126.

Thompson, D. (1999). Democratic Theory and Global Society, *Journal of Political Philosophy*, 7(2): 111–25.

Thym, D. (2016). Competing Models for Understanding Differentiated Integration in B. de Witte, A. Ott, and E. Vos (eds.), *Between Flexibility and Disintegration: The State of EU Law Today* (Cheltenham: Edward Elgar), pp. 28–75.

Treaty on the European Union (TEU).(2012). http://eur-lex.europa.eu/legal-content/EN/TXT/?uri=celex%3A12012 M%2FTXT.

Treaty on the Functioning of the European Union (TFEU). (2012). http://eur-lex.europa.eu/legal-content/EN/TXT/?uri=celex%3A12012E%2FTXT.

Troper, M. (2010). The Survival of Sovereignty in H. Kalmo and Q. Skinner (eds.), *Sovereignty in Fragments: The Past, Present and Future of a Contested Concept*, Cambridge: Cambridge University Press, pp. 132–50.

Tsoukalis, L. (2016). *In Defence of Europe: Can the European Project Be Saved?*, Oxford: Oxford University Press.

Tuck, R. (2016). The Left Case for Brexit, *Dissent*, 6 June, www.dissentmagazine.org/online_articles/left-case-brexit.

Tushnet, M. (2006). Weak-Form Judicial Review and 'Core' Civil Liberties. *Harvard Civil Rights-Civil Liberties Law Review*, 41(1): 1–22.

Ulaş, L. (2017). Transforming (but not Transcending) the State System? On Statist Cosmopolitanism, *Critical Review of International Social and Political Philosophy*, 20(6): 657–76.

Usherwood, S. and Startin, N. (2013). Euroscepticism as a Persistent Phenomenon, *Journal of Common Market Studies*, 51(1): 1–16.

Valentini, L. (2012a). Assessing the Global Order: Justice, Legitimacy, or Political Justice?, *Critical Review of International Social and Political Philosophy*, 15(5): 593–612.

(2012b). Ideal vs. Non-ideal Theory: A Conceptual Map, *Philosophy Compass*, 7(9): 654–64.

(2013). Justice, Disagreement and Democracy, *British Journal of Political Science*, 43(1): 177–99.

(2014). No Global Demos, No Global Democracy? A Systematization and Critique, *Perspectives on Politics*, 12(4): 789–807.

Van Parijs, P. (2013). *Just Democracy: The Rawls–Machiavelli Programme*, Colchester: ECPR Press.

(2016). Thatcher's Plot and How to Defeat It, *Social Europe*, www.socialeurope.eu/thatchers-plot-defeat.

Viehoff, J. (2017). Maximum Convergence on a Just Minimum: A Pluralist Justification for European Social Policy, *European Journal of Political Theory*, 16(2): 164–87.

von Bogdandy, A. (2000). The European Union as a Human Rights Organization? Human Rights and the Core of the European Union, *Common Market Law Review*, 37(5): 1307–38.

(2005). The Prospect of a European Republic: What European Citizens are Voting On, *Common Market Law Review*, 42: 913–41.

(2012). The European Lesson for International Democracy: The Significance of Articles 9–12 EU Treaty for International Organizations, *European Journal of International Law*, 23(2): 315–34.

von Rompuy, H. (2012). Interview on June 2011, as reported in *The Guardian*, 4 November 2012. www.guardian.co.uk/politics/2012/nov/08/alex-salmond-scotland-independence.

Waldron, J. (1990). *The Law*, London: Routledge.

(1993). Special Ties and Natural Duties, *Philosophy & Public Affairs*, 22 (1): 3–30.

(1999). *Law and Disagreement*, Oxford: Oxford University Press.

Walker, N. (2016). Constitutional Pluralism Revisited, *European Law Journal*, 22 (3): 333–55.

Walzer, M. (1981). Philosophy and Democracy, *Political Theory*, 9(3): 379–99.

(1983). *Spheres of Justice: A Defence of Pluralism and Equality*, Oxford: Martin Robertson.

(1994). *Thick and Thin: Moral Argument at Home and Abroad*, Notre Dame: University of Notre Dame Press.

Warleigh, A. (2001). Europeanizing Civil Society: NGOs as Agents of Political Socialization, *Journal of Common Market Studies*, 39(4): 619–39.

Weiler, J.H.H. (1995). Does Europe Need a Constitution? Reflections on Demos, Telos and the German Maastricht Decision, *European Law Journal*, 1(3): 219–58.

(1998a). Bread and Circus: The State of the European Union, *Columbia Journal of European Law*, 4(2): 223–48.

(1998b). Europe: The Case against the Case for Statehood, *European Law Journal*, 4(1): 43–62.

(1999). *The Constitution of Europe: 'Do the New Clothes Have an Emperor?' and Other Essays on European Integration*, Cambridge: Cambridge University Press.

(2001). Federalism without Constitutionalism: Europe's *Sonderweg* in K. Nicolaïdis and R. Howse (eds.), *The Federal Vision*, Oxford: Oxford University Press, pp. 54–70.

(2003). In Defence of the Status Quo: Europe's Constitutional *Sonderweg* in J.H.H. Weiler and M. Wind (eds.), *European Constitutionalism beyond the State*, Cambridge: Cambridge University Press, pp. 7–25.

(2012). In the Face of Crisis: Input Legitimacy, Output Legitimacy and the political Messianism of European integration, *Journal of European Integration*, 34(7): 825–41.

Weiner, A. (1998). *European' Citizenship Practice: Building Institutions of a Non-State*, Boulder, CO: Westview.

Wenar, L. (2006). Why Rawls Is Not a Cosmopolitan Egalitarian in R. Martin and D. Reidy (eds.), *Rawls's Law of Peoples: A Realistic Utopia?*, Oxford: Blackwell, pp. 95–114.

Wendler, F. (2014). Justification and Political Polarization in National Parliamentary Debates on EU Treaty Reform, *Journal of European Public Policy*, 21(4): 549–67.

White, J. (2011). *Political Allegiance after European Integration*, Basingstoke: Palgrave.

White, S. (2011). New Labour and the Politics of Ownership in P. Diamond and M. Kenny (eds.), *Reassessing New Labour: Market, State and Society under Blair and Brown*, Oxford: Blackwell, pp. 140–51.

Williams, B. (2005). Realism and Moralism in Political Theory in G. Hawthorn (ed.), *In the Beginning Was the Deed*, Princeton, NJ: Princeton University Press, pp. 1–17.

Winch, D. (1978). *Adam Smith's Politics: An Essay in Historiographic Revision.* Cambridge: Cambridge University Press.

Wincott, D. (1995). Political Theory, Law and European Union in J. Shaw and G. More (eds.), *New Legal Dynamics of European Union*, Oxford: Clarendon Press, pp. 293–311.

Winzen, T. (2012). National Parliamentary Control of European Union Affairs: A Crossnational and Longitudinal Comparison, *West European Politics*, 35 (3): 657–72.

(2013). European Integration and National Parliamentary Oversight Institution, *European Union Politics*, 14: 297–323.

(2016). From Capacity to Sovereignty: Legislative Politics and Differentiated Integration in the European Union, *European Journal of Political Research*, 55 (1): 100–19.

Wolff, R.P. (1970). *In Defense of Anarchism*, New York: Harper and Row.

Young, I.M. (1989). Polity and Group Difference: A Critique of the Ideal of Universal Citizenship, *Ethics*, 99(2): 250–74.

(2000). *Inclusion and Democracy*, Oxford: Oxford University Press.

Ypi, L. (2008a). Statist Cosmopolitanism, *Journal of Political Philosophy*, 16(1): 48–71.

(2008b). Sovereignty, Cosmopolitanism, and the Ethics of European Foreign Policy, *European Journal of Political Theory*, 7(3): 349–64.

(2010). On the Confusion between Idea and Non-Ideal in Recent Debates on Global Justice, *Political Studies*, 58(3): 536–55.

(2011). *Global Justice and Avant-Garde Political Agency*, New York: Oxford University Press.

Zolo, D. (1995). *Cosmopolis: La prospettiva del governo mondiale*, Milan: Feltrinelli.

Zürn, M. (2016). Four Models of a Global Order with Cosmopolitan Intent: An Empirical Assessment, *Journal of Political Philosophy*, 24(1): 88–119.

Index